SINFULLY VEGAN

SINFULLY VEGAN

More than 160 Decadent Desserts to Satisfy Every Sweet Tooth

LOIS DIETERLY

Da Capo
LIFE
LONG

A Member of the Perseus Books Group

Designed by Trish Wilkinson
Set in 11 point Minion Pro

Cataloging-in-Publication data for this book is available from the Library of Congress.

ISBN: 978-0-7382-1488-7
E-book ISBN: 978-0-7382-1498-6

Published by Da Capo Press
A Member of the Perseus Books Group
www.dacapopress.com

Note: The information in this book is true and complete to the best of our knowledge. This book is intended only as an informative guide for those wishing to know more about health issues. In no way is this book intended to replace, countermand, or conflict with the advice given to you by your own physician. The ultimate decision concerning care should be made between you and your doctor. We strongly recommend you follow his or her advice. Information in this book is general and is offered with no guarantees on the part of the authors or Da Capo Press. The authors and publisher disclaim all liability in connection with the use of this book. The names and identifying details of people associated with events described in this book have been changed. Any similarity to actual persons is coincidental.

Da Capo Press books are available at special discounts for bulk purchases in the U.S. by corporations, institutions, and other organizations. For more information, please contact the Special Markets Department at the Perseus Books Group, 2300 Chestnut Street, Suite 200, Philadelphia, PA, 19103, or call (800) 810-4145, ext. 5000, or e-mail special.markets@perseus books.com.

10 9 8 7 6 5 4 3 2 1

CONTENTS

INTRODUCTION

Nothing will benefit human health and increase chances
for survival of life on Earth as much as the evolution to a
vegetarian diet.

—ALBERT EINSTEIN

I decided to become vegan about fifteen years ago. It was not a quick
transformation—it took me about two years to complete. I have always had a
sweet tooth, and the one thing that I missed was good desserts. Other than that,
I loved being vegan. I loved the new foods that I was eating—kale and tahini
with hot pepper sauce, TVP stroganoff (stroganoff made with chunks of textured vegetable protein to replace the meat), and veggie stir-fries replaced heavy
meals like chicken with dumplings and roast beef and mashed potatoes. I was
much happier . . . except for the desserts. All the vegan desserts that I tried were
either tasteless or dry. And all of them were very expensive. Was I destined to
live out the rest of my life without indulging in a few decadent treats every once
in a while? Of course not! The logical solution was to make homemade vegan
goodies! And so began my vegan baking adventure. You may notice that some
of the ingredients used in the recipes in this book may cost more than their nonvegan counterparts. However, it is still cheaper to make your own delicious
vegan desserts than to buy them from a vegan bakery.

I was born with a love of cooking, especially baking. My mother was a home
economics teacher who allowed me to work side by side with her from the time I

was very small. I was never satisfied using somebody else's recipe; I always liked to create my own. One of my first memories is of making "chocolate pudding" when I was about four years old. I used flour, cocoa powder, milk, and many other ingredients. I don't think anyone else appreciated my efforts, but I was pleased! By becoming vegan, I provided myself with a vast area in which to experiment. Because I could not find many decent vegan baked goods, I set out to create my own. I worked with recipes that I had enjoyed as a nonvegan first. I looked at creations in gourmet cookbooks and magazines and attempted to "veganize" them, and I created many of my own recipes from scratch. I found that I love to create new culinary masterpieces. I also discovered that not only are vegan baked goods healthier for you but they can taste delicious, too! If you are like the majority of Americans, you made eating more healthfully or losing a few pounds one of your New Year's resolutions. But, as the year progresses, that resolution becomes harder and harder to keep. You see gooey candy and creamy chocolate on TV, smell buttery popcorn at movie theaters, salivate over the dessert cart at business lunches. So you're faced with either another failed resolution or a year of deprivation. Neither choice sounds appealing, but what are you to do? If only you could have your cake and eat it, too. . . . Well, perhaps you can. Sinfully Vegan will show you how to make decadent cakes and treats that will satisfy your sweet tooth without totally blowing your diet or your resolution to eat more healthfully.

In the years that have passed since I first worked on this book, many changes have occurred in the vegan community. There are many more vegan restaurants, or at least vegan dishes at restaurants; many more commercially made vegan desserts; and many more choices of ingredients to use in vegan baking. Being vegan has entered the mainstream of American life. Maybe it still isn't embraced by the majority of people, but our numbers are increasing. Being vegan now is more exciting than ever! There are delicious new products being made available all the time. I have also grown in my outlook on creating vegan treats. I have tried to meet the changing palates of people by including a few raw recipes, gluten-free/sugar-free treats, muffin tops, cupcakes, and desserts made to appeal specifically to children (though adults will love them, too!) I had a lot of fun creating more than twenty new recipes for this book!

As you go through this book, take note of the ♡ icon. This icon designates my favorite recipes.

Why Vegan Desserts Can Be Healthy and Delicious

Of course, cakes and pies alone will never provide us with all the vitamins, minerals, and nutrients we need, but they can be made healthier so that indulging in a piece once in a while is not a sin. Traditional cake and icing recipes are rich in cholesterol and fat (eggs, milk, and butter) and refined sugar. You probably already know that cholesterol is not good for your body. Too much of it clogs your arteries and makes it harder for your heart to pump blood to the rest of your body. Your liver is capable of producing on its own all the cholesterol you need—you don't need to get it from an outside source. Therefore, if your resolution is to eat healthier, you should be trying to avoid cholesterol. To quote Dr. Charles Glueck, director of the Jewish Hospital Cholesterol Center in Cincinnati, Ohio, "For every one percent reduction in total cholesterol level, there is a two percent reduction of heart disease risk."

Fat is another nutritional bad boy, although it is highly misunderstood. All fat is not bad. Our bodies do need some fats, such as omega-3 fatty acids found in fish and flax oils and monounsaturated fats found in olive and canola oil. It's the hydrogenated fats found in solid shortenings, which make piecrusts flaky and cakes fluffy, that you should avoid at all costs. Hydrogenated fats are fats to which more hydrogen has been artificially added. Our bodies don't know what to do with this "fake" fat, so it is deposited in our arteries. Most of the recipes in this book use monounsaturated fats—fats necessary (in small amounts) for healthy hair, skin, and hearts. If a vegan butter or butter spread is required, a brand such as Spectrum or Earth Balance, which is nonhydrogenated, is suggested. Spectrum and Earth Balance also make a good nonhydrogenated vegan shortening. To eat more healthfully, you must learn to be an avid label reader.

The eggs that are used to bind ingredients together in most traditional recipes are also a large source of dietary cholesterol. Each egg contains 215 milligrams of cholesterol, and many traditional recipes, such as carrot cake, for example, usually require several eggs. If a cake contains four eggs, that means it has 860 mg of cholesterol or about 108 mg per slice! Compare this to xanthan gum, a natural carbohydrate made from a tiny microorganism called *Xanthomonas campestris*. Xanthan gum works as a wonderful substitute for eggs. It contains no cholesterol, only 8 calories, and provides 9 grams of fiber, or 36 percent of the daily amount recommended by the USDA—all in a tiny 1-tablespoon serving! What a great ingredient!

Flax powder is another substitute that can be used for eggs. I use 1 teaspoon of flax powder mixed with ¼ cup of water for each egg called for in a recipe. If 4 teaspoons of flax powder is used to replace the four eggs in the carrot cake example, you would have 0 grams cholesterol and less than 5 grams of total fat, none of which is saturated (the bad kind). The total calories from the 4 teaspoons of flax flour would equal 52, while the total number of calories in 4 (medium-size) eggs would be 252, and if you opt for large eggs, that amount jumps to 284! So now you see how much sense it makes to replace eggs in recipes if you are trying to eat more healthfully.

The milk used in most traditional cake recipes is loaded with fat and cholesterol. Think of it this way: A newborn calf weighs about 60 pounds. In one year, eating only cow's milk, it will grow to weigh between 300 and 600 pounds. Now that's powerful stuff! Even one cup of reduced-fat 2% milk still has 120 calories and 5 grams of fat, 3 of those grams being saturated, as well as 20 milligrams of cholesterol. True, it has 30 percent of the recommended daily percentage of calcium that a person needs, but compare that to 1 cup of soy milk, which can be used as a milk substitute in all recipes. Soy milk has 80 calories per cup, 6 grams of fat, 0.1 gram of that being saturated, and no cholesterol! And it has 30 percent of the recommended daily percentage of calcium. Soy milk is just one alternative to dairy milk. Explore the nondairy "milk" section at your local store. Many new vegan products are being introduced all the time. Some are new and some are changes/improvements to old standbys. I love using almond milk, although when cooking for a family member with a nut allergy, I use rice milk.

In addition to the nutrition angle, dairy milk has many undesirable side effects. Some studies have shown allergies to milk and dairy products can cause many uncomfortable symptoms, including irritability, restlessness, hyperactivity, muscle pain, mental depression, abdominal pain, cramps or bloating, gas, diarrhea, bad breath, headaches, lack of energy, constipation, poor appetite, nasal stuffiness, runny nose, sinusitis, asthma, shortness of breath, rashes, eczema, and hives. Milk and dairy products may also be linked to diabetes in children, several types of cancer, benign breast conditions, acne, fibroids, chronic intestinal upset, and heart disease. Do you still want milk and dairy products in your dessert? Take a look at the chart below and compare the nutritional facts of dairy milk (2%) to other vegan milk choices (note that the chart information is based on an 8-ounce serving). As always, learn to be an avid label-reader.

	2% dairy milk	Soy milk Unsweetened, added calcium	Almond milk unsweetened	Rice milk (Heartwise Original)
Calories	137	80	40	130
Calories from fat	43	35	30	20
Total fat	5 g	6 g	3 g	2 g
Saturated fat	3 g	1 g	0	0
Cholesterol	20 mg	0	0	0
Sodium	145 mg	90 mg	180 mg	80 mg
Total carbohydrates	12 g	4 g	2 g	27 g
Dietary fiber	0	1 g	1 g	3 g
Protein	10 g	7 g	1 g	1 g
Calcium	35 %	30 %	20 %	30 %

Butter is another high-cholesterol ingredient—30 milligrams per 1 tablespoon portion with 100 percent of its calories derived from fat. It can easily be replaced with applesauce, mashed bananas, canola oil, whipped tofu, or prune butter, depending on the recipe. Besides the substitution of healthier ingredients for unhealthy ones, several of the cakes in this book already include fruits and vegetables as one of the ingredients. Bananas, a fruit high in niacin, are a main ingredient in the Bold Banana Cake (page 63) and carrots, high in vitamin A, are found in abundance in the Hold the Wheat Carrot Cake (page 61) and Ten-Carat Gold Cake (page 88). Zucchini can be found in some of the chocolate cake recipes such as Nuts About Chocolate Cake (page 50) and Cherry, Cherry Not Contrary Cake (page 45). What better way to "sneak" veggies to your kids than in a cake? They'll never know it! And, remember, all is fair when trying to eat healthier!

Another way to substitute for butter is to use some of the newer vegan butter spreads that are now available. The change in the quality of the available vegan butter spreads since the publication of the first addition of this book is tremendous. Keep your eyes open as newer products become available. If you decide to use vegan butter spread, understand that the recipe won't be as healthy as a recipe that uses fruit for most or all the fat. But decide what your goal is: Are you trying to make a vegan recipe that is very similar to a regular dessert, but that should still be eaten in small amounts, or are you looking for something to satisfy your sweet tooth that is healthy enough that you can eat it for breakfast . . . or every day, if you want to? Take a look at the chart below to compare the nutritional values of 1 tablespoon of dairy butter, vegan butter (I like to use Earth Balance Natural Buttery Spread), and canola oil.

Many of the desserts in this book should still be viewed as snack foods to be eaten in moderation; however, they are much healthier than their full-fat,

	Dairy butter	Earth Balance Natural Buttery Spread	Canola oil
Calories	100	100	119
Calories from fat	100	100	119
Total fat	11 g	11 g	14 g
Saturated fat	7 g	3.5 g	1 g
Cholesterol	30 mg	0	0
Sodium	81 mg	120 mg	0
Total carbohydrates	0	0	0
Dietary fiber	0	0	0
Protein	0	0	0
Calcium	0	0	0

cholesterol-laden counterparts. You will be pleasantly surprised by the delectable confections you can create with these recipes.

A Guide to Deciphering Fats

One of the most confusing aspects of reading food labels and trying to eat more healthfully is trying to understand the differences between types of fats. All fats are not created equal. Fats have gotten a bad rap in the last few years as consumers have gone from eating a lot of fat, to eating no fat, and back to eating a lot of fat again. Somewhere in the middle is the key to eating healthfully, but how are you to know? To start, you must become familiar with the major types of fat. The fats defined here are listed in descending order of healthiness. You should try to eat as close to the top of the list as you can and avoid the fats at the bottom of the list. Not only is the type of fat that you eat important, but the amount of fat is critical as well. You will find a section on how to calculate the amount of fat that you should consume and information on where to find equations to calculate your own BMR (basal metabolic rate).

Unsaturated fats: These are fats that help lower blood cholesterol if used in place of saturated fats. There are two types: monounsaturated and polyunsaturated. Most (but not all) liquid vegetable oils are unsaturated. The exceptions include coconut, palm, and palm kernel oils.

Monounsaturated fats: This is one of the two healthiest fats, the other being polyunsaturated fat. Examples include olive, canola, and peanut oil. It is known to reduce the levels of LDL (bad) cholesterol.

Polyunsaturated fats: These fats are also considered relatively healthy. Examples include safflower, sesame, corn, and soybean oil. There is a special group of polyunsaturated fats called omega-3 oils that have been thought to lower LDL (bad) cholesterol and elevate HDL (good) cholesterol. Omega-3 oils are found in cold-water fish such as mackerel and herring. They are also found in plant sources. Flax and chia seeds are two great plant sources of this nutrient.

Saturated fats: These are a big dietary cause of high LDL levels (bad cholesterol). When looking at a food label, pay very close attention to the percent of saturated fat and avoid or limit any foods that are high (over 20 percent saturated fat is considered high). Saturated fats are found in animal products such as butter, cheese, whole milk, ice cream, cream, and fatty meats, none of which are found in the recipes in this book. Saturated fats are also found in some vegetable oils such as coconut, palm, and palm kernel oils. Most other vegetable oils contain unsaturated fat and are healthier.

Trans-fatty acids: These fats are formed when vegetable oil is hardened, through either full or partial hydrogenation. They are synthetically created saturated fats. Trans-fatty acids raise LDL levels, and they can also lower HDL (good cholesterol) levels. They are difficult to eliminate from the body and are a low quality source of energy. Trans-fatty acids can be found in fried foods, commercial baked goods (doughnuts, cookies, crackers), processed foods, and margarines. They are listed on food labels as partially hydrogenated or hydrogenated oil. New nutrition labels, instituted in January 2006, list trans fats as a separate category. Look for it . . . and avoid it!

Partially hydrogenated: This term refers to oils that have become partially hardened but not completely solid. Foods made with partially hydrogenated oils contain high levels of trans-fatty acids (formed by the hydrogenation process), which are linked to heart disease. Most commercially produced cookies, crackers, snack foods, and some cereals contain partially hydrogenated oils.

Hydrogenated: This term refers to oils that have become hardened (such as hard shortening and margarine) through the addition of hydrogen molecules. Foods made with hydrogenated oils also contain high levels of trans-fatty acids. Again, most commercially prepared baked goods contain hydrogenated oils.

How Much Fat Is Too Much?

Your ideal amount of fat intake is unique and depends on the amount of calories you consume. As a rule of thumb, no more than 25 to 35 percent of your total daily calories should come from fat, with less than 7 percent coming from saturated fat. For example, if you consume 2,000 calories per day, no more than 500 to 700 calories should come from fat and no more than 140 calories from saturated fat. Trans fats are an even bigger fat bad boy. You should eliminate them completely or limit them to 1 percent of your total caloric intake (according to the American Heart Association). To put this in numbers, if you eat 2,000 calories per day, no more than 20 calories should come from trans fats. If you look at this in terms of grams on a nutritional label, that would correspond to 2 grams. The following foods are foods that you should be careful when using and always read labels to ensure that you aren't getting too many trans fats.

- Stick margarine (2.8 grams of trans fat per tablespoon, and 2.1 grams of saturated fat)
- Tub margarine (0.6 grams of trans fat per tablespoon, and 1.2 grams of saturated fat)
- Regular shortening (4.2 grams of trans fat per tablespoon, and 3.4 grams of saturated fat)—look for such shortening brands as Spectrum that has 0 trans fats.
- Dairy butter (0.3 grams of trans fat per tablespoon, and 7.2 grams of saturated fat)—you may substitute vegan buttery spread such as that made by Earth Balance. This spread also comes in stick form—no trans fats!
- Baked goods. Even worse news—more trans fats are used in commercially baked products than any other foods. Doughnuts contain shortening in the dough and are cooked in trans fat.
- Cookies and cakes (with shortening-based frostings) from supermarket bakeries have plenty of trans fat. Some higher-quality baked goods use butter instead of margarine, so they contain less trans fat but more saturated fat.
- Commercially prepared doughnuts have about 5 grams of trans fat apiece, and nearly 5 grams of saturated fat. Try instead the Fasnachts (these taste like glazed doughnuts) on page 237, Jelly-Filled Doughnuts on page 239, and Boston Cream–Filled Doughnuts on page 241.
- Commercially prepared cream-filled cookies have 1.9 grams of trans fat, and 1.2 grams of saturated fat. Healthier choice: Check out the cookie section starting on page 23.

- Commercially prepared pound cake has 4.3 grams of trans fat per slice, and 3.4 grams of saturated fat. Healthier choice: Check out the Lemon Loaf on page 43 or Just Loafing Around on page 51.

Beware: Even if a label says "low fat," it may still have trans fats!

To sum up the discussion on fats, the American Heart Association's Nutrition Committee (www.heart.org/heartorg) strongly advises these fat guidelines for healthy Americans over the age of two:

- Limit total fat intake to less than 25 to 35 percent of your total calories each day;
- Limit saturated fat intake to less than 7 percent of total daily calories;
- Limit trans fat intake to less than 1 percent of total daily calories;
- The remaining fat should come from sources of monounsaturated and polyunsaturated fats such as nuts, seeds, fish, and vegetable oils; and
- Limit cholesterol intake to less than 300 mg per day, for most people. If you have coronary heart disease or your LDL cholesterol level is 100 mg/dL or greater, limit your cholesterol intake to less than 200 milligrams a day.

The nutrition and fat in coconut oil is a topic that's really come to the fore in recent years. Coconut oil is classified as a saturated fat. It is actually made up of around 90 percent saturated fat, 6 percent monounsaturated fat, and 2 percent polyunsaturated fat. Coconut oil, unlike other highly saturated fats, is mostly made up of medium chain fatty acids (MCFAs). Am I sounding very smart here? Well, I have to admit that I wouldn't know an MCFA from an IRA or a PDA! So, I did what all good Americans do and ran to my computer and Googled it. Supposedly, MCFAs are more easily digested and absorbed in the body than other fats. And what does that mean? Is coconut oil good or bad for your body? If you can definitively answer that question, there are many who would like to hear about it! Numerous studies have come up with recommendations for and against coconut oil. Until more research is done, probably the best action, as in everything, is moderation. If this interests you, feel free to surf the Web. There are many interesting postings that discuss this topic!

Following you will find a chart that will give you an idea of how much fat you can eat. Unlike some nutrients where you want to eat at least that amount, with fat, you will be very healthy if you don't even come close to these numbers!

Total calories per day	Total fat calories per day (30%)	Total fat per day (30%) (grams)	Total saturated fat calories per day (7%)	Total saturated fat per day (7%) (grams)
1,200	360	40	84	9
1,500	450	50	105	11
1,800	540	60	126	14
2,000	600	66	140	15

How many calories should you be eating per day? On average, men should consume between 2,000 and 3,000 calories, and women should consume between 1,600 and 2,400 calories. Children would have different numbers as well. Many factors—such as age, height, lean body mass, environmental temperature, and activity level—can affect these numbers. To estimate the number of calories that you should consume, you can look up a chart and find the category in which you would fall. Or, with the easy availability of online resources, you can go to a site on the Internet that will do the calculation for you. One such site is www.shapefit.com/dailycalorie-calc.html. This site, like many others, only provides an estimate, but it is a helpful basic guide to use. On the other hand, you can get as complicated as you want with this. If you like, you can determine your basal metabolic rate (BMR), which is the number of calories you'd burn if you stayed in bed all day (wouldn't we all like to do that once in awhile!). To calculate your BMR and personal calories per day, you can try the following site: www.bmi-calculator.net/bmr-calculator/. Once you know your BMR, you can then use the online calculator to find out how many calories you can eat per day.

You will notice that as you age, you can eat less and less (not fair!)! But you can do some things to change this. For one, you can increase the amount of exercise that you do and thus increase your BMR, and/or you can get "more bang for the buck" and eat desserts that taste delicious but have fewer calories.

Ultimately the key to eating healthfully is being informed. You only have one body—take care of it. Be aware of what you put into it. As the saying goes, "You are what you eat!"

Nutritional Comparisons

How do the recipes in this book stack up nutritionally? Let's compare them to traditional recipes and see. As you look at this chart, keep in mind that you do not need to (and should not) consume any cholesterol. As you can see, the vegan recipes all have 0 milligrams of cholesterol, and the regular recipes have quite a lot of cholesterol, varying from 24 milligrams per serving of All-American Apple Crumb Pie (page 156) to 176 milligrams per serving of Caramel Apple Streusel Cheesecake (page 201). Look at it this way: A 1,500-calorie diet should not contain more than 11 grams of saturated fat per day. One serving of the regularly prepared Raised Sugar Cake (page 90) uses up that total allotment by itself with a whopping 13 grams! And the Caramel Apple Streusel Cheesecake is way over that amount for just one serving. But fortunately, the vegan version of the cheesecake comes in at only 4 grams of saturated fat per serving, thus allowing you to indulge in this treat once in a while without ruining your healthy diet!

How to "Veganize" Your Own Recipes

Once you have become comfortable with making some of the recipes in this book, you may want to try to "veganize" some of your own favorite recipes. Here are some easy substitutions you can make to accomplish this.

You can replace any milk in a recipe with a vegan milk of your choice. There are many kinds. I like to use almond milk the best. But there's also rice, hemp, and soy, to name some major contenders. If these aren't to your liking, there are others as well. Research on the Internet and check with a local health food store. You would use the same amount of vegan milk as dairy milk when baking. In

Food	Calories per serving	Total fat (g) per serving	Cholesterol (mg) per serving	Saturated fat (g) per serving
Raised Sugar Cake—Vegan*	656	25	0	2
Raised Sugar Cake—Regular	745	32	81	13
Caramel Apple Streusel Cheesecake—Vegan*	541	26	0	4
Caramel Apple Streusel Cheesecake—Regular	551	35	176	21
Brownies—Vegan*	126	<1	0	<1
Brownies—Regular	141	7	40	3
Hot Cocoa—Vegan*	136	5	0	<1
Hot Cocoa—Regular	441	8	35	5
Apple Crumb Pie—Vegan*	268	9	0	3
Apple Crumb Pie—Regular	440	20	24	9

*Vegan Recipes

pudding recipes, you may have to add an additional thickener such as arrowroot to achieve the desired consistency.

Butter can be replaced with a variety of ingredients such as applesauce, mashed bananas, canola oil, whipped tofu, or prune butter, depending on the recipe. The texture of the finished product will vary, depending on which substitute you choose. You may want to experiment with several choices until you get the results you want. Another consideration when substituting butter is how healthy you want your cake to be. Applesauce, prune butter, tofu, or bananas will produce the healthiest dessert, but will be different in texture and taste. If you are making something chocolate, which has a strong flavor of its own, the taste of the applesauce, prune butter, or bananas might not make much of a difference. Using whipped tofu will not alter the flavor, but the texture will be different. If you want to stay close to the taste and texture of the original cake, you can substitute vegan butter spread or shortening—just remember to read the label and try to buy a brand that is nonhydrogenated.

Eggs are another ingredient that should be replaced. I use flax powder, xanthan gum, or commercial egg replacer, depending on the recipe. I suggest using the xanthan gum in a non-wheat-based recipe because it also helps the product rise and replaces the gluten as well. In most wheat-based desserts, I mix 1 teaspoon of flax powder with ¼ cup of water for every egg. If the dessert that I am making is light colored or a lighter cake, such as My Grandmother's Crumb Cake recipe (page 70), I opt for a commercial egg replacer such as Ener-G. I use the same ratio as the flax powder—1 teaspoon of egg replacer and ¼ cup of water for each egg. Whipped egg whites may be replaced in some recipes by commercial egg replacer. (Follow the directions on the back of the box.) When making meringue with commercial egg replacer, I have found that the pie must be eaten immediately or the meringue deflates. This type of meringue does not work for making crispy meringue cookies, and it is only marginally successful for angel food cakes.

Buying Vegan Ingredients

The quality of your finished product is directly related to the quality of the ingredients that you put into it. Be selective when choosing ingredients. I encourage you to always read ingredient labels to make sure you're choosing the healthiest products. You'll see that I mention several brand names throughout this book, but this does not in any way mean that these are the only products you should use. There are probably several other brands available that are equally healthy and would work just as well. These are just the brands that I use—I'm familiar with them and I like the results they produce, and they appear to be generally available at most supermarkets or health food stores. For example, I use Tofutti cream cheese for the cheesecakes. It has a creamy texture that is almost indistinguishable from regular cream cheese. If you choose to use another brand of cream cheese, be sure to test the texture and taste before you take the time and effort to make a cheesecake. If you do not like either the taste or texture of the cream cheese straight from the container, you will not like it in the cheesecake. I threw away several early attempts at desserts just because I didn't use the best vegan products to make them.

When buying vegan milk, look for a brand that is made from non-genetically modified ingredients. Vanilla vegan milk works well in many dessert recipes. If you can't find any vanilla-flavored product, you can simply add a teaspoon of vanilla extract to each cup of vegan milk.

I buy organic ingredients whenever possible. Not only do they taste better, but some studies indicate that they retain more of their natural nutrients than their chemically produced counterparts. Be sure to buy only the freshest ingredients. I try to use fresh in-season fruit whenever possible. That means that I can't make the Tropical Fruit Cake (page 67) in the winter because strawberries are not available locally where I live until the summer.

Stocking Your Vegan Pantry

To successfully make delicious vegan baked goods, you must be fully prepared, which means you should stock your pantry with several staples. Most of these ingredients can be purchased in large grocery stores or health food stores. If you can't find the ingredients in a store, I recommend that you do an Internet search and buy the ingredients directly from the manufacturer or from a large site. Searching for ingredients online is easy: Simply type the name of the ingredient that you are trying to find into your Internet browser and go from there. I can't stress strongly enough that your finished product will only be as good as the ingredients you put into it, so make sure that you take the time to select the proper ingredients. The ingredients listed below are common to many of the recipes in this book, and it's a good idea to be familiar with them.

Agar (also called agar-agar): This substance can be found in powder or flake form. It is made from red seaweed (although it is white in color when you buy it). It is the vegetarian form of gelatin and is used as a thickener. (Note: Agar is made from seaweed, whereas gelatin is derived from the collagen inside animals' skin and bones. Although both are used as a thickener, obviously agar is the way to go for vegan baked goods!)

Agave nectar: Agave nectar is an all-natural liquid sweetener created from the extract of the agave plant. Proponents of its use say that it doesn't spike blood sugar the way natural sugar does. However, when buying agave nectar, be aware of the type that you are purchasing. Many brands sold in the supermarket claim to be organic but are nothing more than refined fructose.

Almond milk: Almond milk is a creamy beverage made from ground almonds. Because it comes from a nonanimal source, it contains no cholesterol or lactose. It has a rich, creamy texture and can be substituted for dairy milk in an even swap.

Arrowroot flour: This flour is also known as arrowroot starch or simply arrowroot. It can be purchased in some grocery stores in the baking section or in most health food stores. It works as a thickener, has no taste of its own, and is easily digestible. Be careful not to boil arrowroot—continued heating tends to break down the arrowroot and diminish its thickening ability.

Barley flour: Barley is a hardy grain that was first cultivated in the Stone Age. Barley flour is made from ground pearl barley and is combined with a gluten-containing flour for use in baking. Therefore, it is low in gluten but not gluten free. It is easily digestible, wheat free, and is a good source of dietary fiber.

Brown rice syrup: This syrup is made by cooking brown rice flour or brown rice starch with enzymes. The syrup is filtered, and excess water is evaporated to thicken it. The sweetness can be adjusted. It is used as an alternative sweetener to replace sugar.

Carob (also known as carob powder): This is a chocolate alternative made from the pod of the honey locust tree that grows in the Mediterranean region. The pod is dried, roasted, and pulverized. It is naturally sweeter than chocolate.

Coconut oil: Rich in lauric acid, coconut oil is used primarily to make piecrusts tender and flaky. Coconut oil has no hydrogenated fat in it. It is naturally solid under 76°F. (Vegetable shortening is made from hydrogenated fat so that it is a solid at room temperatures.) It is high in saturated fat, and the jury is still out on the health benefits of this oil.

Ener-G Egg Replacer: This is a commercial egg replacer. The main ingredients are potato starch, tapioca flour, and leavening.

Flax powder: This powder is made from ground flaxseeds and is one of the only plant sources of omega-3 fatty acids. Flax powder has 540 milligrams of omega-3 per serving and is also high in fiber and lignans. It is mixed with water to replace eggs in vegan recipes. The ratio is ¼ cup of water to 1 teaspoon of flax powder.

Garbanzo bean flour (also known as chickpea flour): This flour is made from the garbanzo bean, a legume. Garbanzo beans, also called chickpeas, are high in protein and are a helpful source of zinc, folate, protein, and fiber.

Hemp milk: This vegan milk is made from the seeds of the edible part of the same plant (Cannabis sativa L.) used to make marijuana; however, the seeds and products made from them don't contain any THC delta-9-tetrahydrocannabinol (the psychotomimetic component of marijuana). Basically, this just means that you can't get high from hemp milk! People who are allergic to soy or dairy should be able to safely consume hemp milk. The taste of this "milk" is more creamy and nutty than either soy or rice milk. Furthermore, it is usually thicker.

Lignans: These are potential anticancer substances found in higher-order plants. Flaxseeds are high in lignans.

Maple syrup: This is a syrup made from the sap of several varieties of maple trees. The sap is collected and heated to concentrate the syrup. It is used as a substitute for white cane sugar. Items made with maple sugar have more of a brown sugar taste to them. Use only pure maple syrup, not maple-flavored pancake syrup that contains mostly corn syrup.

Rice flour: This flour can be used to thicken soups and stews and to provide an alternative to wheat flour in cakes and biscuits. It may be made from either white or brown rice.

Rice milk: Another vegan milk, this is a kind of grain milk made mostly from brown rice. It is commonly unsweetened because it has a naturally slightly sweet flavor. Some types of rice milk may nevertheless be sweetened with sugar cane syrup or other sugars, so read the label to be sure to get the type that you want. Rice milk is a great nondairy, nut-free milk alternative that may be substituted for dairy milk in an even swap.

Sea salt: Sea salt is higher in trace minerals than is table salt and additive-free.

Soy cream cheese: Cream cheese made with soy milk instead of cow's milk. There are many brands of soy cream cheese on the market, so be sure to read the labels. Many contain casein, a dairy-derived ingredient that should be avoided. Also, before you use it, be sure to test the soy cream cheese that you choose for flavor and texture. It should be pleasing in taste and similar in texture to Philadelphia Cream Cheese, or you may not be happy with the results of the recipe that you are making. I like to use Tofutti Brand soy cream cheese.

Soy milk: Many kinds of soy milk are on the market today, often available at local grocery stores. You'll probably need to experiment to find the type that you like the best. Again, read labels. Be sure to purchase a brand that is made with non-genetically engineered soybeans. Brands such as Edensoy are nuttier in taste and have a slightly brownish tint to them. They work well in all these recipes, but you may want a soy milk that more closely resembles the color of cow's milk. Silk brand soy milk and 8th Continent soy milk are both nearly white like cow's milk. If you want a sweeter end product, use vanilla soy milk. If you have plain soy milk and the recipe calls for vanilla soy milk, simply add 1 teaspoon of vanilla extract for every cup of soy milk. Other nondairy milks may be substituted for soy milk. Feel free to explore the many options that are available. Any vegan milk will work in most of these recipes. In the rare case that a certain type is better, I will recommend it.

Spelt flour: This is a flour that is more quickly and easily digested than most grains because of its high water solubility. It is considered a high-energy grain because it has more protein, fiber, fat, iron, zinc, copper, and vitamins B_1 and B_2 than does wheat. Spelt flour contains gluten, but it's tolerated by many people with gluten allergies.

Stevia: Stevia is an extraordinarily sweet herb (200 to 300 times sweeter than sugar) used as a sugar substitute. In the past few years it has become much more common. Because of its extreme sweetness it is a little difficult to use in baking. I did use a baking form, which I found on the Internet, in a cookie recipe in the sugar-free/gluten-free/vegan section.

Sucanat: Sucanat stands for "sugar cane natural." It is a sweetener made from dried, granulated cane sugar. The mineral salts and vitamins naturally present in sugar cane are preserved because only the water and fiber are removed in the processing of this product. It is coarsely granular, dark in color like brown sugar, and tastes a little like molasses.

Tahini: This is a paste made from ground sesame seeds commonly used in savory dishes like hummus; you can also use it in sweet recipes.

Textured vegetable protein (TVP): TVP is a food product produced from soybeans that makes an excellent meat substitute. It has a long shelf life if stored properly and is an excellent source of protein and fiber.

Tofu: Tofu is a vegan staple. If you have not discovered this wonder food, it's about time that you do! There are two different types of tofu. Japanese-style tofu, also called silken tofu, is usually sold in 12-ounce aseptic boxes on store shelves. It can be found in most grocery stores. It has a creamy texture when processed in a food processor and is best suited for the recipes in this book. It works well to make puddings, cream sauces, frostings, and as an egg replacer in baking. The other type of tofu is Chinese style. It is usually packed in 1-pound tubs of water and has a spongier texture. It is much better suited for stir-fries, where the tofu needs to hold its shape. If you try to use this type of tofu for making puddings, cream sauces, or frostings you will probably be disappointed with the results. The texture will be grainy rather than smooth. Also remember to read labels and be sure to buy tofu made with non-genetically modified soybeans.

Vegan butter spread: This is used to replace butter in vegan baking recipes when you want to retain the same texture as the original recipe. Be sure to read the labels on butter spreads before buying them. Most nondairy margarines are vegan; however, not all are healthy. Choose one that is made with a healthy oil such as canola and does not contain any hydrogenated or partially hydrogenated fats. I prefer to use Spectrum or Earth Balance brand.

Vegan cream cheese: There are many vegan nondairy products these days; vegan cream cheese is made from a nondairy base. Most vegan cream cheeses are soy based.

Vegetable shortening: You probably have a can of vegetable shortening sitting in your pantry right now. To ensure a healthier vegan product, don't use it until you read the label. Chances are that it is made with hydrogenated fats. Spectrum and Earth Balance make good nonhydrogenated shortening. Prior to finding these products I didn't make recipes that used shortening. Life just keeps getting better!

Xanthan gum: Xanthan gum is made from a tiny microorganism called *Xanthomonas campestris*. It can be used to replace gluten in wheat-free recipes (gluten is what helps the baked good rise), and it can also be added to recipes as a stabilizer. It can be found in the baking section of some grocery stores. If you can't find xanthan gum and do not wish to purchase it over the Internet, you may substitute powdered pectin (equal substitution for xanthan gum). The taste and texture will vary slightly, but the end product will still be good.

Suggested Kitchen Equipment

To bake, all you really need are a few simple tools; the list below will help you outfit your own baker's kitchen with ease.

Blender: A good blender is useful to use to make smoothies and some of the creamed recipes. I splurged on a Vita-Mix blender and use it for either a food processor or a blender.

Electric mixer: You can use one to mix some of the recipes if you like. I mix most of my cakes by hand.

Food processor: I encourage you to invest in a good food processor (if you don't already have one) to process the silken tofu into a smooth, creamy consistency. Small food processors (1-cup capacity) are nice for pureeing small amounts of tofu or chopping nuts for a garnish, but a larger (3-quart capacity) food processor is necessary for the cheesecakes and frostings.

Immersion blender (a.k.a. stick blender or hand blender): This is a cheaper alternative to the food processor and can be used to cream the tofu in these recipes. It will take longer to cream the tofu, and you must stand and hold it the entire time rather than allowing the food processor to do it on its own, but the result will be the same. It can be purchased in most kitchen supply stores.

Parchment paper: Parchment paper is useful because it keeps food from coming in direct contact with the baking pan, thus preventing sticking. There is no need to grease a cookie sheet ever again if you use parchment paper. I use it to line pans, roll out crusts, and place doughnuts on to rise.

Pie weights: These are clay or metal balls that are placed in a piecrust while it bakes to prevent it from shrinking or bubbling up. You can find them in most kitchen supply stores.

Springform pan: This is a round, straight-sided baking pan that has sides that can be unclamped and removed. It works well for making cheesecakes, Boston cream pies, and other types of cakes that you do not want to flip out of a pan.

Peaceful Vegans

> Eating vegetables and tofu will keep you in peace.
> —CHINESE FOLK SAYING

> "Spare Me," says the animal
> When a small animal is killed
> and trembling. It wants to say "Spare Me" but who is hearing!
> I beg all the mankind who wants peace
> try to have great compassion and stop killing!
> —MENCIUS CA. 372–289 BC,
> CHINESE PHILOSOPHER

> For as long as man continues to be the ruthless destroyer
> of lower living beings, he will never know health or peace.
> For as long as men massacre animals, they will kill each other.
> Indeed, he who sows the seeds of murder and pain
> cannot reap joy and love.
> —PYTHAGORAS
> 6TH CENTURY BC, GREEK PHILOSOPHER
> AND MATHEMATICIAN

Many people strongly believe that by becoming vegan you become more aware of other living things around you. You develop empathy for living creatures, no matter how small. If this is true, would this make a more peaceful world in which to live? Would we be as quick to solve differences with war—the senseless killing of human beings—if we did not even condone the senseless killing of animals for food? What do you think?

Gone Vegan? You're Not Alone

You might be surprised to know the vast number of past and present famous vegans. For example, respected American pediatrician Benjamin Spock was raised as a vegetarian until the age of twelve. This is all the more interesting because he was born in 1903, long before being a vegetarian was the "in" thing to do. He grew to be 6 feet 4 inches tall on this diet and even earned a spot on the Olympic rowing crew that won a gold medal in the 1924 Olympic Games. Not too shabby! At some point during young adulthood, Dr. Spock began to eat a SAD (Standard American Diet) diet composed of typical high-fat fare. He continued this dietary regimen until he had a mild stroke at the age of eighty-eight, at which point he returned to vegetarianism. He eventually became vegan and lived to the ripe old age of ninety-five. There are many famous people—actors, actresses, athletes, and singers—who are vegan. If you're curious who's vegan, try typing "famous vegans" into your computer's browser for a current list. Not only are famous people finding the benefits that come with a vegan diet, but many others are as well. It's getting easier (and tastier) to be vegan all the time!

COOKIES AND BROWNIES

VANILLA SPRITZ COOKIES

This recipe is easy to use in a cookie press and makes dainty and delicious vanilla cookies. I like to include them in my cookie tray assortment during the holiday season.

Makes about 6 dozen cookies

Preparation time: 15 minutes ▼ **Baking time:** 8 minutes per tray

1 cup soft vegan butter spread, preferably tub style, at room temperature. (If using stick butter, soften it in the microwave until it is the consistency of tub butter. Do not melt!)

½ cup vegetable shortening

1 cup granulated sweetener

1 teaspoon egg replacer (such as Ener-G)

¼ cup water

¼ cup vegan milk

1 teaspoon vanilla extract

4 cups unbleached all-purpose flour

1 teaspoon baking powder

▶ Preheat the oven to 400°F. Line cookie sheets with parchment paper.

▶ Cream the butter, shortening, and sweetener together in a medium-size bowl. In a small cup, mix the egg replacer and ¼ cup of water. Add the egg replacer mixture, milk, and vanilla to the butter mixture and stir to combine. Mix the flour and baking powder in a separate bowl and add slowly to the butter mixture.

▶ The batter will be stiff and should form a ball in the bowl. (If the batter is too sticky, add a little flour. If the mixture is too dry, add more milk.) Do not chill the dough. Place the dough in a cookie press and press out cookies onto the prepared cookie sheet. If you do not have a cookie press, chill the dough for about 1 hour, then roll it between two pieces of waxed paper until it is ¼ inch thick. Cut it into shapes using cookie cutters. You can use the rim of a drinking glass as an alternative to a cookie cutter. The amount of cookies that this recipe makes will vary, depending on the size of the cookie cutter that you use. Cookies made using a cookie press are generally small, so count on fewer cookies if you roll them out and cut them into shapes.

▶ Bake for 8 minutes. Let cool on a wire rack.

PER SERVING: 64 calories, 3 g fat (<1 g saturated), 8 g carbohydrate, <1 g dietary fiber, <1 g protein, 0 mg cholesterol, 16 mg sodium, 9 mg potassium. Calories from fat: 44 percent.

Variation: Try melting vegan chocolate chips and dip each cookie halfway into the chocolate for black-and-white cookies. Or, add 2 teaspoons of lemon or orange extract for lemon or orange spritz cookies. These fruit-flavored cookies are also delicious dipped in chocolate.

SNAPPY GINGER COOKIES

These cookies remind me of the ones I used to buy at the grocery store around Halloween—crispy and spicy. They taste great dunked in cold vegan milk or hot coffee.

> Makes about 5 dozen cookies

Preparation time: 15 minutes ▼ **Baking time:** 6 minutes per tray

1 cup vegetable shortening (preferably nonhydrogenated, such as Spectrum or Earth Balance)

1 cup brown sugar

1 teaspoon flax powder

¼ cup water

1 cup molasses

3 tablespoons grated fresh ginger, or 1 tablespoon ground

2 tablespoons white vinegar

2½ cups unbleached all-purpose flour

2½ cups whole wheat flour

1½ teaspoons baking soda

½ teaspoon salt

1 teaspoon ground cinnamon

1 teaspoon ground cloves

PER SERVING: 90 calories, 4 g fat (1 g saturated), 14 g carbohydrate, <1 g dietary fiber, 1 g protein, 0 mg cholesterol, 35 mg sodium, 118 mg potassium. Calories from fat: 34 percent.

▶ Preheat the oven to 375°F. Line cookie sheets with parchment paper or grease lightly.

▶ Cream the shortening and sugar together in a large bowl. In a cup, combine the flax powder and ¼ cup of water. Add the flax mixture, molasses, fresh ginger, and vinegar to the shortening mixture. Beat until combined.

▶ Sift together the dry ingredients, including all the spices, in another bowl. Add to the shortening mixture and stir to combine. Roll out the dough ¼ inch thick between two pieces of waxed paper. Remove the top piece of waxed paper and cut the cookies into shapes. You may use decorative cookie cutters, or if you do not have cookie cutters, you may use the top edge of an 8-ounce drinking glass to cut the cookies. The number of cookies that you make will vary, depending on the size of the cookie cutter(s) that you use. I based the number of cookies in this recipe on 2-inch round cookies. (If the dough is hard to work with, refrigerate until it is stiffer—about 2 hours.)

▶ Place on the prepared cookie sheets. Bake for 5 to 6 minutes. Allow to cool slightly, transfer to a wire rack, and let cool completely.

HOME-STYLE
CHOCOLATE CHIP COOKIES

These cookies are a real favorite at my house and disappear fast! But they're so easy to make that I don't mind.

(Makes about 4 dozen cookies)

Preparation time: 10 minutes ▼ **Baking time:** 20 minutes per tray

2½ cups pure maple syrup

1 cup canola oil

2 cups vegan chocolate chips

2 teaspoons vanilla extract

7 cups barley flour

▸ Preheat the oven to 350°F. Line cookie sheets with parchment paper or grease lightly.

▸ Combine the maple syrup, canola oil, chocolate chips, and vanilla in a medium-size bowl. Add the barley flour and stir to combine. Drop teaspoon-size amounts onto the prepared cookie sheets.

▸ Bake for 20 minutes (or until the cookies just begin to brown).

▸ Allow to cool for 5 minutes. Transfer to a wire rack and let cool completely.

Variation: Try substituting 1 teaspoon of peppermint extract for the 1 of the teaspoons of vanilla, for an interesting-tasting mint chocolate chip cookie.

PER SERVING: 254 calories, 9 g fat (2 g saturated), 42 g carbohydrate, 2 g dietary fiber, 14 g sugar, 3 g protein, 0 mg cholesterol, 6 mg sodium, 105 mg potassium. Calories from fat: 31 percent.

Hint: If you measure out the oil before the maple syrup, the maple syrup will come out of the measuring cup more easily.

LITTLE OATIES

Same delicious taste as traditional oatmeal cookies, but much quicker and easier to make!

Makes 3½ dozen cookies

Preparation time: 10 minutes ▼ **Baking time:** 15 minutes per tray

2½ cups pure maple syrup

½ cup brown sugar or Sucanat

¼ cup unsweetened applesauce (preferably organic)

1 cup canola oil

2 teaspoons vanilla extract

3 cups barley flour

6 cups rolled oats

1 teaspoon baking soda

▸ Preheat the oven to 350°F. Line cookie sheets with parchment paper or grease lightly.

▸ Combine the maple syrup, sugar, apple sauce, canola oil, and vanilla in a medium-size bowl and stir. Add the barley flour, oats, and baking soda, and mix. Drop teaspoon-size amounts onto the prepared cookie sheets.

▸ Bake for 15 minutes (or until the cookies just begin to brown).

▸ Allow to cool for 5 minutes. Transfer to a wire rack and let cool completely.

Variations: Try adding 1 cup of chocolate chips for oatmeal chocolate chip cookies. Or replace 1 cup of oats with 1 cup of unsweetened coconut and add 1 cup of chocolate chips for a deliciously rich-tasting cookie.

PER SERVING: 160 calories, 6 g fat (<1 g saturated), 26 g carbohydrate, 1 g dietary fiber, 12 g sugar, 2 g protein, 0 mg cholesterol, 45 mg sodium, 88 mg potassium. Calories from fat: 31 percent.

Hint: If you measure out the oil before the maple syrup, the maple syrup will come out of the measuring cup more easily!

MOM'S WARM
PEANUT BUTTER COOKIES

My husband loves peanut butter cookies and he's always asking me to make them.
Since I (like all moms) have a busy schedule, I created this recipe to be tasty, healthy,
and very easy to make. It has only five ingredients—how's that for simple?

Makes about 4 dozen cookies

Preparation time: 10 minutes ▼ **Baking time:** 20 minutes per tray

1 cup pure maple syrup

½ cup canola oil

1 cup natural peanut butter

2 teaspoons vanilla extract

2 cups unbleached all-purpose
flour

▶ Preheat the oven to 350°F. Line cookie sheets with parchment paper or grease lightly.

▶ Combine the maple syrup, canola oil, peanut butter, and vanilla in a medium-size bowl. Add the flour and stir to combine. Form the dough into teaspoon-size balls with your hands.

▶ Place the balls ½ to 1 inch apart on the prepared cookie sheets. Crisscross the tines of a fork across the top of each cookie to make perpendicular imprints.

▶ Bake for 20 minutes. Allow to cool for 5 minutes. Transfer to a wire rack and let cool completely.

Variations: Roll the dough into balls. Instead of pressing down with a fork, make a hole in the center of each ball with your fingertip or knuckle, being careful not to press all the way through the cookie. Bake as directed above. When the cookies are completely cool, fill the hole with grape jelly for peanut butter and jelly cookies. Or you can melt vegan chocolate chips and fill the hole with the melted chocolate for chocolate peanut butter cookies. Chill before serving.

PER SERVING: 89 calories, 5 g fat (<1 g saturated), 10 g carbohydrate, <1 g dietary fiber, 4 g sugar, 2 g protein, 0 mg cholesterol, 26 mg sodium, 55 mg potassium. Calories from fat: 49 percent.

SNICKERDOODLES

I grew up eating these delicious cookies with a funny name. They're crispy vanilla cookies rolled in cinnamon and sugar, then baked. Guaranteed not to last long!

Makes about 3 dozen cookies

Preparation time: 15 minutes ▼ **Baking time:** 20 minutes per tray

½ cup vegan butter spread, such as Spectrum or Earth Balance (I use tub style. If you choose to use stick style, be sure to soften but not melt it.)

½ cup vegetable shortening (preferably nonhydrogenated, such as Spectrum)

1 cup granulated sweetener

2 teaspoons vanilla extract

¼ teaspoon salt

½ cup water

2 teaspoons flax powder

3 cups unbleached all-purpose flour

½ cup sugar

½ teaspoon ground cinnamon

▶ Preheat the oven to 375°F. Coat cookie sheets with non-stick cooking spray or line with parchment paper.

▶ Cream the butter spread, shortening, and granulated sweetener together. Add the vanilla and salt and stir to combine. In a small cup, mix the ½ cup of water and the flax powder, add to the shortening mixture, and stir to combine. Add the flour and mix well.

▶ In a small, wide bowl, mix the sugar and cinnamon. Form the dough into 1-inch balls. Roll in the cinnamon mixture. Place ½ to 1 inch apart on the prepared cookie sheets.

▶ Flatten the balls with the floured bottom of a drinking glass and bake for 20 minutes. Remove from the oven immediately and transfer to a wire rack to cool.

Variation: Try rolling the cookies in plain sugar for vegan sugar cookies.

PER SERVING: 113 calories, 5 g fat (1g saturated), 16 g carbohydrate, <1 g dietary fiber, 1 g protein, 0 mg cholesterol, 13 mg sodium, 16 mg potassium. Calories from fat: 37 percent.

CHOCOLATE-COCONUT CRISPS

I had leftover chocolate cookie dough from the crust of a cheesecake I was making and wondered what it would taste like with coconut mixed in. I tried it and liked it, so I worked to adjust the recipe and voilà—Chocolate-Coconut Crisps.

Makes about 3 dozen cookies

Preparation time: 15 minutes ▼ **Baking time:** 20 minutes per tray

½ cup vegan butter spread, such as Spectrum or Earth Balance (I use tub style. If you choose to use stick style, be sure to soften but not melt it.)

½ cup vegetable shortening (preferably nonhydrogenated, such as Spectrum)

1 cup granulated sweetener

½ cup pure maple syrup

2 teaspoons coconut extract

¼ teaspoon salt

½ cup water

2 teaspoons flax powder

2½ cups unbleached all-purpose flour

½ cup unsweetened cocoa powder

½ cup unsweetened shredded coconut

▶ Preheat the oven to 375°F. Coat cookie sheets with non-stick cooking spray or line with parchment paper.

▶ Cream together the butter spread, shortening, granulated sweetener, and maple syrup. Add the coconut extract and salt and stir to combine. In a small cup, mix the ½ cup of water and the flax powder, add to the shortening mixture, and stir to combine. Add the flour and cocoa powder and mix well.

▶ Place the coconut in a shallow bowl. Form the dough into 1-inch balls and roll in the coconut.

▶ Place ½ to 1 inch apart on the prepared baking sheets. Flatten the balls with the floured bottom of a drinking glass.

▶ Bake for 20 minutes. Remove from the oven immediately and transfer to a wire rack to cool.

PER SERVING: 113 calories, 5 g fat (2 g saturated), 16 g carbohydrate, <1g dietary fiber, 3 g sugar, 1 g protein, 0 mg cholesterol, 14 mg sodium, 43 mg potassium. Calories from fat: 40 percent.

Gluten-Free/Sugar-Free Vegan Cookies

The following four cookies are gluten free.

....

Peanut Butter Cookies Extraordinaire ♡

This cookie recipe is chock-full of healthy ingredients. Its base is teff flour, a gluten-free flour that may be used to substitute for other flours. Its nutty flavor adds a pleasant sweetness to any recipe. Flax oil boosts the nutritional power of this cookie, and agave nectar adds just a touch of sweetness. With all the nutritional goodness, it's hard to believe they taste yummy!

Makes 1½ dozen cookies

Preparation time: 5 minutes ▼ **Baking time:** 15 minutes

½ cup peanut butter

⅓ cup agave nectar

⅓ cup flax oil

¼ teaspoon vanilla extract

2 cups teff flour

PER SERVING: 144 çalories, 7.9 g fat (0 g saturated fat), 15.9 g carbohydrate, <1 g dietary fiber, 4.2 g sugar, 3.2 g protein, 0 mg cholesterol, 34 mg sodium. Calories from fat: 12 percent.

▶ Preheat the oven to 350°F. Line cookie sheets with parchment paper.

▶ Put the peanut butter in a bowl. Add the agave nectar and flax oil and cream together. Add the vanilla and mix. Add the teff flour and stir to combine.

▶ Roll dough into walnut-sized balls and then flatten with the floured bottom of a drinking glass or drop teaspoon-size plops onto the prepared cookie sheets. Bake at 350°F for 15 minutes. Transfer to a wire rack and let cool completely. The cookies will have a tender texture.

OATMEAL FREEBIES ♡

I was inspired to make these cookies by a woman who e-mailed me from Florida, wanting a gluten-free, sugar-free oatmeal cookie recipe. We both worked on it and here is the result. These cookies are so tasty you'll forget they're good for you, too! Thank you, Florida gluten-free vegan!

Makes 2½ dozen cookies

Preparation time: 5 minutes ▼ **Baking time:** 30 minutes

⅓ cup flax oil

1 cup vegan milk

1 teaspoon vanilla extract

⅔ cup agave nectar

1 cup brown rice flour

4 cups gluten-free rolled oats

1 teaspoon xanthan gum

½ teaspoon baking soda

¾ cup stevia (see Note)

► Preheat the oven to 350°F. Line cookie sheets with parchment paper.

► In a large bowl, mix the flax oil, milk, vanilla, and agave nectar. In a smaller bowl, combine the brown rice flour, oats, xanthan gum, baking soda, and stevia.

► Slowly pour the dry ingredients into the wet, stirring as you do this. Stir to combine completely.

► Drop tablespoon-size portions onto the prepared cookie sheets. Flatten with the back of a spoon. Bake for 30 minutes. Allow to cool for 5 minutes on the cookie sheets, then transfer to a wire rack and let cool completely.

PER SERVING: 87 calories, 3.5 g fat (0 g saturated fat), 11.9 g carbohydrate, 1.4 g dietary fiber, 0.4 g sugar, 2.1 g protein, 0 mg cholesterol, 27 mg sodium. Calories from fat: 5 percent.

Note: Use baking stevia (I used Stevia Baking Blend, available at https://nunaturals.com/product/94).

NO-BAKE OATMEAL COOKIES

This nutrient-packed snack cookie is good any time of the day!

Makes 1 dozen cookies

Soaking time: 8 hours
Preparation time: 5 minutes ▼ **Dehydration time:** 4 hours

2 cups raw cashews (soaked for 8 hours)

4 pitted dates

½ teaspoon vanilla extract

2 teaspoons water

⅔ cups gluten-free rolled oats

PER SERVING: 157 calories, 10.9 g fat (2.1 g saturated fat), 12.6 g carbohydrate, 1.4 g dietary fiber, 3 g sugar, 4.2 g protein, 0 mg cholesterol, 4 mg sodium. Calories from fat: 17 percent.

▸ Preheat your oven to its lowest temperature (I have an electric range and put it on the WARM setting) or, if you have a dehydrator, follow the manufacturer's directions for the appropriate temperature setting. Line a cookie sheet or the dehydrator tray with parchment paper.

▸ Put all the ingredients in a food processor or Vita-Mix blender and puree until smooth.

▸ Form the dough into teaspoon-size balls and flatten on the prepared cookie sheet.

▸ Leave in the oven for 4 hours at the lowest temperature, or follow the manufacturer's directions for your dehydrator.

NO-BAKE CHOCOLATE COOKIES

These no-bake goodies are also packed with nutrients—and chocolate!

Makes 1 dozen cookies

Soaking time: 8 hours
Preparation time: 5 minutes ▼ **Dehydration time:** 4 hours

2 cups raw cashews
   (soaked for 8 hours)

4 pitted dates

¼ teaspoon vanilla extract

4 teaspoons water

1 tablespoon unsweetened
   cocoa powder

PER SERVING: 140 calories, 10.7 g fat
(2.1 g saturated fat), 9.8 g
carbohydrate, 1 g dietary fiber, 2.9 g
sugar, 3.6 g protein, 0 mg cholesterol,
4 mg sodium. Calories from fat: 16
percent.

▶ Preheat your oven to its lowest temperature (I have an electric range and put it on the WARM setting) or, if you have a dehydrator, follow the manufacturer's directions for the appropriate temperature setting. Line a cookie sheet or the dehydrator tray with parchment paper.

▶ Put all the ingredients in a food processor or Vita-Mix blender and puree until smooth.

▶ Form the dough into teaspoon-size balls and flatten on the prepared cookie sheet.

▶ Leave in the oven for 4 hours at the lowest temperature, or follow the manufacturer's directions for your dehydrator.

I Can't Believe They're Not Sinful Brownies

This was one of the first recipes I ever "veganized." There are times when I simply must have chocolate! I can even eat the batter of these brownies before they are baked. That's an added bonus for vegan recipes—you don't have to worry about the health hazards of raw eggs in the batter, so you can sneak batter to your heart's content.

Makes 9 servings

Preparation time: 10 minutes ▼ **Baking time:** 40 to 47 minutes
Freezes well

1⅓ cups granulated sweetener

¾ cup unsweetened applesauce (preferably organic)

½ cup + 2 tablespoons water

2 teaspoons flax powder

2 teaspoons vanilla extract

1⅓ cups unbleached all-purpose flour

¾ cup unsweetened cocoa powder

½ teaspoon baking powder

¼ teaspoon salt

▶ Preheat the oven to 350°F. Coat an 8-inch square baking pan with nonstick cooking spray.

▶ Stir together the granulated sweetener, applesauce, and 2 tablespoons of the water in a medium-size bowl. In a small cup, mix the flax powder with the remaining ½ cup of water. Add to the applesauce mixture and stir to combine. Add the vanilla and stir.

▶ In another small bowl, combine the flour, cocoa powder, baking powder, and salt. Add the applesauce mixture to the flour mixture. Stir just to combine and pour into the prepared pan.

▶ Bake for 40 minutes for chewy brownies, 45 to 47 minutes for cakelike brownies.

▶ Allow to cool in the pan before serving.

PER SERVING: 225 calories, 1 g fat (<1 g saturated), 54 g carbohydrate, 3 g dietary fiber, 3 g protein, 0 mg cholesterol, 29 mg sodium, 146 mg potassium. Calories from fat: 4 percent.

Hint: Brownies are difficult to test for doneness. Using the toothpick-in-the-center method is not a reliable measure. I usually do the touch test. When you touch the top of the brownies, it should not leave an indentation. If it does, the batter is still soft. You may want to experiment with baking times, and when you have made brownies that are the exact doneness that you like, write that time on the recipe. Oven temperatures vary and everyone likes brownies baked to a different doneness. I like brownies gooey and moist. If you like them cakelike, you will have to adjust the baking time.

DEATH BY CHOCOLATE BROWNIES

Warning: These brownies are for the serious chocolate lover only! They are not quite as healthy as the I Can't Believe They're Not Sinful Brownies (page 35), but they are my favorite brownie recipe. I could live on these brownies!

Makes 16 servings

Preparation time: brownies, 10 minutes; topping, 10 minutes
Baking time: 40 to 47 minutes ▾ **Freezes well**

1⅓ cups granulated sweetener

¾ cup unsweetened applesauce
(preferably organic)

½ cup + 2 tablespoons water

2 teaspoons flax powder

2 teaspoons vanilla extract

1⅓ cups unbleached all-purpose
flour

¾ cup unsweetened cocoa powder

½ teaspoon baking powder

¼ teaspoon salt

1 cup vegan chocolate chips

Chocolate topping:

1 cup powdered sugar

¼ cup canola oil

½ teaspoon vanilla extract

⅙ cup unsweetened cocoa powder
(fill a ⅓-cup measuring cup
only half full)

3½ tablespoons arrowroot

½ cup water

- ▶ Preheat the oven to 350°F. Coat an 8-inch square baking pan with nonstick cooking spray.
- ▶ Stir together the granulated sweetener, applesauce, and 2 tablespoons of the water in a medium-size bowl. In a small cup, mix the flax powder with the remaining ½ cup of water. Add to the applesauce mixture and stir to combine. Add the vanilla and stir.
- ▶ In another small bowl, combine the flour, cocoa powder, baking powder, and salt. Add the applesauce mixture to the flour mixture. Stir just to combine. Add the chocolate chips and stir to combine. Pour into the prepared pan.
- ▶ Bake for 40 minutes for chewy brownies, 45 to 47 minutes for cakelike brownies (or until middle brownie is set when you touch it, meaning you don't leave finger imprint but it's not too springy and cakelike).
- ▶ To make the chocolate topping: While the brownies are baking, place the powdered sugar, canola oil, vanilla, cocoa powder, and arrowroot in a small saucepan. Stir to combine, using a wire whisk for best results. Stir in the ½ cup of water. Place over medium-high heat and keep stirring until the mixture starts to thicken, but do not boil.
- ▶ Pour the hot topping over the brownies and smooth out evenly. Allow to cool in the pan completely before serving.

PER SERVING: 223 calories, 8 g fat (3 g saturated), 40 g carbohydrate, 3 g dietary fiber, 3 g protein, 0 mg cholesterol, 18 mg sodium, 107 mg potassium. Calories from fat: 29 percent.

Hint: When making the topping, I hold the pan over the heat. As I allow the topping to thicken, I don't have it sitting directly on the burner. This enables it to thicken more quickly, but still keeps it from coming to a boil. The thickening power of arrowroot is destroyed if it boils. The topping will thicken more as it cools, which is why it should be spread on the brownies immediately and then allowed to cool.

SWIRLY BERRY BROWNIES

I created these brownies to add a little variety to plain brownies. Sometimes I cut them up into bite-size pieces and put them on my cookie tray at holiday time.

Makes 9 servings

Preparation time: 10 minutes ▼ **Baking time:** 45 to 50 minutes
Freezes well

1⅓ cups granulated sweetener

¾ cup unsweetened applesauce (preferably organic)

½ cup + 2 tablespoons water

2 teaspoons flax powder

2 teaspoons vanilla extract

1⅓ cups unbleached all-purpose flour

¾ cup unsweetened cocoa powder

½ teaspoon baking powder

¼ teaspoon salt

½ cup raspberry preserves

PER SERVING: 280 calories, 2 g fat (<1 g saturated), 66 g carbohydrate, 4 g dietary fiber, 4 g protein, 0 mg cholesterol, 37 mg sodium, 178 mg potassium. Calories from fat: 6 percent.

▶ Preheat the oven to 350°F. Coat an 8-inch square baking pan with nonstick cooking spray.

▶ Stir together the granulated sweetener, applesauce, and 2 tablespoons of the water in a medium-size bowl. In a small cup, mix the flax powder with the remaining ½ cup of water. Add to the applesauce mixture and stir to combine. Add the vanilla and stir.

▶ In another small bowl, combine the flour, cocoa powder, baking powder, and salt. Add the applesauce mixture to the flour mixture. Stir just to combine and pour into the prepared pan. Drop spoonfuls of raspberry preserves on top of the brownie batter. Using a knife, swirl the preserves into the batter. Do not mix in completely.

▶ Bake for 45 minutes for chewy brownies, 50 minutes for cakelike brownies.

▶ Allow to cool in the pan before serving.

HEAVENLY BROWNIE TORTE

I created this dessert to dress up plain old brownies when I was baking for a restaurant. I saw one like it at an exclusive bakery that wasn't vegan. It looked so good that I just had to give it a shot.

> Makes 12 servings

Preparation time: brownies, 10 minutes; caramel, 10 minutes; chocolate candy coating, 10 minutes
Baking time: 40 to 47 minutes ▼ **Assembly:** 10 minutes

1⅓ cups granulated sweetener

¾ cup unsweetened applesauce (preferably organic)

½ cup + 2 tablespoons water

2 teaspoons flax powder

2 teaspoons vanilla extract

1⅓ cups unbleached all-purpose flour

¾ cup unsweetened cocoa powder

½ teaspoon baking powder

¼ teaspoon salt

½ cup vegan chocolate chips

Caramel sauce:
(make the day before if possible)

⅓ cup corn syrup

⅓ cup brown sugar

2 teaspoons vanilla extract

¼ teaspoon salt

3½ tablespoons vegan milk

▶ Preheat the oven to 350°F. Coat an 8-inch round baking pan with nonstick cooking spray. Line the bottom of the pan with parchment or waxed paper.

▶ Stir together the granulated sweetener, applesauce, and the 2 tablespoons of water in a medium-size bowl. In a small cup, mix the flax powder with the remaining ½ cup of water. Add to the applesauce mixture and stir to combine. Add the vanilla and stir.

▶ In another small bowl, combine the flour, cocoa powder, baking powder, and salt. Add the applesauce mixture to the flour mixture. Stir just to combine. Add the chocolate chips and stir to combine. Pour into the prepared pan and bake for 40 minutes for chewy brownies, 45 to 47 minutes for cakelike brownies. Allow to cool for 10 minutes in the pan. Remove from the pan and let cool completely on a wire rack before assembling.

▶ To make the caramel sauce: While the brownies are baking, place the corn syrup and brown sugar in a small pan. Heat over medium-high heat until boiling. Simmer until the sugar reaches the soft-ball stage, or 240°F. Add the vanilla, salt, and milk, stir, and remove from the heat. Allow the mixture to cool completely at room temperature. (Do not refrigerate before assembling the torte—the caramel will thicken as it cools.)

continues

continued

▸ To assemble the torte: Place the completely cooled, unsliced brownie upside down on a wire rack placed atop a bowl that has a diameter larger than that of the brownie. Gently pour the caramel sauce over the brownie, leaving about a ½-inch margin without caramel around the outer edge of the brownie, to keep it from dripping down the side of the brownie when you pour the chocolate onto it. (You may want to reserve a little caramel to drizzle on each serving plate before placing the cut brownies on it.) Place the pecans in an evenly spaced pattern around the top of the brownie on the caramel, spacing them close together so that all the caramel is covered. Refrigerate to harden the caramel while you heat the chocolate.

Chocolate candy topping:

½ teaspoon vanilla extract

½ cup vegan creamer

2 cups vegan chocolate chips

1 cup whole pecans

▸ To make the chocolate candy topping: Heat the vanilla and vegan creamer in a small pan over medium heat until hot but not boiling. Slowly stir in the vegan chocolate chips. Stir until the chips are completely melted and the mixture is smooth. While the mixture is hot, gently pour over the brownie, nuts, and caramel, being careful not to dislodge the nuts or caramel. Allow the excess chocolate to drip into the bowl under the brownie. When the brownie is completely covered with chocolate, place the bowl, wire rack, and torte in the refrigerator until the chocolate hardens, about 10 minutes. Remove from the refrigerator and remove any hard drips of chocolate that formed when the chocolate ran off the torte through the wire rack (kitchen shears work well for this). Place the torte on a serving plate. When serving, drizzle the reserved caramel on each individual serving plate (optional) and place a slice of torte on top.

PER SERVING: 493 calories, 19 g fat (7 g saturated), 85 g carbohydrate, 6 g dietary fiber, <1 g sugar, 5 g protein, 0 mg cholesterol, 46 mg sodium, 194 mg potassium. Calories from fat: 31 percent.

Hint: If the caramel is too hard, allow it to set at room temperature for about 10 minutes before serving.

PEANUT BUTTER TWIST BROWNIES

For Reese's Peanut Butter Cup lovers everywhere: Brownies with peanut butter swirled in them. Be careful not to overbake these brownies, or they will be dry.

Makes 16 servings

Preparation time: brownies, 10 minutes; peanut butter filling, 5 minutes
Baking time: 45 to 50 minutes ▼ **Freezes well**

1⅓ cups granulated sweetener

¾ cup unsweetened applesauce (preferably organic)

½ cup + 2 tablespoons water

2 teaspoons flax powder

2 teaspoons vanilla extract

1⅓ cups unbleached all-purpose flour

¾ cup unsweetened cocoa powder

½ teaspoon baking powder

¼ teaspoon salt

½ cup vegan chocolate chips

½ cup natural peanut butter

½ cup pure maple syrup

3 ounces (¼ [12-ounce] package) firm silken tofu

PER SERVING: 235 calories, 7 g fat (2 g saturated), 42 g carbohydrate, 3 g dietary fiber, 6 g sugar, 5 g protein, 0 mg cholesterol, 56 mg sodium, 187 mg potassium. Calories from fat: 24 percent.

▶ Preheat the oven to 350°F. Coat an 8-inch square baking pan with nonstick cooking spray.

▶ Stir together the granulated sweetener, applesauce, and 2 tablespoons of the water in a medium-size bowl. In a small cup, mix the flax powder with the remaining ½ cup of water. Add to the applesauce mixture and stir to combine. Add the vanilla and stir.

▶ In another small bowl, combine the flour, cocoa powder, baking powder, and salt. Add the applesauce mixture to the flour mixture. Stir just to combine. Add the chocolate chips and stir to combine. Pour into the prepared pan.

▶ Place the peanut butter, maple syrup, and tofu together in a food processor. Process until smooth. Drop by spoonfuls onto the brownie batter. With a knife, swirl the peanut butter into the batter. (Be careful not to mix completely.)

▶ Bake for 45 minutes for chewy brownies, 50 minutes for cakelike brownies.

▶ Allow to cool in the pan before serving.

CAKES AND
QUICK BREADS

In this chapter you will find many different types of vegan cakes and quick breads. Explore many taste sensations including chocolate cakes, pineapple upside down cake, and pumpkin cake as well as banana bread and fruity pumpkin bread. Have fun tickling your vegan sweet tooth!

....

LEMON LOAF

This is simply a delectable lemon pound cake. The name pound cake comes from a time when each ingredient in the recipe weighed a pound! How times have changed.

Makes 12 servings

Preparation time: cake, 15 minutes; glaze, 5 minutes; raspberry sauce, 10 minutes
Baking time: 1 hour ▾ **Freezes well**

2 cups unbleached all-purpose flour

1 teaspoon baking powder

½ teaspoon baking soda

½ cup pure maple syrup

¾ cup vanilla vegan milk

⅓ cup soft vegan butter spread, preferably tub style, at room temperature. (If using stick butter, soften it in the microwave until it is the consistency of tub butter. Do not melt!)

4 teaspoons egg replacer (such as Ener-G)

¾ cup water

3½ teaspoons lemon extract

Lemon glaze or raspberry sauce (recipes follow)

▶ Preheat the oven to 350°F. Lightly coat an 8 by 3½ by 2½-inch loaf pan with nonstick cooking spray.

▶ In a bowl, combine the flour, baking powder, and baking soda. Using an electric mixer, in a separate medium-size bowl, combine the maple syrup, milk, and butter.

▶ In a small bowl, mix the egg replacer with the ¾ cup of water. Add to the maple syrup mixture along with the lemon extract, and mix. Slowly add the flour mixture to the liquid mixture. Mix until just combined and pour the batter into the prepared pan.

▶ Bake for 1 hour, or until a toothpick inserted into the center comes out clean. Allow to cool completely before removing from the pan.

▶ Top with the lemon glaze or raspberry sauce.

Variation: Add ¾ cup of poppy seeds to the batter for lemon poppy seedcake.

Per serving (cake only): 287 calories, 6 g fat (1 g saturated), 28 g carbohydrate, <1 g dietary fiber, 8 g sugar, 30 g protein, 0 mg cholesterol, 542 mg sodium, 448 mg potassium. Calories from fat: 17 percent.

continues

continued

Lemon glaze:

¾ cup powdered sugar

2 tablespoons lemon juice
(freshly squeezed will give
the best flavor)

Raspberry sauce:

1 (12-ounce) package frozen
raspberries

¼ cup water

⅓ cup granulated sweetener

1 tablespoon arrowroot

2 tablespoons water

▸ Mix the sugar and lemon juice together. Pour over the cake before slicing.

▸ Bring the first three ingredients to a boil in a medium-size saucepan. Dissolve the arrowroot in the 2 tablespoons of water and add to the hot raspberry mixture. Heat until just thickened—do not boil. (The mixture will thicken more as it cools.) Allow to cool.

▸ Slice the cake and place on individual plates. Spoon the sauce over the cake slices. Serve immediately.

Per serving (lemon glaze): 31
calories, <1 g fat (0 g saturated),
8 g carbohydrate, <1 g dietary fiber,
<1 g protein, 0 mg cholesterol,
<1 mg sodium, 12 mg potassium.
Calories from fat: 0 percent.

Per serving (raspberry sauce):
19 calories, <0.1 g fat (0 g saturated),
5 g carbohydrate, <1 g dietary fiber,
<1 g protein, 0 mg cholesterol,
<1 mg sodium, 6 mg potassium.
Calories from fat: 0 percent.

CHERRY, CHERRY NOT CONTRARY CAKE

Tender, moist chocolate cake filled with fresh cherry filling and topped with fluffy chocolate icing is sure to please your guests every time. And they'll never guess the secret ingredient that makes it so moist—zucchini!

Makes 12 servings

Preparation time: cake, 20 minutes; filling, 15 minutes; frosting, 10 minutes
Baking time: 1½ hours ▼ **Cooling time:** 30 minutes in the oven
Assembly/frosting: 15 minutes ▼ **Chilling time:** at least 8 hours

1 cup rice flour

1¼ cups garbanzo bean flour

2 teaspoons xanthan gum

½ cup unsweetened cocoa powder

1 tablespoon baking powder

1½ teaspoons baking soda

¼ teaspoon salt

¼ cup unsweetened applesauce (preferably organic)

½ cup soft vegan butter spread, preferably tub style, at room temperature. (If using stick butter, soften it in the microwave until it is the consistency of tub butter. Do not melt!)

2 cups granulated sweetener

1 tablespoon flax powder or egg replacer (such as Ener-G)

1¼ cups water

2 teaspoons vanilla extract

2 cups shredded zucchini

8 to 10 pitted, stemmed fresh cherries or cherries with stems, for garnish

▶ Preheat the oven to 325°F. Coat a 9-inch round spring-form pan with nonstick cooking spray.

▶ Combine the flours, xanthan gum, cocoa powder, baking powder, baking soda, and salt in a bowl and set aside. In another bowl, combine the applesauce, butter, and granulated sweetener, mix until fluffy, and set aside. In a small bowl, mix the flax powder with ¾ cup of the water. Add to the applesauce mixture and stir to combine. Add the vanilla, zucchini, and the remaining ½ cup of water. Slowly add the flour mixture to the liquid ingredients and stir to combine. Pour the batter into the prepared pan.

▶ Bake at 325°F for 1½ hours, or until a toothpick inserted into the center comes out clean. Allow to cool in the oven for 30 minutes with the heat turned off and the door open. Remove from the oven and allow to cool completely in the pan.

continues

continued

Cherry Filling, page 265

Whipped Chocolate Frosting,
    page 266

½ cup vegan chocolate chips, for
    garnish (optional)

Vegan Chocolate Syrup, page 267
    (optional)

PER SERVING: 523 calories, 19 g fat
(6 g saturated), 89 g carbohydrate,
6 g dietary fiber, 6 g sugar, 9 g
protein, 0 mg cholesterol, 914 mg
sodium, 450 mg potassium.
Calories from fat: 29 percent.

▸ While the cake is cooling, make the Cherry Filling and set aside. When the cake is cool, remove the collar of the pan and cut the cake in half horizontally to make two layers. Remove the top layer and set aside. Put the collar back on the bottom of the pan. Spread the cherry filling over the bottom layer of the cake. Replace the top of the cake upside down (so that flat, cut side is on top) on top of the cherries and gently press down. Frost with Whipped Chocolate Frosting.

▸ Place the pitted, stem-free cherries around the outside of the cake, if desired.

▸ For a fancier look, leave the stems on the cherries, pit from below, melt ½ cup of vegan chocolate chips, and dip the bottom half of each cherry in the chocolate. Place the chocolate-covered cherries in the refrigerator to harden. Drizzle Vegan Chocolate Syrup on top of the cake in a lattice pattern and place the chocolate cherries around the outside edge of the cake just before serving. The number of cherries that you will need will vary, depending on the size of the cherries and how closely you space them. Eight to ten cherries are usually enough.

CHOCOLATE RASPBERRY CELEBRATION LOAF

Impress your friends with this luscious blend of chocolate and raspberry. It's easy to make and looks quite festive. Use your imagination to decorate it with a combination of fluffy chocolate icing, fresh raspberries, and mint leaves.

Makes 12 servings

Preparation time: cake, 15 minutes; frosting, 10 minutes
Baking time: 45 minutes ▼ **Assembly/frosting/decoration:** 20 minutes

1½ cups unbleached all-purpose flour

⅓ cup unsweetened cocoa powder

1 tablespoon baking powder

3 ounces (¼ [12-ounce] package) firm silken tofu

½ teaspoon vanilla extract

¼ cup unsweetened applesauce (preferably organic)

¾ cup water or apple juice

¾ cup pure maple syrup

Standard Chocolate Frosting, page 269

½ cup fresh raspberries, for garnish (optional)

8 to 10 fresh mint leaves, for garnish (optional)

Vegan chocolate bar(s), for garnish (optional)

Filling:
¾ cup raspberry jam

PER SERVING: 351 calories, 10 g fat (4 g saturated), 62 g carbohydrate, 3 g dietary fiber, 14 g sugar, 9 g protein, 0 mg cholesterol, 19 mg sodium, 327 mg potassium. Calories from fat: 23 percent.

▶ Preheat the oven to 350°F. Lightly coat an 8 by 3½ by 2½-inch loaf pan with nonstick cooking spray.

▶ In a large bowl, combine the flour, cocoa powder, and baking powder. Mix with a whisk. In a food processor, puree the tofu until smooth. Add the vanilla and applesauce and blend. Add the water and maple syrup and blend. Slowly add the liquid ingredients to the flour mixture and mix with the whisk until combined. Do not overmix. Pour the batter into the prepared pan.

▶ Bake for 45 minutes, or until a toothpick inserted into the center comes out clean. While the cake is baking, make the frosting. (If possible, it is best to make the frosting the day before.)

▶ Allow the cake to cool for 10 minutes, then remove from the pan and let cool completely on a wire rack. When cool, cut the rounded top off the cake, with a sharp knife or wire cake cutter, to make it almost flat. Cut the cake into thirds lengthwise to make three layers. Place the top layer upside down on a serving plate. Spread with ⅓ cup of the raspberry jam. Top with the next layer. Spread with the rest of the jam. Place the last layer on top. This will be the smallest layer because the cake tapers to the top. Place this layer on upside down so that the top is completely flat.

continues

continued

▶ Frost the cake top and sides with Standard Chocolate Frosting. Pipe the frosting around the bottom edge of the cake. If in season, align fresh raspberries along the long edges on the top of the cake. Garnish with several fresh mint leaves. If vegan chocolate candy bars are available, use a potato peeler to make chocolate curls to place in the middle of the cake between the rows of raspberries.

Hint: If you don't have a loaf pan, you may bake this cake in an 8-inch square cake pan. Adjust the baking time to about 35 minutes. When the cake has cooled, cut the rounded top off the cake and discard (or eat!) it. Cut the cake in half vertically to make two rectangular pieces. With a sharp knife or wire cake cutter, cut each rectangle in half horizontally to make four thin layers. Alternate cake and raspberry filling. Frost the top and sides and decorate.

MOCHA MADNESS CAKE

Coffee shops selling lattes and mocha drinks are springing up all over the place, proving that people adore coffee and chocolate! I developed this cake to mimic the taste of a chocolate cappuccino.

Makes 12 servings

Preparation time: cake, 15 minutes; frosting, 10 minutes
Baking time: 35 to 40 minutes ▼ **Frosting/decoration:** 5 minutes

2¼ cups unbleached all-purpose flour

1¾ cups granulated sweetener

¾ cup unsweetened cocoa powder

1½ teaspoons baking powder

¾ teaspoon baking soda

¼ teaspoon salt

2 cups vegan milk

2 teaspoons apple cider vinegar

1 teaspoon vanilla extract

½ cup canola oil

Coffee Frosting, page 270

½ cup vegan chocolate chips, ground, or chocolate-covered espresso beans, for garnish (optional)

▶ Preheat the oven to 375°F. Coat an 8 x 11-inch cake pan with nonstick cooking spray.

▶ In a medium-size bowl, combine the flour, sweetener, cocoa powder, baking powder, baking soda, and salt. In another bowl, combine the milk and vinegar. Add the vanilla and oil. Slowly pour the liquid mixture into the dry mixture and stir to combine. Beat one hundred strokes, until the batter is smooth and glossy.

▶ Pour into the prepared pan and bake for 35 to 40 minutes, or until a toothpick inserted into the center comes out clean. Allow the cake to cool completely in the pan before frosting.

▶ Frost with Coffee Frosting and garnish with ground chocolate chips or chocolate-covered espresso coffee beans, if desired.

PER SERVING (CAKE ONLY): 314 calories, 10.7 g fat (1.2 g saturated), 52.9 g carbohydrate, 2.5 g dietary fiber, 31 g sugar, 4.7 g protein, 0 mg cholesterol, 153 mg sodium. Calories from fat: 16 percent.

NUTS ABOUT CHOCOLATE CAKE

This cake evokes images of hot fudge sundaes with its combination of chocolate cake, creamy chocolate icing, chocolate syrup, and nuts. I take it along when I am going to a dinner or picnic where there are a lot of nonvegan people. I always have to make sure that I get a piece first, though, or else it disappears! In addition to being sinfully delicious, it contains a good amount of healthy zucchini and is wheat free.

Makes 12 servings

Preparation time: cake, 20 minutes; syrup, 5 minutes; frosting, 10 minutes
Baking time: 1 ½ hours ▼ **Cooling time:** 30 minutes in the oven

1 cup rice flour

1 ¼ cups garbanzo bean flour

2 teaspoons xanthan gum

½ cup unsweetened cocoa powder

1 tablespoon baking powder

1 ½ teaspoons baking soda

¼ teaspoon salt

¼ cup unsweetened applesauce (preferably organic)

½ cup soft vegan butter spread, preferably tub style, at room temperature. (If using stick butter, soften it in the microwave until it is the consistency of tub butter. Do not melt!)

2 cups granulated sweetener

1 tablespoon flax powder or egg replacer (such as Ener-G)

1 ¼ cups water

2 teaspoons vanilla extract

2 cups shredded zucchini

Whipped Chocolate Frosting, page 266

¾ cup chopped pecans, for garnish (optional)

Vegan Chocolate Syrup, page 267

▶ Preheat the oven to 325°F. Coat a 9-inch round spring-form pan with nonstick cooking oil.

▶ Combine the flours, xanthan gum, cocoa powder, baking powder, baking soda, and salt in a bowl and set aside. Combine the applesauce, butter, and granulated sweetener and mix until fluffy. Mix the flax powder with ¾ cup of the water in a small bowl, add to the applesauce mixture, and stir to combine. Add the vanilla, zucchini, and remaining ½ cup of water. Slowly add the flour mixture to the liquid ingredients. Stir to combine. Pour the batter into the prepared pan.

▶ Bake at 325°F for 1½ hours, or until a toothpick inserted into the center comes out clean. Allow to cool in the oven for 30 minutes with the heat turned off and the door open. Allow to cool completely in the pan. Prepare the Whipped Chocolate Frosting.

▶ After the cake is completely cooled, frost. Sprinkle with the chopped pecans. Prepare the Vegan Chocolate Syrup. Drizzle the chocolate syrup in a zigzag over the nuts.

▶ Refrigerate the cake overnight before serving, if possible.

PER SERVING: 542 calories, 25 g fat (6 g saturated), 78 g carbohydrate, 8 g dietary fiber, 7 g sugar, 11 g protein, 0 mg cholesterol, 210 mg sodium, 409 mg potassium. Calories from fat: 37 percent.

Just Loafing Around

This pound cake tastes great plain, but can be used as a base for a variety of creations. It is scrumptious topped with fresh fruit—strawberries, raspberries, peaches, or cherries. Drizzle the chocolate sauce over the fresh fruit mounded on this firm yet moist cake and you have a truly memorable dessert. You could also serve it with a scoop of nondairy frozen dessert, such as Tofutti, and Vegan Chocolate Syrup (page 267) for a wonderful taste experience.

Makes 12 servings

Preparation time: cake, 15 minutes; glaze, 5 minutes; chocolate sauce, 10 minutes
Baking time: 1 hour ▼ **Freezes well**

2 cups unbleached all-purpose flour

1 teaspoon baking powder

½ teaspoon baking soda

½ cup brown sugar

½ cup pure maple syrup

¾ cup vanilla vegan milk

⅓ cup soft vegan butter spread, preferably tub style, at room temperature. (If using stick butter, soften it in the microwave until it is the consistency of tub butter. Do not melt!)

4 teaspoons egg replacer (such as Ener-G)

½ cup water

2 tablespoons vanilla extract

Vanilla Glaze, page 268, or Vegan Chocolate Syrup, page 267

▶ Preheat the oven to 350°F. Lightly coat an 8 by 3½ by 2½-inch loaf pan with nonstick cooking spray.

▶ In a large bowl, combine the flour, baking powder, and baking soda. Using an electric mixer, in a separate bowl, combine the maple syrup, milk, and butter.

▶ In small bowl, mix the egg replacer with the ½ cup of water. Add to the maple syrup mixture along with the vanilla and mix. Slowly add the flour mixture to the liquid mixture and mix until just combined. Pour the batter into the prepared pan.

▶ Bake for 1 hour, or until a toothpick inserted into the center comes out clean. Allow the cake to cool completely before removing from the pan.

▶ Top the cake with Vanilla Glaze, or top each slice with a drizzle of Vegan Chocolate Syrup.

Variation: Add ¾ cup of vegan chocolate chips to the batter just before pouring into the prepared pan, for a delicious chocolate chip pound cake.

PER SERVING (CAKE ONLY): 178 calories, 7 g fat (<1 g saturated), 26 g carbohydrate, <1 g dietary fiber, 8 g sugar, 3 g protein, 0 mg cholesterol, 94 mg sodium, 74 mg potassium. Calories from fat: 32 percent.

MOCHA GOOBER CAKE ♡

I got so many requests for desserts made with chocolate and peanut butter when I was doing commercial baking that I created several variations on that theme, so that the desserts were always a bit different. This treat consists of dark chocolate cake smothered in creamy peanut butter frosting. Here's a helpful hint: The Creamy Peanut Butter Frosting tastes best if you prepare it the day before and allow it to set.

Makes 12 servings

Preparation time: cake, 15 minutes; frosting, 10 minutes
Baking time: 35 to 40 minutes ▼ **Frosting/decoration:** 5 minutes

2¼ cups unbleached all-purpose flour

1¾ cups granulated sweetener

¾ cup unsweetened cocoa powder

1½ teaspoons baking powder

¾ teaspoon baking soda

¼ teaspoon salt

2 cups vegan milk

2 teaspoons apple cider vinegar

1 teaspoon vanilla extract

½ cup canola oil

Creamy Peanut Butter Frosting, page 270, or Peanut Butter Buttercream Frosting, page 282

¼ cup vegan chocolate chips, ground, for garnish (optional)

▶ Preheat the oven to 375°F. Coat an 8 x 11-inch cake pan with nonstick cooking spray.

▶ In a medium-size bowl, combine the flour, sweetener, cocoa powder, baking powder, baking soda, and salt. In another bowl, combine the milk and vinegar. Add vanilla and oil. Slowly pour the liquid mixture into the dry mixture and stir to combine. Beat one hundred strokes, until the batter is smooth and glossy.

▶ Pour into the prepared pan and bake for 35 to 40 minutes, or until a toothpick inserted into the center comes out clean. Allow the cake to cool completely in the pan before frosting.

▶ Frost with Creamy Peanut Butter Frosting or Peanut Butter Buttercream Frosting and garnish with ground chocolate, if desired.

PER SERVING (CAKE ONLY): 314 calories, 10.7 g fat (1.2 g saturated), 52.9 g carbohydrate, 2.5 g dietary fiber, 31 g sugar, 4.7 g protein, 0 mg cholesterol, 153 mg sodium. Calories from fat: 16 percent.

CHOCOLATE-COVERED GOLD

This cake is a traditional American favorite. Its delicate vanilla flavor is the perfect complement for the rich, creamy chocolate icing. It's a sure crowd-pleaser.

Makes 12 servings

Preparation time: cake, 15 minutes; icing, 10 minutes
Baking time: 50 minutes ▼ **FROSTING/GARNISH:** 5 minutes

¾ cup soft vegan butter spread, preferably tub style, at room temperature. (If using stick butter, soften it in the microwave until it is the consistency of tub butter. Do not melt!)

1¼ cups pure maple syrup

1 tablespoon vanilla extract

4½ cups unbleached all-purpose flour

1½ tablespoons baking powder

¼ teaspoon salt

2½ cups vegan milk

Whipped Chocolate Frosting, page 266, or Chocolate Buttercream Frosting, page 281

¼ cup vegan dark chocolate chips, ground (optional)

PER SERVING: 548 calories, 17 g fat (6 g saturated), 89 g carbohydrate, 4 g dietary fiber, 22 g sugar, 13 g protein, 0 mg cholesterol, 48 mg sodium, 394 mg potassium. Calories from fat: 25 percent.

▶ Preheat the oven to 350°F. Coat a 9 by 11-inch cake pan with nonstick cooking spray.

▶ Place the butter in a bowl and cream. Slowly add the maple syrup and beat until light and fluffy, then add the vanilla and mix. In another bowl, combine the flour, baking powder, and salt. Alternately add the flour mixture and the milk to the butter mixture and mix well.

▶ Pour into the prepared pan and bake for about 50 minutes, or until a toothpick inserted into the center comes out clean. Allow the cake to cool completely in the pan before frosting.

▶ While the cake is baking, prepare the Whipped Chocolate Frosting or Chocolate Buttercream.

▶ Frost the cake and garnish with ground chocolate chips, if desired. Refrigerate the cake before serving and store in the refrigerator.

MELLOW YELLOW CAKE

I like to make fruity cakes in the summer. For this treat, I layered yellow cake with raspberry jam and topped it off with a light raspberry frosting.

Makes 12 servings

Preparation time: cake, 15 minutes; icing, 10 minutes
Baking time: 50 minutes ▼ **Frosting/garnish:** 5 minutes

¾ cup soft vegan butter spread, preferably tub style, at room temperature. (If using stick butter, soften it in the microwave until it is the consistency of tub butter. Do not melt!)

1¼ cups pure maple syrup

1 tablespoon vanilla extract

4½ cups unbleached all-purpose flour

1½ tablespoons baking powder

¼ teaspoon salt

2½ cups vegan milk

Light Raspberry Frosting, page 271

Filling:

¾ cup raspberry jam

PER SERVING: 486 calories, 9 g fat (<1 g saturated), 91 g carbohydrate, 2 g dietary fiber, 22 g sugar, 12 g protein, 0 mg cholesterol, 211 mg sodium, 415 mg potassium. Calories from fat: 15 percent.

▶ Preheat the oven to 350°F. Coat a 9 by 11-inch cake pan with nonstick cooking spray.

▶ Place the butter in a bowl and cream. Slowly add the maple syrup and beat until light and fluffy. Add the vanilla and mix. In another bowl, combine the flour, baking powder, and salt. Alternately add the flour mixture and the milk to the butter mixture and stir well.

▶ Pour into the prepared pan and bake for about 50 minutes, or until a toothpick inserted into the center comes out clean. While the cake is baking, prepare the Light Raspberry Frosting. Allow the cake to cool completely in the pan before frosting.

▶ When the cake is completely cooled, carefully invert onto a wire rack. With a long, sharp knife, cut the cake in half lengthwise, making two layers. Return the bottom layer to the pan and top with raspberry jam. Place the top layer on the layer of jam.

▶ Mound the frosting onto the cake and decorate with fresh raspberries, if desired. Store in the refrigerator.

CITRUS ORANGE CAKE

I created this cake to be completely different from the dark chocolate creations with which I usually work. This is a light vanilla cake covered with orange frosting. It makes a lovely spring or summer dessert garnished with fresh fruit!

Makes 12 servings

Preparation time: cake, 15 minutes; icing, 10 minutes
Baking time: 50 minutes ▼ **Frosting/garnish:** 5 minutes

¾ cup soft vegan butter spread, preferably tub style, at room temperature. (If using stick butter, soften it in the microwave until it is the consistency of tub butter. Do not melt!)

1¼ cups pure maple syrup

1 tablespoon vanilla extract

4½ cups unbleached all-purpose flour

1½ tablespoons baking powder

¼ teaspoon salt

2½ cups vegan milk

Fluffy Orange Frosting, page 271

Fresh orange wedges or mandarin orange sections, for garnish (optional)

PER SERVING (YELLOW CAKE WITH ORANGE FROSTING): 422 calories, 9 g fat (<1 g saturated), 74 g carbohydrate, 2 g dietary fiber, 22 g sugar, 11 g protein, 0 mg cholesterol, 45 mg sodium. Calories from fat: 17 percent.

▶ Preheat the oven to 350°F. Coat a 9 by 11-inch cake pan with nonstick cooking spray.

▶ Place the butter in a bowl and cream. Slowly add the maple syrup and beat until light and fluffy. Add the vanilla and mix. In another bowl, combine the flour, baking powder, and salt.

▶ Alternately add the flour mixture and the milk to the butter mixture. Mix well. Pour into the prepared pan and bake for 50 minutes, or until a toothpick inserted into the center comes out clean.

▶ Allow the cake to cool completely in the pan before frosting. While the cake is baking, prepare the Fluffy Orange Frosting.

▶ Mound onto the cake and swirl or make peaks in the frosting. Decorate with fresh orange wedges or mandarin orange sections, if desired. Chill before serving. Store in the refrigerator.

continues

continued

Variations:

- Substitute 2½ cups of orange juice for the 2½ cups of milk—this will make a delicious orange cake. You can also top this cake with Fluffy Orange Frosting for a tasty orange treat.

- Substitute orange juice for the milk in the cake recipe and frost with Fluffy Orange Frosting, as in variation above, but bake in two 9-inch round cake pans coated with nonstick cooking spray and lined with waxed or parchment paper. Adjust the baking time to 30 to 35 minutes. Cut each cake layer in half horizontally so that you have four layers. Spread each layer with ⅓ cup of raspberry preserves and then mound Fluffy Orange Frosting just on the top of the cake, allowing the preserves to peek out between the layers of cake. Because the soft frosting and preserves do not make a sturdy cake, you may want to insert a wooden skewer, which is available at most grocery stores or kitchen supply stores, into the middle of the cake. If you cut it so that the skewer cannot be seen, no one but you will know it's there.

PER SERVING (ORANGE CAKE WITH ORANGE FROSTING): 447 calories, 11 g fat (<1 g saturated), 78 g carbohydrate, 1 g dietary fiber, 22 g sugar, 11 g protein, 0 mg cholesterol, 100 mg sodium, 425 mg potassium. Calories from fat: 20 percent.

PER SERVING (ORANGE CAKE WITH ORANGE FROSTING AND RASPBERRY FILLING): 607 calories, 23 g fat (1 g saturated), 96 g carbohydrate, 2 g dietary fiber, 22 g sugar, 11 g protein, 0 mg cholesterol, 176 mg sodium, 445 mg potassium. Calories from fat: 30 percent.

Toasted Coconut Pecan Cake ♡

Even as a child, I loved to cook. My favorite recipe was for a toasted coconut pecan cake—a yellow cake mix to which pecans were added, topped with a cream cheese icing mixed with coconut toasted in butter. I loved that cake. As I got older and started thinking about my health, I realized that I could make the same cake, only healthier. So here's the new and improved version. Because of the vegan cream cheese frosting, pecans, and coconut, it is still higher in calories than the other cakes in this book. The coconut raises the amount of saturated fat as well. But, it contains no cholesterol. Sometimes we all have to splurge!

Makes 12 servings

Preparation time: cake, 20 minutes; icing, 10 minutes
Baking time: 30 minutes ▼ **Frosting/garnish:** 5 minutes

1 cup unsweetened shredded coconut

¾ cup soft vegan butter spread, preferably tub style, at room temperature. (If using stick butter, soften it in the microwave until it is the consistency of tub butter. Do not melt!)

1¼ cups pure maple syrup

1 tablespoon vanilla extract

1 cup chopped pecans

4½ cups unbleached all-purpose flour

1½ tablespoons baking powder

¼ teaspoon salt

2½ cups vegan milk

Toasted Coconut Pecan Frosting, page 272

Garnish (optional): reserve ¼ cup toasted coconut to sprinkle on top of the cake

▶ Preheat the oven to 350°F. Coat three 8-inch cake pans with nonstick cooking spray. Line the bottom of each pan with waxed or parchment paper.

▶ To toast the coconut for the cake and frosting, line a cookie sheet with aluminum foil. Coat with nonstick cooking spray. Spread the coconut in a thin layer on the cookie sheet and place under the broiler. Stir as the coconut begins to brown. When golden brown, remove from the broiler immediately and set aside.

▶ Place the butter in a bowl and cream. Slowly add the maple syrup and beat until light and fluffy. Add the vanilla and mix. Add the toasted coconut and pecans.

▶ In another bowl, combine the flour, baking powder, and salt. Alternately add the flour mixture and the milk to the butter mixture and stir well. Pour into the prepared pans and bake for about 30 minutes, or until a toothpick inserted into the center comes out clean. While the cake is baking, prepare the Toasted Coconut Pecan Frosting.

continues

continued

PER SERVING: 830 calories, 60 g fat (31 g saturated), 69 g carbohydrate, 4 g dietary fiber, 22 g sugar, 10 g protein, 0 mg cholesterol, 177 mg sodium, 284 mg potassium. Calories from fat: 53 percent. (Some of these figures are higher than in the other recipes in this book because this cake contains both nuts and coconut. Both these foods are healthy, but they're also quite high in fat, some of it saturated.)

▸ Allow the cake to cool for 10 minutes in the pans and then remove from the pans. Remove the paper from the bottom of the cake. Let cool completely on wire racks before frosting.

▸ Frost only the tops of the cakes. Do not frost the sides. Stack and allow the icing to ooze out from between the layers.

▸ If you reserved toasted coconut, sprinkle it on top of the cake.

TROPICAL MANGO CAKE

This cake got rave reviews from my taste testers! It tastes great made with mango juice, but if you can't find any at your local health food store or grocery store, any juice that sounds good to you may be substituted. Just be sure that it is 100 percent juice.

Makes 12 servings

Preparation time: cake, 15 minutes; icing, 10 minutes
Baking time: 55 minutes ▼ **Frosting/garnish:** 5 minutes

¾ cup soft vegan butter spread, preferably tub style, at room temperature. (If using stick butter, soften it in the microwave until it is the consistency of tub butter. Do not melt!)

1¼ cups pure maple syrup

1 teaspoon vanilla extract

4½ cups unbleached all-purpose flour

1½ tablespoons baking powder

¼ teaspoon salt

2½ cups mango juice

Whipped Coconut Cream Frosting, page 273 (reserve extra coconut, for garnish)

▶ Preheat the oven to 350°F. Coat a 9 by 11-inch cake pan with nonstick cooking spray.

▶ Place the butter in a bowl and cream. Slowly add the maple syrup and beat until light and fluffy. Add the vanilla and mix.

▶ In another bowl, combine the flour, baking powder, and salt. Alternately add the flour mixture and mango juice to the butter mixture and stir well.

▶ Pour into the prepared pan and bake for 55 minutes, or until a toothpick inserted into the center comes out clean. While the cake bakes, prepare the Whipped Coconut Cream Frosting. Allow the cake to cool completely in the pan, then mound the frosting onto the cake and swirl or make peaks in the frosting.

▶ Sprinkle with the reserved coconut.

PER SERVING: 507 calories, 21 g fat (12 g saturated), 71 g carbohydrate, 1 g dietary fiber, 22 g sugar, 10 g protein, 0 mg cholesterol, 84 mg sodium, 319 mg potassium. Calories from fat: 35 percent.

You Can't Catch Me I'm the Gingerbread . . . Cake

Warm, spicy gingerbread cake is great to eat while wrapped in a fuzzy blanket snuggled in front of a fire with a cup of hot coffee or warm mulled apple cider. What could be better for the holidays?

Makes 12 servings

Preparation time: cake, 15 minutes; icing, 10 minutes
Baking time: 30 minutes ▼ **Frosting/garnish:** 5 minutes

¾ cup pure maple syrup

¾ cup molasses

⅓ cup canola oil

1 tablespoon vanilla extract

4½ cups unbleached all-purpose flour

1½ tablespoons baking powder

2 teaspoons ground ginger

1 teaspoon ground cinnamon

1 teaspoon ground nutmeg

¼ teaspoon ground cloves

¼ teaspoon ground allspice

¼ teaspoon salt

2½ cups vegan milk

Cream Cheese Frosting, page 274, or Vanilla Glaze, page 268

- ▶ Preheat the oven to 350°F. Coat a 9 by 11-inch cake pan or Bundt pan with nonstick cooking spray.
- ▶ Combine the maple syrup and molasses and add to the oil. Add the vanilla and mix. In another bowl, combine the flour, baking powder, spices, and salt. Alternately add the flour mixture and the milk to the maple mixture and mix well. Pour into the prepared pan and bake for 30 minutes (the Bundt cake will take longer to bake—about 45 minutes), or until a toothpick inserted into the center comes out clean.
- ▶ Allow the cake to cool completely in the pan before frosting with either the Cream Cheese Frosting or Vanilla Glaze.

Hint: I found that the Cream Cheese Frosting works well on a 9 x 11-inch cake, and the Vanilla Glaze works well on Bundt cake.

PER SERVING (CAKE ONLY): 406 calories, 14 g fat (1 g saturated), 65 g carbohydrate, 2 g dietary fiber, 12 g sugar, 6 g protein, 0 mg cholesterol, 67 mg sodium, 471 mg potassium. Calories from fat: 29 percent.

PER SERVING (FROSTED OR GLAZED): 540 calories, 21 g fat (3 g saturated), 78 g carbohydrate, 2 g dietary fiber, 14 g sugar, 11 g protein, 0 mg cholesterol, 152 mg sodium, 622 mg potassium. Calories from fat: 26 percent.

HOLD THE WHEAT
CARROT CAKE

My husband loves carrot cake, and I experimented with many carrot cake recipes trying to get just the right texture and taste. This gluten-free recipe did the trick.

> **Makes 12 servings**

Preparation time: cake, 20 minutes; icing, 10 minutes ▼ **Baking time:** 80 minutes
Frosting/garnish: 5 minutes ▼ **Freezes well without frosting**

¾ cup garbanzo bean flour

1¼ cups rice flour

2 teaspoons xanthan gum

2 teaspoons baking soda

¼ teaspoon salt

2 teaspoons ground cinnamon

4 teaspoons flax powder

1 cup water

½ cup unsweetened applesauce (preferably organic)

1 cup canola oil

1 teaspoon vanilla extract

1¼ cups pure maple syrup

2 cups grated carrots (preferably organic)

Cream Cheese Frosting, page 274

▶ Preheat the oven to 325°F. Coat a 9 by 13-inch pan, 9-inch round springform pan, or 9½-inch Bundt pan with non-stick cooking spray.

▶ Mix together the bean flour, rice flour, xanthan gum, baking soda, salt, and cinnamon.

▶ In a small bowl, make a slurry (see Note) with the flax powder and 1 cup of water, then add the applesauce, oil, vanilla, and maple syrup.

▶ Add the wet ingredients to the dry ingredients and mix until just combined. Add the carrots, then pour into the prepared pan. Bake at 325°F for 75 to 80 minutes.

PER SERVING (CAKE ONLY): 354 calories, 19 g fat (1 g saturated), 43 g carbohydrate, 4 g dietary fiber, 21 g sugar, 3 g protein, 0 mg cholesterol, 233 mg sodium, 184 mg potassium. Calories from fat: 47 percent.

Note: A slurry is a thin mixture of liquid, usually water, mixed with a finely ground substance.

continues

continued

PER SERVING (CAKE WITH CREAM CHEESE FROSTING): 493 calories, 26 g fat (3 g saturated), 56 g carbohydrate, 4 g dietary fiber, 23 g sugar, 8 g protein, 0 mg cholesterol, 318 mg sodium, 340 mg potassium. Calories from fat: 39 percent.

PER SERVING (CREAM CHEESE GLAZE): 133 calories, 7 g fat (1 g saturated), 13 g carbohydrate, <0.1 g dietary fiber, 1 g sugar, 5 g protein, 0 mg cholesterol, 85 mg sodium, 152 mg potassium. Calories from fat: 15 percent.

▶ While the cake is baking, prepare the Cream Cheese Frosting. Allow the cake to cool completely in the pan before frosting. If made in the 9 by 13-inch pan or springform pan, frost in the pan; remove the sides of the springform pan before serving. If using a Bundt pan, remove the cake from the pan when it is cool (to do this, run a rubber spatula carefully around the edges of the cake) and invert onto a serving plate. Ice the top with Cream Cheese Frosting. You may want to sprinkle ground walnuts or pecans on top of the iced cake.

▶ Store in the refrigerator.

Variation: You can also use the Vegan Cream Cheese Glaze, page 275, instead of the Cream Cheese Frosting. Either way, this cake is delicious.

BOLD BANANA CAKE

*This is a heavy, rich-tasting, gluten-free cake that works best as only one layer.
You can either frost and serve it right from the pan, or remove it from the pan and
frost and decorate it as a one-layer torte. I like to arrange vegan chocolate chips
around the outside edge and along the bottom of the cake before serving. It gives it
a professional look.*

Makes 10 servings

Preparation time: cake, 20 minutes; icing, 10 minutes
Baking time: 30 to 35 minutes ▼ **Frosting/garnish:** 5 minutes

3 medium-size bananas (the riper, the sweeter)

½ cup pure maple syrup

½ cup unsweetened applesauce (preferably organic)

2 tablespoons whipped tofu (see Note on page 64)

1 teaspoon vanilla extract

1 tablespoon flax powder

¾ cup water

2½ cups gluten-free rolled oats, ground into a fine flour in a blender or food processor

2 teaspoons baking powder

1 teaspoon baking soda

1 teaspoon xanthan gum (optional—but it helps the cake rise by taking the place of gluten that is in wheat flour)

½ cup grain-sweetened vegan chocolate chips (available at health food stores), plus another ½ cup, if also using for a garnish

Maple Cocoa Frosting, page 275

▶ Preheat the oven to 375°F. Coat an 8-inch round cake pan or 8-inch round springform pan with nonstick cooking spray. If you are using the 8-inch round cake pan and will be taking the cake out of the pan to serve, cover the bottom of the pan with waxed or parchment paper.

▶ Mash the bananas in a medium-size bowl with a fork. Add the maple syrup, applesauce, whipped tofu, and vanilla. In a separate small bowl, make a slurry (see Note) with the flax powder and ¾ cup of water, and add to the banana mixture.

▶ In another bowl, mix the oat flour, baking powder, baking soda, and xanthan gum, if using. Add the wet ingredients to the dry ingredients and mix to just combine. Add ½ cup of the chocolate chips and stir again, just to mix. Do not overmix. Pour the batter into the prepared pan.

continues

continued

▸ Bake for 30 to 35 minutes, or until the sides pull away from the edge of the pan and a toothpick inserted into the center comes out clean. While the cake is baking, prepare the Maple Cocoa Frosting. Allow the cake to cool completely in the pan if you will be serving it from the pan. If you are going to serve it like a torte and are using the 8-inch round pan, allow the cake to cool for 10 minutes in the pan, then carefully invert it onto a wire cake rack and allow it to cool completely before frosting with Maple Cocoa Frosting. If you bake the cake in the springform pan, you may allow it to cool completely in the pan. Just remember to remove the metal collar before serving the cake. Garnish with the extra ½ cup of chocolate chips, if desired.

PER SERVING: 216 calories, 5 g fat (2 g saturated), 46 g carbohydrate, 6 g dietary fiber, 20 g sugar, 4 g protein, 0 mg cholesterol, 100 mg sodium, 390 mg potassium. Calories from fat: 17 percent.

Notes:
• Use a mini food processor or blender to whip a small slice of soft tofu from a 12-ounce package. Measure out 2 tablespoons after it is whipped.
• A slurry is a thin mixture of liquid, usually water, combined with a finely ground substance.

APPLESAUCE APPLAUSE CAKE

This moist applesauce cake tastes wonderful on a cool autumn day. Actually, it tastes great anytime! I like to make it as a two-layer cake iced with fluffy vanilla vegan cream cheese icing and pipe a decorative edging of apple butter around the top edge and the bottom of the cake. I make sure that I buy the unsweetened, thick apple butter, such as Bauman's, to use for the edging.

Makes 12 servings

Preparation time: cake, 15 minutes; icing, 10 minutes ▼ **Baking time:** 30 to 35 minutes
Frosting/garnish: 10 minutes ▼ **Freezes well without icing**

3½ cups unbleached all-purpose flour

2 teaspoons baking soda

2 teaspoons ground cinnamon

¼ teaspoon salt

⅓ cup canola oil

1 cup Sucanat or brown sugar

2 teaspoons flax powder

½ cup apple cider, apple juice, or water

2 cups unsweetened applesauce (preferably organic)

Whipped Cream Cheese Frosting, page 276 (should be made the day before serving, if possible)

PER SERVING: 421 calories, 20 g fat (3 g saturated), 54 g carbohydrate, 2 g dietary fiber, 6 g sugar, 7 g protein, 0 mg cholesterol, 319 mg sodium, 170 mg potassium. Calories from fat: 29 percent.

▶ Preheat the oven to 350°F. Coat two 8-inch round baking pans with nonstick cooking oil and line the bottom of the pans with waxed or parchment paper.

▶ In a large bowl, combine the flour, baking soda, cinnamon, and salt and set aside. Using an electric mixer in another bowl, beat the oil and Sucanat until combined. Mix the flax powder and apple cider together in a small bowl, add to the oil mixture, and mix until combined. Beat in the applesauce. On low speed, add the dry ingredients to the oil mixture and beat until just combined. Pour the batter into the prepared pans.

▶ Bake for 30 to 35 minutes, or until a toothpick inserted into the center comes out clean.

▶ If you have not made the frosting the day before, prepare the Whipped Cream Cheese Frosting while the cake is baking.

▶ Allow the cake to cool in the pans for 10 minutes and then remove from the pans. Remove the paper from the bottom of the cakes. Let cool completely on wire racks before frosting.

ORANGE CREAMSICLE CAKE

Who can forget those delicious orange Creamsicles that we ate as kids? This cake brings back memories of lazy summer days spent enjoying the combined flavors of orange and vanilla.

> **Makes 12 servings**

Preparation time: cake, 15 minutes; icing, 10 minutes ▼ **Baking time:** 55 minutes
Frosting/garnish: 5 minutes ▼ **Freezes well without icing**

¾ cup soft vegan butter spread, preferably tub style, at room temperature. (If using stick butter, soften it in the microwave until it is the consistency of tub butter. Do not melt!)

1¼ cups pure maple syrup

1 tablespoon orange extract

4½ cups unbleached all-purpose flour

1½ tablespoons baking powder

¼ teaspoon salt

2½ cups orange juice

Whipped Cream Cheese Frosting, page 276, or Vanilla Buttercream Frosting, page 283

PER SERVING: 481 calories, 16 g fat (2 g saturated), 77 g carbohydrate, 1 g dietary fiber, 21 g sugar, 8 g protein, 0 mg cholesterol, 216 mg sodium, 300 mg potassium. Calories from fat: 15 percent.

▶ Preheat the oven to 350°F. Coat an 8 by 11-inch cake pan with nonstick cooking spray.

▶ Place the butter in a bowl and cream. Slowly add the maple syrup and beat until light and fluffy. Add the orange extract and mix. In another bowl, combine the flour, baking powder, and salt. Alternately add the flour mixture and orange juice to the butter mixture and mix well.

▶ Pour into the prepared pan and bake for 55 minutes, or until a toothpick inserted into the center comes out clean. While the cake is baking, prepare the Whipped Cream Cheese or Vanilla Buttercream Frosting. Allow the cake to cool completely before frosting.

TROPICAL FRUIT CAKE

I used to love strawberry cake with coconut cream frosting before I became vegan. I wanted to be able to continue to enjoy that same taste, so I "veganized" it. This cake is a combination of strawberry cake, strawberry jam, and fluffy coconut cream cheese frosting.

Makes 12 servings

Preparation time: cake, 15 minutes; frosting, 10 minutes ▼ **Baking time:** 30 to 35 minutes
Frosting/garnish: 5 minutes ▼ **Freezes well without frosting**

¾ cup soft vegan butter spread, preferably tub style, at room temperature. (If using stick butter, soften it in the microwave until it is the consistency of tub butter. Do not melt!)

1¼ cups pure maple syrup

10 large strawberries

1 tablespoon vanilla extract

4½ cups unbleached all-purpose flour

1½ tablespoons baking powder

¼ teaspoon salt

2½ cups vegan milk

Coconut Cream Cheese Frosting, page 273 (best if prepared the day before)

½ cup unsweetened shredded coconut, for garnish (optional)

Filling:

¾ cup strawberry preserves

PER SERVING: 561 calories, 26 g fat (10 g saturated), 74 g carbohydrate, 2 g dietary fiber, 21 g sugar, 10 g protein, 0 mg cholesterol, 223 mg sodium, 289 mg potassium. Calories from fat: 28 percent.

▶ Preheat the oven to 350°F. Coat two 9-inch round pans with nonstick cooking spray. Line the bottom of each pan with waxed or parchment paper.

▶ In a bowl, cream the butter, slowly add the maple syrup, and beat until light and fluffy. Puree the strawberries and stir into the butter mixture. Add the vanilla and mix.

▶ In another bowl, combine the flour, baking powder, and salt and mix. Alternately add the flour mixture and the milk to the butter mixture and mix well.

▶ Pour into the prepared pans and bake for about 30 minutes, or until a toothpick inserted into the center comes out clean. Allow the cake to cool for 10 minutes in the pans. Remove the cakes from the pans, remove the paper, and let the cakes cool completely on wire racks before frosting.

▶ If you did not prepare the Coconut Cream Cheese Frosting the day before, prepare it while the cake is baking.

▶ To assemble and frost: With a sharp knife or wire cake cutter, cut the rounded top off both cake layers. Then cut each layer in half lengthwise to form four thin layers. Place the bottom layer on a serving plate and spread with strawberry preserves. Place two more layers on top, spreading each with strawberry preserves. Place the top layer upside down on top of the preserves, so that the side facing up is completely flat. Frost the top and sides of the cake with Coconut Cream Cheese Frosting. Sprinkle the coconut over the top and sides of the cake and refrigerate.

GRANNY'S CRANBERRY CAKE

Chocolate and cranberry teamed together make an interesting duo. This cake is a great way to usher in the Christmas season, and it provides a way to use up some of those Thanksgiving leftovers—you can use your leftover cranberry relish as the filling.

> **Makes 12 servings**

Preparation time: cake, 15 minutes; frosting, 10 minutes ▾ **Baking time:** 30 minutes

2¼ cups unbleached all-purpose flour

1¾ cups granulated sweetener

¾ cup unsweetened cocoa powder

1½ teaspoons baking powder

¾ teaspoon baking soda

¼ teaspoon salt

2 cups vegan milk

2 teaspoons apple cider vinegar

1 teaspoon vanilla extract

½ cup canola oil

Whipped Cream Cheese Frosting, page 276

Fresh cranberries and mint leaves, for garnish (optional)

Filling:

¾ cup cranberry relish (check the label to make sure it is vegan)

▶ Preheat the oven to 375°F. Coat two 8-inch round cake pans with nonstick cooking spray. Line the bottom of each pan with waxed or parchment paper

▶ In a medium-size bowl, combine the flour, sweetener, cocoa powder, baking powder, baking soda, and salt. In another bowl, combine the milk and vinegar. Add the vanilla and oil. Slowly pour the liquid mixture into the dry mixture and stir to combine. Beat one hundred strokes, until the batter is smooth and glossy.

▶ Pour into the prepared pan and bake for 30 minutes, or until a toothpick inserted into the center comes out clean. Allow the cake to cool for 10 minutes in the pans. Remove the cakes from the pans, remove the paper, and let the cakes cool completely on wire racks before frosting.

▶ If you have not prepared the Whipped Cream Cheese Frosting the day before, prepare it while the cake is baking.

▶ To assemble and decorate: When the cake is completely cool, level off the top of the cake layers with a long, sharp knife or wire cake cutter. Cut each layer in half horizontally to form four thin layers. Place the bottom layer on a serving plate. Spread with ¼ cup of cranberry relish. Place the next layer on top and spread with ¼ cup of relish. Repeat with the next layer and the remaining ¼ cup of relish. Frost the top and sides of the cake with Whipped Cream Cheese Frosting and decorate with fresh cranberries and mint leaves, if desired.

PER SERVING (CAKE ONLY): 314 calories, 10.7 g fat (1.2 g saturated), 52.9 g carbohydrate, 2.5 g dietary fiber, 31 g sugar, 4.7 g protein, 0 mg cholesterol, 153 mg sodium. Calories from fat: 16 percent.

CHOCOLATE-COVERED MINT

Have you ever dipped a candy cane in your hot chocolate? As a child, being a creative young chocoholic, I did just that and found that chocolate and mint flavors were natural companions.

Makes 12 servings

Preparation time: cake, 15 minutes; frosting, 10 minutes
Baking time: 30 minutes ▼ **Frosting/garnish:** 5 minutes

2¼ cups unbleached all-purpose flour

1¾ cups granulated sweetener

¾ cup unsweetened cocoa powder

1½ teaspoons baking powder

¾ teaspoon baking soda

¼ teaspoon salt

2 cups vegan milk

2 teaspoons apple cider vinegar

1 teaspoon peppermint extract

½ cup canola oil

Whipped Chocolate Frosting, page 266, or Chocolate Buttercream Frosting, page 281

Garnish (optional):

½ cup hard peppermint candies, ground very fine—read the label to get candies with natural ingredients

Mini vegan candy canes (however many you choose to put on the cake!)

▶ Preheat the oven to 375°F. Coat an 8 by 11-inch cake pan with nonstick cooking spray.

▶ In a medium-size bowl, combine the flour, sweetener, cocoa powder, baking powder, baking soda, and salt. In another bowl, combine the milk and vinegar. Add the peppermint extract and oil. Slowly pour the liquid mixture into the dry mixture and stir to combine. Beat one hundred strokes, until the batter is smooth and glossy.

▶ Pour into the prepared pan and bake for 30 minutes, or until a toothpick inserted into the center comes out clean. Allow the cake to cool completely in the pan before frosting. If you did not prepare the Whipped Chocolate Frosting the day before, or if you are using the Chocolate Buttercream Frosting, prepare it while the cake is baking.

▶ Mound the frosting onto the completely cooled cake and garnish with ground peppermint candies and/or mini candy canes, if desired. (Be sure to check ingredients on the label to be sure they are vegan, if you intend to eat them.)

▶ Refrigerate before serving.

PER SERVING (CAKE ONLY): 314 calories, 10.7 g fat (1.2 g saturated), 52.9 g carbohydrate, 2.5 g dietary fiber, 31 g sugar, 4.7 g protein, 0 mg cholesterol, 153 mg sodium. Calories from fat: 16 percent.

MY GRANDMOTHER'S CRUMB CAKE ♥

This is one of my favorite recipes. It has been handed down through my family for generations, and I was able to veganize it without sacrificing any of the good taste. My kids absolutely love it and ask me to make it all the time. It doesn't last long! We usually eat it for breakfast, but it is equally good for dessert (or even a snack). It's a real crowd-pleaser—vegan and nonvegan! I like to add some fruit spread in the middle when fresh fruit is available in the summer. See page 167 for a recipe for fruit spread.

Makes 9 servings

Preparation time: 15 minutes ▼ **Baking time:** 45 minutes

1½ cups granulated sweetener (see Note)

2 cups unbleached all-purpose flour

2 teaspoons baking powder

½ cup vegetable shortening (preferably nonhydrogenated, such as Spectrum or Earth Balance)

1 teaspoon egg replacer (such as Ener-G)

¼ cup water

1 teaspoon vanilla extract

¾ cup vanilla vegan milk

▶ Preheat the oven to 350°F. Coat an 8-inch square baking pan with nonstick cooking spray.

▶ In a bowl, combine the sugar, flour, and baking powder. Cut the shortening into the flour mixture with two knives until the dough forms pieces no larger than a pea. Remove 1 cup of the dry mixture and reserve to use as the crumb topping.

▶ In a measuring cup, mix the egg replacer with the ¼ cup of water and add the vanilla. Fill the cup the rest of the way with the milk until it measures 1 cup (about ¾ cup of milk). Add the liquid ingredients to the dry ingredients and mix until just combined.

▶ Pour the batter into the prepared pan and sprinkle with the reserved dry mixture. Bake for 45 minutes, or until a toothpick inserted into the center comes out clean.

▶ Allow the cake to cool completely in the pan before serving.

Variations: Add 1 cup of fresh peaches, blueberries, or cherries to the batter before pouring into the pan and adding the crumbs. Bake as directed.

PER SERVING: 336 calories, 12 g fat (5 g saturated), 55 g carbohydrate, 1 g dietary fiber, 3 g protein, 0 mg cholesterol, 84 mg sodium, 61 mg potassium. Calories from fat: 29 percent.

Note: I usually use organic sugar due to the light color and delicate flavor of the cake. Some other sweeteners may change the color and will have more of a molasses flavor.

OOPS, I DROPPED MY CAKE

This tender cake dripping with pineapple and sugar is guaranteed to disappear in a snap!

> **Makes 12 servings**

Preparation time: 5 minutes ▼ **Baking time:** 55 minutes ▼ **Freezes well**

Topping:

1 can (15½ ounces) crushed
  pineapple, drained
  (reserve juice)

1 cup brown sugar (firmly packed)

¼ cup canola oil

4 Bing cherries, pitted and cut in
  half, if in season

Batter:

1½ cups granulated sweetener
  (see Note)

2 cups unbleached all-purpose
  flour

2 teaspoons baking powder

½ cup vegetable shortening
  (preferably nonhydrogenated,
  such as Spectrum)

1 teaspoon egg replacer (such as
  Ener-G)

¼ cup water

1¼ cups reserved pineapple juice

1 teaspoon vanilla extract

- ► Preheat the oven to 375°F. Coat a 9-inch round baking pan with nonstick cooking spray.

- ► To make the topping: Drain the pineapple and reserve the juice. (If the juice does not measure 1¼ cups, add water to make up the difference.) In a small bowl, combine the pineapple, brown sugar, and canola oil. Pour the topping into the prepared pan. If using fresh cherries, arrange the halves at equal distances around the pan. Push them through topping so they are on the bottom of the pan, which will eventually be the top of the cake.

- ► To make the batter: In a bowl, combine the sugar, flour, and baking powder. Cut the shortening into the flour water. Add the 1¼ cups of reserved pineapple juice to the mixture with two knives until the dough forms pieces no larger than a pea.

- ► In a small bowl, mix the egg replacer with the ¼ cup of egg replacer mixture, then add the vanilla. Pour the liquid ingredients into the dry ingredients and mix until just combined. Spoon the batter into the prepared pan onto the topping mixture.

- ► Bake for 55 minutes, or until a toothpick inserted into the center comes out clean.

- ► Invert the cake onto a heatproof serving plate immediately upon removing from the oven. Allow the cake to cool completely before serving.

> **Hint:** This cake tends to drip sticky pineapple juice, so it is a good idea to place a sheet of aluminum foil on the bottom oven rack to make your cleanup easier.

PER SERVING: 308 calories, 13 g fat (4 g saturated), 50 g carbohydrate, <1 g dietary fiber, <1 g protein, 0 mg cholesterol, 66 mg sodium, 127 mg potassium. Calories from fat: 36 percent.

Note: I usually use organic sugar due to the light color and delicate flavor of the cake. Some other sweeteners may change the color and will have more of a molasses taste.

BANANA SPLIT CAKE

This gluten-free cake takes a bit more work because there are several parts to it, but it is definitely worth the extra time. It mimics the taste of a banana split—who can resist that?

> ### Makes 10 servings

Preparation time: cake, 15 minutes; cherry topping, 10 minutes; whipped topping, 10 minutes; chocolate syrup, 5 minutes ▾ **Baking time:** 40 minutes

3 medium-size bananas (the riper, the sweeter)

½ cup pure maple syrup

½ cup unsweetened pineapple

2 tablespoons whipped tofu (see Note)

½ teaspoon vanilla extract

1 tablespoon flax powder

¾ cup pineapple juice

2½ cups gluten-free rolled oats (ground into a fine flour in a blender or food processor)

2 teaspoons baking powder

1 teaspoon baking soda

1 teaspoon xanthan gum (optional—but it helps the cake rise by taking the place of gluten that is in wheat flour)

Vanilla Tofu Whipped Topping, page 268

Cherry Topping, page 265

Vegan Chocolate Syrup, page 267

½ banana, for garnish (optional)

- ▶ Preheat the oven to 375°F degrees. Coat an 8-inch round cake pan or 8-inch round springform pan with nonstick cooking spray.
- ▶ Mash the bananas in a medium-size bowl with a fork. Add the maple syrup, pineapple, whipped tofu, and vanilla. Make a slurry (see Note) with the flax powder and the ¾ cup of pineapple juice, and add to the banana mixture.
- ▶ In another bowl, mix the oat flour, baking powder, baking soda, and xanthan gum, if using. Add the wet ingredients to the dry ingredients and mix to combine. Pour the batter into the prepared pan.
- ▶ Bake for 40 minutes, or until the sides pull away from the edge of the pan and a toothpick inserted into the center comes out clean. Allow the cake to cool completely in the pan.
- ▶ While the cake is baking, make the Vanilla Tofu Whipped Topping, the Cherry Topping, and the Vegan Chocolate Syrup.

Notes:
- Use a mini food processor or blender to whip a small slice of soft tofu from a 12-ounce package. Measure out 2 tablespoons after it is whipped.
- A slurry is a thin mixture of liquid, usually water, combined with a finely ground substance.

PER SERVING: 223 calories, 3 g fat (<1 g saturated), 46 g carbohydrate, 3 g dietary fiber, 16 g sugar, 5 g protein, 0 mg cholesterol, 225 mg sodium, 441 mg potassium. Calories from fat: 11 percent.

continues

continued

▶ To assemble: When the cake is completely cool (and immediately before serving), use a spoon to drop Vanilla Tofu Whipped Topping around the outside edge of the cake. Spoon the cooled Cherry Topping inside the ring of whipped topping. Slice the half banana and stand a slice in each mound of whipped topping. Drizzle Vegan Chocolate Syrup over the cake in a lattice pattern. Serve immediately.

LONG ON FLAVOR SHORTCAKE

When I became vegan, I was faced with the challenge of finding shortcake to use for one of my favorite desserts—strawberry shortcake. None of the commercial shortcakes were vegan, and I had never really liked their spongy consistency anyway. So I came up with this vegan version of strawberry shortcake, which is long on flavor and short on fat and cholesterol.

Makes 9 servings

Preparation time: cake, 15 minutes; strawberries, 15 minutes; whipped topping, 5 minutes
Baking time: 45 minutes

1½ cups granulated sweetener (I usually use organic sugar)

2 cups unbleached all-purpose flour

2 teaspoons baking powder

½ cup vegetable shortening (preferably nonhydrogenated, such as Spectrum or Earth Balance)

1 teaspoon egg replacer (such as Ener-G)

¼ cup water

1 teaspoon vanilla extract

¾ cup vanilla vegan milk

2 pints fresh strawberries (organic if possible)

2 recipes Vanilla Tofu Whipped Topping, page 268

9 fresh mint leaves, for garnish (optional)

▶ Preheat the oven to 350°F. Coat an 8-inch square baking pan with nonstick cooking spray.

▶ In a bowl, combine the sweetener, flour, and baking powder. Cut the shortening into the flour mixture with two knives until the dough forms pieces no larger than a pea. Remove 1 cup of the dry mixture and reserve to use as a crumb topping.

▶ In a measuring cup, mix the egg replacer with the ¼ cup of water and add the vanilla. Fill the cup the rest of the way with the milk until it measures 1 cup (about ¾ cup of milk). Add the liquid ingredients to the dry ingredients and mix until just combined. Pour the batter into the prepared pan. Sprinkle with the reserved dry mixture.

▶ Bake for 45 minutes, or until a toothpick inserted into the center comes out clean. While the cake is baking, prepare a double recipe of Vanilla Tofu Whipped Topping. Allow the cake to cool completely in the pan before serving.

▶ Hull the strawberries, place in a bowl, and crush into a sauce with a fork. Refrigerate until ready to use.

▶ To assemble: Place a spoonful of strawberry sauce on an individual plate. Top with a slice of cake. Top with more strawberry sauce. Spoon on a dollop of Vanilla Tofu Whipped Topping. Drizzle a small amount of strawberry juice from the sauce over the whipped topping, if desired. Garnish with a fresh mint leaf, if desired. Repeat for the remaining servings. Serve immediately.

PER SERVING: 524 calories, 16 g fat (6 g saturated), 86 g carbohydrate, 5 g dietary fiber, 2 g sugar, 12 g protein, 0 mg cholesterol, 94 mg sodium, 631 mg potassium. Calories from fat: 26 percent.

LEMON TIMES TWO CAKE

By now, you're well aware of my love for chocolate (If it were up to me, everything would have chocolate in it!), but I also enjoy the tangy sweet flavor of lemon.

Makes 12 servings

Preparation time: cake, 15 minutes; frosting, 10 minutes
Baking time: 50 minutes ▼ **Frosting/garnish:** 5 minutes

¾ cup soft vegan butter spread, preferably tub style, at room temperature. (If using stick butter, soften it in the microwave until it is the consistency of tub butter. Do not melt!)

1¼ cups pure maple syrup

½ teaspoon lemon extract

4½ cups unbleached all-purpose flour

1½ tablespoons baking powder

¼ teaspoon salt

2½ cups lemon juice

Whipped Lemon Frosting, page 272

½ fresh lemon, thinly sliced, for garnish (optional)

Fresh mint leaves, for garnish (optional)

▶ Preheat the oven to 350°F. Coat an 8 by 11-inch cake pan with nonstick cooking spray.

▶ Place the butter in a bowl. Slowly add the maple syrup and beat until light and fluffy. Add the lemon extract and mix. In another bowl, combine the flour, baking powder, and salt. Alternately add the flour mixture and lemon juice to the butter mixture and mix well.

▶ Pour into the prepared pan and bake for about 50 minutes, or until a toothpick inserted into the center comes out clean. Allow the cake to cool completely in the pan before frosting.

▶ If you did not make the Whipped Lemon Frosting the day before, prepare while the cake is baking. Mound onto the cake and swirl or make peaks in the frosting.

▶ To garnish: Make a cut starting at the middle of each lemon slice through to the outer edge (the radius of the slice). Twist each lemon slice and arrange on the cake top. Place a mint leaf with each lemon twist. Chill before serving. Store in the refrigerator.

PER SERVING: 429 calories, 11 g fat (<1 g saturated), 76 g carbohydrate, 1 g dietary fiber, 22 g sugar, 10 g protein, 0 mg cholesterol, 100 mg sodium, 383 mg potassium. Calories from fat: 20 percent.

CINN-SATIONAL APPLE CAKE

Cinnamon sticks in apple cider were my inspiration for this cake. I make it in the fall when apples are abundant and at their best. The homey smell of cinnamon and apples wafts through the house as the cake bakes. This cake makes a wonderful dessert, but you can eat it for breakfast as well.

Makes 15 servings

Preparation time: cake, 15 minutes; glaze, 5 minutes
Baking time: 1 hour ▼ **Freezes well**

2 cups unbleached all-purpose flour

1½ cups whole wheat flour

2 teaspoons baking soda

2 teaspoons ground cinnamon

¼ teaspoon salt

⅓ cup canola oil

1 cup Sucanat or brown sugar

2 teaspoons flax powder

½ cup apple cider, apple juice, or water

⅓ cup unsweetened applesauce (preferably organic)

¾ cup vanilla vegan milk

2 cups baking apples (such as Macintosh), cored, peeled, and grated

Cinnamon maple glaze:

½ cup pure maple syrup

1 teaspoon ground cinnamon

▶ Preheat the oven to 350°F. Coat a Bundt pan with non-stick cooking spray.

▶ In a large bowl, combine the flours, baking soda, cinnamon, and salt. In a separate bowl, using an electric mixer, beat the oil and Sucanat until combined. Mix the flax powder with the apple cider in a small bowl, add to the oil mixture, and mix until combined. Add the applesauce and milk to the oil mixture and stir to combine. On low speed, add the dry ingredients to the oil mixture and beat until just combined. Stir in the grated apples by hand.

▶ Pour the batter into the prepared pan. Bake for 60 minutes, or until a toothpick inserted into the center comes out clean. Allow the cake to cool completely in the pan. Remove from the pan and place on a serving plate.

▶ To make the glaze: In a small saucepan, heat the maple syrup until it is hot but not boiling. Add the cinnamon and stir to combine. Pour the warm glaze over the cake and serve.

PER SERVING: 255 calories, 10 g fat (<1 g saturated), 38 g carbohydrate, 3 g dietary fiber, 11 g sugar, 4 g protein, 0 mg cholesterol, 176 mg sodium, 156 mg potassium. Calories from fat: 35 percent.

"P" Is for Pumpkin Cake

This is a wonderful cake to make in the fall when pumpkins and chrysanthemums are everywhere, the air is crisp, and the leaves are turning red and gold. For those of you who do not live in a changing climate and have never experienced the splendid colors and tastes of fall in the northeast United States, you can still appreciate this cake. It's like pumpkin pie in cake form!

Makes 15 servings

Preparation time: cake, 15 minutes; frosting, 10 minutes ▼ **Baking time:** 80 minutes

1½ cups unbleached all-purpose flour

1½ cups whole wheat flour

2 teaspoons ground cinnamon

2 teaspoons baking soda

½ teaspoon salt

2 cups pure maple syrup

1 (15-ounce) can pure pumpkin puree

½ cup canola oil

½ cup unsweetened applesauce (preferably organic)

4 teaspoons flax powder

¾ cup water

Pumpkin Whipped Topping, page 269

▶ Preheat the oven to 350°F. Coat a Bundt cake pan with nonstick cooking spray.

▶ Combine the flours, cinnamon, baking soda, and salt in a large bowl. Combine the maple syrup, pumpkin, oil, and applesauce in another bowl. In a small bowl, combine the flax powder and ¾ cup of water. Add to the liquid ingredients and stir. Slowly add the flour mixture to the liquid ingredients, mixing to just combine.

▶ Pour the batter into the prepared pan. Bake for about 80 minutes, or until a toothpick inserted into the center comes out clean. Let the cake cool completely in the pan before serving. Remove from the pan.

▶ While the cake is baking, make the Pumpkin Whipped Topping.

▶ To serve: Cut the cake and place on individual plates. Top each slice with a dollop of whipped topping and a sprinkle of cinnamon, if desired.

PER SERVING: 367 calories, 10 g fat (<1 g saturated), 62 g carbohydrate, 3 g dietary fiber, 28 g sugar, 7 g protein, 0 mg cholesterol, 285 mg sodium, 371 mg potassium. Calories from fat: 25 percent.

RICHER THAN
FORT KNOX CAKE

This moist chocolate cake filled with chocolate pudding and coated with a thin chocolate candy covering is a chocolate lover's dream. If you feel ambitious and want to impress your friends, go ahead and take the extra time to garnish this cake to make it look truly spectacular.

Makes 15 servings

Preparation time: cake, 15 minutes; filling, 10 minutes; candy coating, 10 minutes; whipped chocolate topping, 15 minutes ▼ **Baking time:** 50 minutes ▼ **Frosting/garnish:** 15 minutes

2¼ cups unbleached all-purpose flour

1¾ cups granulated sweetener

¾ cup unsweetened cocoa powder

1½ teaspoons baking powder

1¼ teaspoons baking soda

½ teaspoon salt

2 cups vegan milk

1 teaspoon vanilla extract

¼ cup soy mayonnaise (such as Nayonaise)

½ cup unsweetened applesauce (preferably organic)

15 fresh cranberries, or 5 long-stemmed cherries, for garnish (optional)

1 tablespoon granulated sugar, for garnish (optional)

5 mint leaves, for garnish (optional)

10 fresh orange wedges or mandarin orange sections, patted dry, for garnish (optional)

Chocolate Decorative Topping, page 277 (see Note on page 79)

▶ Preheat the oven to 375°F. Coat a Bundt pan with non-stick cooking spray.

▶ In a medium-size bowl, combine the flour, sweetener, cocoa powder, baking powder, baking soda, and salt. In another bowl, combine the milk, vanilla, mayonnaise, and applesauce. Slowly pour the liquid mixture into the dry mixture. Stir to combine.

▶ To make the filling: Place the tofu in a food processor and blend until smooth and creamy. Add the powdered sugar and vanilla and continue to blend. Add the melted chocolate and blend to combine.

▶ Pour half of the batter into the prepared pan. Spoon the filling over the batter. Top with the remaining batter, being careful not to mix the layers together. Bake for 50 minutes, or until the edges pull away from the sides of the pan. Remove from the oven and allow to cool completely in the pan.

continues

continued

Pudding filling:

1 pound (16 ounces, or 1⅓ [12-ounce] packages) firm silken tofu

1 cup powdered sugar

2 teaspoons vanilla extract

2 cups vegan chocolate chips, melted (use a microwave or double boiler)

Candy coating:

¼ cup vegan milk

2 cups vegan chocolate chips

- ▶ To make the candy coating: When the cake is cool, heat the milk over low heat. Add the chocolate chips to the milk and stir until smooth. Place the cooled cake on a wire rack set onto a bowl with a diameter larger than that of the cake, so that any extra chocolate sauce will drip into the bowl. Pour the chocolate topping over the cake to coat it completely. Refrigerate it until the topping hardens into a chocolate shell. Remove from the refrigerator and break off any hard points that have formed by the chocolate's dripping through the wire rack, so the cake will sit flat on a serving plate. (Kitchen shears work well for this.)

- ▶ To garnish: Place the Chocolate Decorative Topping in a pastry bag fit with a (large star) #2D decorating tip. If you don't have a decorating bag, you can cut the corner off the bottom of a plastic bag and insert the decorating tip into the corner of the bag instead. Pipe five evenly spaced mounds of Chocolate Decorative Topping around the top of the cake. Dip the cranberries in water and roll in sugar to coat them. Place three sugared cranberries on top of each mound of chocolate. Place one mint leaf with each set of cranberries. Arrange the orange slices in a fan shape between the mounds of chocolate. Serve immediately. (If not serving immediately, wait to add the orange slices and store in refrigerator.)

PER SERVING: 590 calories, 23 g fat (11 g saturated), 93 g carbohydrate, 5 g dietary fiber, 2 g sugar, 12 g protein, 0 mg cholesterol, 212 mg sodium, 363 mg potassium. Calories from fat: 30 percent.

Note: Prepare the Chocolate Decorative Topping the day before you make this cake, if you want to use it to garnish the finished cake. The cake is delicious without it, but looks spectacular if fully garnished.

White on White Tropical Cake

I call this cake "white on white" because it truly is a vision in white—rich-tasting white coconut cake covered in white coconut frosting.

> **Makes 12 servings**

Preparation time: cake, 20 minutes; frosting, 10 minutes
Baking time: 40 minutes ▼ **Frosting:** 5 minutes

¾ cup vegetable shortening (preferably nonhydrogenated, such as Spectrum or Earth Balance)

1½ cups granulated sweetener (I use organic sugar because of the white color of this cake)

¾ cup + 2 tablespoons water

1½ teaspoons coconut extract

2¼ cups unbleached all-purpose flour

1 tablespoon baking powder

¼ teaspoon salt

½ cup egg replacer (such as Ener-G)

2 teaspoons cream of tartar

1 (15-ounce) can coconut milk (about 1½ cups)

¾ cup unsweetened shredded coconut

Coconut Cream Cheese Frosting, page 273

▶ Preheat the oven to 375°F. Coat a 9 by 12-inch baking pan with nonstick cooking oil.

▶ In a large bowl, cream together the shortening, sweetener, 2 tablespoons of water, and coconut extract. In a smaller bowl, combine the flour, baking powder, and salt. In a small electric mixer bowl, combine the egg replacer with remaining ¾ cup of water. Beat until soft peaks form. Add the cream of tartar to the whipped egg replacer and beat until combined.

▶ Pour the coconut milk into the shortening mixture, alternating with the flour mixture. Stir to combine. Add the coconut and stir until just combined. Gently fold in the whipped egg replacer.

▶ Pour into the prepared pan. Bake for 40 minutes, or until a toothpick inserted into the center comes out clean. Allow the cake to cool completely in the pan before frosting.

▶ If you did not make the Coconut Cream Cheese Frosting the day before, prepare while the cake is baking. Mound onto the cake after it has cooled completely. Refrigerate before serving.

PER SERVING: 627 calories, 38 g fat (26 g saturated), 65 g carbohydrate, 1 g dietary fiber, 1 g sugar, 9 g protein, 0 mg cholesterol, 129 mg sodium, 432 mg potassium. Calories from fat: 53 percent.

GERMAN CHOCOLATE CAKE

German Chocolate Cake is a traditional favorite that I "veganized" so I did not have to live without it! If you've never tried it, you'll love its unusual blend of chocolate and cooked coconut-pecan frosting.

> **Makes 12 servings**

Preparation time: cake, 10 minutes; frosting, 15 minutes
Baking time: 35 minutes ▼ **Assembly:** 5 minutes

2¼ cups unbleached all-purpose flour

1¾ cups granulated sweetener

¾ cup unsweetened cocoa powder

1½ teaspoons baking powder

1¼ teaspoons baking soda

¼ teaspoon salt

2 cups vegan milk

1 teaspoon vanilla extract

¼ cup soy mayonnaise (such as Nayonaise)

½ cup unsweetened applesauce (preferably organic)

German Chocolate Coconut-Pecan Frosting, page 278

PER SERVING: 632 calories, 42 g fat (26 g saturated), 64 g carbohydrate, 5 g dietary fiber, <1 g sugar, 6 g protein, 0 mg cholesterol, 209 mg sodium, 296 mg potassium. Calories from fat: 58 percent.

▶ Preheat the oven to 375°F. Coat three 8-inch round cake pans with nonstick cooking spray. Line the bottom of each pan with waxed or parchment paper.

▶ In a medium-size bowl, combine the flour, sweetener, cocoa powder, baking powder, baking soda, and salt. In another bowl, combine the milk, vanilla, mayonnaise, and applesauce. Slowly pour the liquid mixture into the dry mixture and stir to combine.

▶ Pour into the prepared pans and bake for 35 minutes, or until a toothpick inserted into the center comes out clean. While the cake is baking, prepare the German Chocolate Coconut-Pecan Frosting. Let the cake cool for 10 minutes in the pans. Invert each layer onto a wire rack, remove the waxed or parchment paper, and allow the cake to cool completely before frosting.

▶ When the cake is completely cool, frost only the tops of layers, stack them, and allow the frosting to drip down between the layers.

PEANUT BUTTER SURPRISE

Remember the taste of peanut butter Tandy Kakes? Perhaps these snack cakes are a regional treat. They are tiny snack cakes with yellow cake and peanut butter, covered with chocolate. Peanut Butter Surprise re-creates this treat in a large, yummy vegan cake creation.

Makes 15 servings

Preparation time: cake, 15 minutes; filling, 10 minutes; candy coating, 10 minutes
Baking time: 50 minutes ▼ **Frosting/garnish:** 10 minutes

1½ cups granulated sweetener

¾ cup soft vegan butter spread, preferably tub style, at room temperature. (If using stick butter, soften it in the microwave until it is the consistency of tub butter. Do not melt!)

1 tablespoon vanilla extract

4½ cups unbleached all-purpose flour

1½ tablespoons baking powder

¼ teaspoon salt

2¾ cups vanilla vegan milk

Filling and whipped garnish:

1 pound (16 ounces, or 1⅓ [12-ounce] packages) firm silken tofu

¾ cup creamy natural peanut butter

1 cup powdered sugar

2 tablespoons unbleached all-purpose flour

½ cup vegan chocolate chips, for garnish (optional)

▶ Preheat the oven to 375°F. Coat a Bundt pan with non-stick cooking spray.

▶ Combine the sweetener and butter in a medium-size bowl and cream until smooth. Add the vanilla and blend. In another bowl, combine the flour, baking powder, and salt. Alternately add the flour mixture and the milk to the butter mixture, stirring to combine. Pour half of the batter into the prepared Bundt pan.

▶ To make the peanut butter pudding filling and whipped garnish: Place the tofu in a food processor and process until smooth, scraping down the sides of the processor bowl as necessary. Add the peanut butter and blend. Add the powdered sugar and flour and blend. Spoon all but ½ cup of the pudding filling onto the batter in the pan, being careful not to touch the sides of the pan. Do not mix the batter with the filling layers. Top with the remaining batter. Refrigerate the reserved ½ cup of peanut butter filling to use for a garnish later on. Bake the cake for 50 minutes, or until the edges pull away from the sides of the pan. Remove from the oven and allow the cake to cool completely in the pan. When the cake is cool, prepare the candy coating.

continues

continued

Candy coating:

¼ cup vegan milk

2 cups vegan chocolate chips

▸ To make the candy coating: Heat the milk over low heat. Add the chocolate chips and stir until they are smooth and creamy. Place the cooled cake on a wire rack set on a bowl with a diameter larger than that of the cake, so any extra candy coating will drip into the bowl. Pour the candy coating over the cake to coat it completely and refrigerate it until the topping hardens into a chocolate shell. Remove from the refrigerator and break off any hard points that have formed by the chocolate's dripping through the wire rack, so that the cake will sit flat on a serving plate (kitchen shears work well for this). Place the cake on a serving plate.

▸ To garnish: Place the reserved peanut butter filling in a pastry bag fit with a #2D (large star) decorating tip. If you don't have a decorating bag, you may cut the corner off the bottom of a plastic bag and insert the decorating tip into the corner of the bag instead. Pipe five evenly spaced mounds of reserved peanut butter filling around the top of the cake. If desired, grind ½ cup of vegan chocolate chips in a food processor, blender, or coffee grinder until fine. Sprinkle onto the mounds of peanut butter filling. Refrigerate until serving.

PER SERVING: 561 calories, 24 g fat (6 g saturated), 79 g carbohydrate, 4 g dietary fiber, 1 g sugar, 14 g protein, 0 mg cholesterol, 117 mg sodium, 354 mg potassium. Calories from fat: 35 percent.

DOUBLE CHOCOLATE DELIGHT ♡

This is the cake that launched my vegan baking career. It's a rich chocolate cake covered in creamy chocolate cream cheese frosting. This is a favorite at my house and the ultimate chocolate lover's treat.

Makes 12 servings

Preparation time: cake, 10 minutes; frosting, 15 minutes
Baking time: 35 minutes ▼ **Assembly/garnish:** 15 minutes

2¼ cups unbleached all-purpose flour

1¾ cups granulated sweetener

¾ cup unsweetened cocoa powder

1½ teaspoons baking powder

¾ teaspoon baking soda

¼ teaspoon salt

2 cups vegan milk

2 teaspoons apple cider vinegar

1 teaspoon vanilla extract

½ cup canola oil

Chocolate Cream Cheese Frosting, page 267

½ cup vegan chocolate chips, for garnish

▶ Preheat the oven to 375°F. Coat two 8-inch cake pans with nonstick cooking spray. Line the bottom of each pan with waxed or parchment paper

▶ In a medium-size bowl, combine the flour, sweetener, cocoa powder, baking powder, baking soda, and salt. In another bowl, combine the milk and vinegar. Add the vanilla and oil. Slowly pour the liquid mixture into the dry mixture and stir to combine. Beat one hundred strokes, until the batter is smooth and glossy.

▶ Pour into the prepared pans and bake for 35 to 40 minutes, or until a toothpick inserted into the center comes out clean. Allow the cake to cool for 10 minutes in the pans. Remove from the pans, remove the paper, and place on wire racks. Allow to cool completely.

▶ If you did not prepare the Chocolate Cream Cheese Frosting the day before, prepare it while the cake is baking.

▶ To assemble and frost: Cut the rounded top off both cake layers. Using a sharp knife or wire cake cutter, cut the cake layers in half horizontally to form four thin layers. Place the bottom layer on a serving plate. Ice the top and add another layer of cake. Continue until you reach the top layer. Place the top layer on upside down so that the bottom of that layer is the top of the cake. This makes the top of the cake completely flat and easier to frost and decorate. Frost the top and sides of the cake.

▶ Grind ½ cup of vegan chocolate chips in a food processor, blender, or coffee grinder. Sprinkle on top of the cake. If desired, pipe the remaining frosting around the bottom and top edges of the cake, using a decorator tip and bag. Refrigerate until ready to serve.

PER SERVING (CAKE ONLY): 314 calories, 10.7 g fat (1.2 g saturated), 52.9 g carbohydrate, 2.5 g dietary fiber, 31 g sugar, 4.7 g protein, 0 mg cholesterol, 153 mg sodium. Calories from fat: 16 percent.

MINT MADNESS

Chocolate and mint are so good together that I created several combinations. In this one, I have taken a chocolate cake and topped it off with a fluffy mint frosting.

Makes 12 servings

Preparation time: cake, 15 minutes; frosting, 10 minutes
Baking time: 35 to 40 minutes ▼ **Frosting:** 5 minutes

2¼ cups unbleached all-purpose flour

1¾ cups granulated sweetener

¾ cup unsweetened cocoa powder

1½ teaspoons baking powder

¾ teaspoon baking soda

¼ teaspoon salt

2 cups vegan milk

2 teaspoons apple cider vinegar

1 teaspoon peppermint extract

½ cup canola oil

Fluffy Mint Frosting, page 279, or Pink Peppermint Buttercream Frosting, page 280

½ cup vegan chocolate chips, for garnish (optional)

▶ Preheat the oven to 375°F. Coat an 8 by 11-inch cake pan with nonstick cooking spray.

▶ In a medium-size bowl, combine the flour, sweetener, cocoa powder, baking powder, baking soda, and salt. In another bowl, combine the milk and vinegar. Add the peppermint extract and oil. Slowly pour the liquid mixture into the dry mixture and stir to combine. Beat one hundred strokes, until the batter is smooth and glossy.

▶ Pour into the prepared pan and bake for 35 to 40 minutes, or until a toothpick inserted into the center comes out clean. Allow the cake to cool completely in the pan before frosting.

▶ While the cake is baking, prepare the Fluffy Mint Frosting or Pink Peppermint Buttercream Frosting. Spread the frosting on the cooled cake. If desired, grind ½ cup of chocolate chips in a food processor, blender, or coffee grinder until fine and sprinkle over the top of the cake. Refrigerate until ready to serve.

PER SERVING (CAKE ONLY): 314 calories, 10.7 g fat (1.2 g saturated), 52.9 g carbohydrate, 2.5 g dietary fiber, 31 g sugar, 4.7 g protein, 0 mg cholesterol, 153 mg sodium. Calories from fat: 16 percent.

CHERRY VANILLA DREAM

I was waiting in line at the grocery store and saw this gorgeous cherry cake on the cover of a magazine. It looked so good that I knew I'd have to try to make a cake like it. I went home and came up with cherry cake with cherry filling in the middle topped with cream cheese frosting.

Makes 12 servings

Preparation time: cake, 15 minutes; frosting, 10 minutes
Baking time: 30 to 35 minutes ▼ **Frosting/garnish:** 5 minutes

¾ cup soft vegan butter spread, preferably tub style, at room temperature. (If using stick butter, soften it in the microwave until it is the consistency of tub butter. Do not melt!)

1½ cups granulated sweetener

1 tablespoon cherry extract

4½ cups unbleached all-purpose flour

1½ tablespoons baking powder

¼ teaspoon salt

2½ cups vanilla vegan milk

½ cup fresh cherries, pitted and chopped

Whipped Cream Cheese Frosting, page 276

6 to 8 whole fresh cherries, for garnish (optional)

Filling:

¾ cup cherry preserves or Cherry Topping, page 265

▸ Preheat the oven to 375°F. Coat two 8-inch round cake pans with nonstick cooking spray. Line the bottom of each pan with waxed or parchment paper.

▸ Place the butter in a bowl. Slowly add the granulated sweetener to the butter and beat until light and fluffy. Add the cherry extract and mix. In another bowl, combine the flour, baking powder, and salt.

▸ Alternately add the flour mixture and the milk to the butter mixture and mix well. Stir in the chopped cherries.

▸ Pour into the prepared pans and bake for 30 to 35 minutes, or until a toothpick inserted into the center comes out clean. While the cake is baking, prepare the Whipped Cream Cheese Frosting. Allow the cake to cool for 10 minutes in the pans. Invert the layers onto a wire rack and allow to cool completely before frosting.

▸ To assemble and frost: Cut the rounded top off both cake layers. Place the bottom layer on a serving plate and spread with cherry preserves. Place the top layer upside down on top of the preserves, so that the top is completely flat. Frost the top and sides of the cake with the cream cheese frosting. Garnish with several fresh cherries, if desired. Refrigerate before serving.

Variation: If you desire, you can make this as a more informal cake. You can still put cherry preserves in the center of the cake, but allow it to ooze out and drizzle down the sides of the cake. Mound the cream cheese frosting on the top of the cake and also allow it to drizzle down the side. Do not frost the sides of the cake. Garnish with cherries.

PER SERVING: 492 calories, 17 g fat (2 g saturated), 77 g carbohydrate, 2 g dietary fiber, <1 g sugar, 9 g protein, 0 mg cholesterol, 209 mg sodium, 215 mg potassium. Calories from fat: 19 percent.

TRIPLE CHERRY TREAT

This is basically a cherry cake with just a hint of chocolate. It is a one-layer cake as opposed to the two-layer Cherry Vanilla Dream Cake. It is the same cherry cake as the Cherry Vanilla Dream, but it is topped with Cherry Filling, which is surrounded by fluffy Whipped Cherry Topping and then drizzled with Vegan Chocolate Syrup.

Makes 12 servings

Preparation time: cake, 15 minutes; cherry whip, 10 minutes; cherry topping, 10 minutes; chocolate syrup, 5 minutes
Baking time: 45 minutes ▼ **Frosting/garnish:** 10 minutes

¾ cup soft vegan butter spread, preferably tub style, at room temperature. (If using stick butter, soften it in the microwave until it is the consistency of tub butter. Do not melt!)

1½ cups granulated sweetener

1 tablespoon cherry extract

4½ cups unbleached all-purpose flour

1½ tablespoons baking powder

¼ teaspoon salt

2½ cups vanilla vegan milk

½ cup fresh cherries, pitted and chopped

Whipped Cherry Topping, page 266

Cherry Filling, page 265

Vegan Chocolate Syrup, page 267

PER SERVING: 493 calories, 14 g fat (1 g saturated), 83 g carbohydrate, 3 g dietary fiber, 6 g sugar, 12 g protein, 0 mg cholesterol, 113 mg sodium, 447 mg potassium. Calories from fat: 23 percent.

▶ Preheat the oven to 350°F. Coat a 10-inch round spring-form pan with nonstick cooking spray.

▶ Place the butter in a bowl. Slowly add the granulated sweetener to the butter and beat until light and fluffy. Add the cherry extract and mix. In another bowl, combine the flour, baking powder, and salt.

▶ Alternately add the flour mixture and the milk to the butter mixture. Mix well. Stir in the chopped cherries. Pour into the prepared pan and bake for about 45 minutes, or until a toothpick inserted into the center comes out clean. Let cool completely in the pan.

▶ While the cake is baking, prepare the Whipped Cherry Topping. Refrigerate until ready to use. Next, make the Cherry Filling.

▶ When the cake is cool, remove the collar of the pan. Remove the cake from the bottom of the pan and cut the rounded top off the cake. Place the cake back in the pan upside down. Put the collar back on the bottom of the pan. Mound Whipped Cherry Topping on top of the cooled cake. Top with Cherry Filling. Drizzle with Vegan Chocolate Syrup. Refrigerate the cake until ready to serve. Remove the collar when the cake is ready to be served. Store in the refrigerator with the collar on.

TEN-CARAT GOLD CAKE

This cake is a rich blend of coconut, cinnamon, and raisins that stays moist and tender because of the carrots. Here's a helpful hint: If you are into using a juicer that extracts juice and leaves the pulp of fruits and vegetables (such as the Champion), you may use the carrot pulp that is left over after juicing carrots for this cake. I like to freeze carrot pulp in three-cup amounts so that when I am ready to make a carrot cake, I just have to get out one bag.

Makes 12 servings

Preparation time: cake, 15 minutes; frosting, 10 minutes
Baking time: 1 hour ▼ **Frosting:** 5 minutes

2¼ cups spelt flour

1 tablespoon baking powder

1 teaspoon xanthan gum (optional—but it helps the cake rise by taking the place of gluten that is in wheat flour)

¾ teaspoon ground cinnamon

1½ cups granulated sweetener

½ cup canola oil

1⅛ cups coconut milk

1 tablespoon vanilla extract

½ teaspoon coconut extract

3 cups grated carrots or carrot pulp

1 tablespoon flax powder

¾ cup water

½ cup raisins (preferably organic)

¾ cup unsweetened shredded coconut

Whipped Cream Cheese Frosting, page 276

2 tablespoons unsweetened shredded coconut, for garnish (optional)

PER SERVING: 504 calories, 26 g fat (11 g saturated), 60 g carbohydrate, 7 g dietary fiber, 1 g sugar, 9 g protein, 0 mg cholesterol, 193 mg sodium, 430 mg potassium. Calories from fat: 38 percent.

▶ Preheat the oven to 350°F. Coat a 9-inch round springform pan with nonstick cooking spray.

▶ In a large bowl, combine the flour, baking powder, xanthan gum, and cinnamon. In a medium-size bowl, combine the granulated sweetener, oil, coconut milk, vanilla and coconut extracts, and carrots. In a cup, combine the flax powder with ¾ cup of water. Add to the sugar mixture and mix to combine. Slowly add the liquid mixture to the flour mixture and stir to just combine. Stir in the raisins and coconut.

▶ Pour into the prepared pan and bake for 60 minutes, or until a toothpick inserted into the center comes out clean. Allow the cake to cool completely in the pan before frosting.

▶ Either the day before or while the cake is baking, prepare the Whipped Cream Cheese Frosting. When the cake is completely cool, mound the frosting onto the cake. Sprinkle with coconut, if desired. Refrigerate until serving. When ready to serve, remove the collar of the pan.

Variation: I wrote this recipe to be wheat free for those people who cannot tolerate wheat flour (but note that spelt is not gluten free); however, if you either can't find spelt flour, or choose not to use it, you may substitute unbleached all-purpose flour for the spelt flour, increase the coconut milk to 1¼ cups, and omit the xanthan gum.

ORANGE YOU GLAD IT HAS CHOCOLATE CHIPS CAKE

This cake is delightfully different with its unique blend of orange cake and dark chocolate chips. I like to make it when I need to bring dessert to a picnic for several reasons. First, it travels well because it does not have frosting. Second, it doesn't need refrigeration, so I don't have to worry about it sitting out on a picnic table for a while. Finally, it's easy to make!

Makes 15 servings

Preparation time: cake, 15 minutes; frosting, 10 minutes ▼ **Baking time:** 55 to 60 minutes
Frosting/garnish: 5 minutes ▼ **Freezes well**

¾ cup soft vegan butter spread, preferably tub style, at room temperature. (If using stick butter, soften it in the microwave until it is the consistency of tub butter. Do not melt!)

1¼ cups pure maple syrup

1 tablespoon orange extract

4½ cups unbleached all-purpose flour

1½ tablespoons baking powder

¼ teaspoon salt

2½ cups orange juice

2 cups vegan chocolate chips

Several fresh orange slices or mandarin orange sections, for garnish

Curls made from vegan chocolate, for garnish

Orange glaze:

¾ cup powdered sugar

2 tablespoons orange juice

▶ Preheat the oven to 350°F. Coat a Bundt cake pan with nonstick cooking spray.

▶ Place the butter in a bowl and cream. Slowly add the maple syrup and beat until light and fluffy. Add the orange extract and mix. In another bowl, combine the flour, baking powder, and salt. Alternately add the flour mixture and orange juice to the butter mixture. Mix well. Stir in chocolate chips.

▶ Pour into the prepared pan and bake for 55 to 60 minutes, or until a toothpick inserted into the center comes out clean. Let the cake cool completely in the pan. Remove from the pan.

▶ To make the glaze: Combine the powdered sugar and orange juice in a small food processor. Pour onto the cake.

▶ Garnish with fresh orange wedges or mandarin orange slices and curls of vegan dark chocolate, if desired.

PER SERVING: 412 calories, 14 g fat (4 g saturated), 71 g carbohydrate, 2 g dietary fiber, 16 g sugar, 5 g protein, 0 mg cholesterol, 85 mg sodium, 180 mg potassium. Calories from fat: 27 percent.

RAISED SUGAR CAKE ♡

This tender yeast cake covered with sugar and butter makes a delicious breakfast or dessert. You need to let the dough rise for a few hours, so I usually make it in the evening, let it rise overnight, and then finish the recipe the next morning. This recipe makes three cakes, so you can store two in the freezer for later use.

Makes 3 cakes, 12 servings each

Preparation time: 15 minutes ▼ **Rising time:** 6 hours
Putting into pans: 10 minutes ▼ **Baking time:** 25 minutes ▼ **Freezes well**

1 cup plain hot mashed potatoes (see Note on page 91)

1 cup granulated sweetener

¼ teaspoon salt

2 teaspoons flax powder

½ cup water

1 (0.7-ounce) packet active dry yeast dissolved in 1 cup of lukewarm water

¾ cup canola oil

4 cups unbleached all-purpose flour

Topping:

¼ pound (1 stick or ½ cup) soft vegan butter spread, preferably tub style, at room temperature. (If using stick butter, soften it in the microwave until it is the consistency of tub butter. Do not melt!)

1 pound light brown sugar

Pinch of ground cinnamon (optional)

▶ Put the mashed potatoes in a large bowl (if using instant potatoes, measure out enough flakes, water, and milk to make 1 cup of mashed potatoes according to the package directions). Add the sweetener and salt to the mashed potatoes and stir to combine. In a small bowl, mix the flax powder with the ½ cup of water. Add the yeast mixture, oil, and flax powder mixture to the mashed potato mixture. Add the flour and stir until smooth. Cover the bowl with a towel and allow the dough to rise for 5 hours in a warm place. (I usually allow the dough to rise overnight—just be sure to put it in a really big bowl so it doesn't climb out!)

▶ Coat three 9-inch round cake pans with nonstick cooking oil. Spoon the dough into the three pans, dividing it evenly among them. Allow the dough to rise for 1 hour, or until puffy. Preheat the oven to 350°F. Using the handle of a wooden spoon, poke holes about an inch apart in the dough. (Don't make the holes too deep or the sugar and butter will go to the bottom of the cake.) Place a small amount of butter (¼ to ½ teaspoon) in each hole and push it down with brown sugar. Sprinkle the rest of the sugar on top of the cakes. Sprinkle the top of the cakes lightly with cinnamon, if desired.

continues

continued

▸ Bake for 25 minutes, or until the top of the cake is nicely browned. Allow to cool completely before serving.

PER SERVING: 185 calories, 35 g fat (1 g saturated), 146 g carbohydrate, 5 g dietary fiber, 8 g protein, 0 mg cholesterol, 166 mg sodium, 362 mg potassium. Calories from fat: 33 percent.

Note: I usually cheat and use instant mashed potatoes. (Use the directions on the box of instant potatoes. With the brand that I use, I have to make 1½ servings of potatoes to make 1 cup. I only add the potato flakes, water, and vegan milk instead of dairy milk—do not add butter.) If you're using real potatoes, 1 to 2 small potatoes will work well. Peel the potatoes, cut into small pieces, and place in a little water in a small pan. Cover and boil until soft. Immediately mash them with an electric mixer. Do not use a hand masher or the cake will be lumpy; and do not use a food processor or the potatoes will have the consistency of glue.

COCONUT-COVERED DELIGHT

This traditional chocolate cake with coconut cream frosting reminds me of a Mounds candy bar.

Makes 12 servings

Preparation time: cake, 15 minutes; frosting, 10 minutes
Baking time: 35 minutes ▼ **Assembly:** 5 minutes

2¼ cups unbleached all-purpose flour

1¾ cups granulated sweetener

¾ cup unsweetened cocoa powder

1½ teaspoons baking powder

¾ teaspoon baking soda

¼ teaspoon salt

2 cups vegan milk

2 teaspoons apple cider vinegar

1 teaspoon vanilla extract

½ cup canola oil

Mega-Coconut Cream Cheese Frosting, page 274

1 cup unsweetened shredded coconut, for garnish (optional)

PER SERVING (CAKE ONLY): 314 calories, 10.7 g fat (1.2 g saturated), 52.9 g carbohydrate, 2.5 g dietary fiber, 31 g sugar, 4.7 g protein, 0 mg cholesterol, 153 mg sodium. Calories from fat: 16 percent.

▸ Preheat the oven to 375°F. Coat two 8-inch round cake pans with nonstick cooking spray. Line the bottom of each cake pan with waxed or parchment paper.

▸ In a medium-size bowl, combine the flour, sweetener, cocoa powder, baking powder, baking soda, and salt. In another bowl, combine the milk and vinegar. Add the vanilla and oil. Slowly pour the liquid mixture into the dry mixture and stir to combine. Beat one hundred strokes, until the batter is smooth and glossy.

▸ Pour into the prepared pans and bake for 35 minutes, or until a toothpick inserted into the center comes out clean. Allow the cake to cool for 10 minutes in the pans, then remove from pans, remove the paper, and let cool completely before frosting. If you did not make the Mega-Coconut Cream Frosting the day before, prepare it while the cake is baking.

▸ To assemble and frost: Cut the rounded top off the cake layers, with a sharp knife or wire cake cutter. Place the bottom layer on a serving plate. Cover with coconut frosting. Place the top layer on upside down, so the top is completely flat. Frost the top and sides of the cake. Sprinkle the top and sides with shredded coconut. Refrigerate until serving.

PEANUT BUTTER KANDY KAKE

For those of you who are familiar with peanut butter Tandy Kakes, this cake tastes just like those yummy snack cakes. If you like this recipe, try the Peanut Butter Surprise, page 82, which is also reminiscent of this childhood favorite.

Makes 12 servings

Preparation time: cake, 10 minutes; peanut butter filling, 10 minutes; chocolate, 10 minutes
Baking time: 50 minutes ▼ **Assembly:** 10 minutes

¾ cup soft vegan butter spread, preferably tub style, at room temperature. (If using stick butter, soften it in the microwave until it is the consistency of tub butter. Do not melt!)

1¼ cups pure maple syrup

1 tablespoon vanilla extract

4½ cups unbleached all-purpose flour

1½ tablespoons baking powder

¼ teaspoon salt

2½ cups vegan milk

Peanut butter filling:

¾ cup smooth natural peanut butter

⅓ cup pure maple syrup

¾ cup vegan milk

▶ Preheat the oven to 350°F. Coat a 10-inch round spring-form pan or 9-inch round cake pan with nonstick cooking spray. Line the bottom of the cake pan with waxed or parchment paper.

▶ Place the butter in a bowl and cream. Slowly add the maple syrup and beat until light and fluffy. Add the vanilla and mix. In another bowl, combine the flour, baking powder, and salt and mix to combine. Alternately add the flour mixture and the milk to the butter mixture and mix well.

▶ Pour into the prepared pan. Bake for 50 minutes, or until a toothpick inserted into the cake comes out clean. Allow the cake to cool completely in the pan if using the spring-form pan. Invert the cake onto a wire rack to cool after 10 minutes if using the round cake pan. Remove the waxed or parchment paper and allow to cool completely before assembling. While the cake is cooling, prepare the peanut butter filling.

▶ To make the peanut butter filling: Place all the filling ingredients in a food processor, process until smooth, and set aside. Cut the rounded top off the cake. Cut the cake in half horizontally with a sharp knife or wire cake cutter. Place the top of the cake upside down on a wire rack set on a bowl with a diameter bigger than that of the cake. Cover the cake layer with peanut butter filling. Place the other layer of cake on the peanut butter with the flat side facing up.

continues

continued

Chocolate candy topping:

¼ cup vegan milk

2 cups vegan chocolate chips

PER SERVING: 411 calories, 21 g fat
(7 g saturated), 54 g carbohydrate,
4 g dietary fiber, 14 g sugar, 9 g
protein, 0 mg cholesterol, 130 mg
sodium, 236 mg potassium. Calories
from fat: 40 percent.

▸ To make the chocolate candy topping: Over low heat, heat the milk until hot but not boiling (just steaming). Add the chocolate chips and stir until smooth. Carefully pour the chocolate over the cake, making sure to cover the whole cake top and sides. Smooth out the chocolate on top of the cake so it is not too thick. Refrigerate it until the topping hardens into a chocolate shell. Remove from the refrigerator and break off any hard points that have formed by the chocolate dripping through the wire rack, so the cake will sit flat on a serving plate. (Kitchen shears work well for this.) Store in the refrigerator.

PEANUT BUTTER KANDY KAKE THE SECOND ♡

This recipe is just a different version of an old favorite. I contemplated deleting the older version but I thought of the old poem: "Make new friends, but keep the old; / One is silver and the other gold." That's how I feel about these two cake recipes. Both are delicious. Try each one and see which one you like better!

> **Makes 10 servings**

Preparation time: cake, 15 minutes; chocolate toppings, 10 minutes ▼ **Baking time:** 45 minutes
Cooling time: (before putting on chocolate): ½ hour ▼ **Assembly:** 5 minutes

½ cup soft vegan butter spread, preferably tub style, at room temperature. (If using stick butter, soften it in the microwave until it is the consistency of tub butter. Do not melt!)

1 cup light brown sugar (firmly packed)

1 teaspoon vanilla extract

2 cups unbleached all-purpose flour

2 teaspoons baking powder

½ teaspoon baking soda

¼ teaspoon salt

1½ cups vegan milk

Peanut butter filling:
¾ cup natural peanut butter

Chocolate topping:
3 tablespoons vegan milk
1 cup vegan chocolate chips

PER SERVING: 362 calories, 19.8 g fat (5 g saturated fat), 38.4 g carbohydrate, 2 g dietary fiber, 16.3 g sugar, 0.4 g protein, 0 mg cholesterol, 301 mg sodium. Calories from fat: 30 percent.

▸ Preheat the oven to 350°F. Coat an 8-inch cake pan with nonstick cooking spray.

▸ Cream the butter, brown sugar, and vanilla together in a large bowl. Mix the flour, baking powder, baking soda, and salt together in another bowl. Alternately add the milk and the flour mixture to the butter mixture. Mix well until a smooth batter is formed (at least one hundred strokes).

▸ Pour into the prepared pan. Bake for 40 to 45 minutes, or until a toothpick inserted into the center of the cake comes out clean.

▸ Immediately after removing the cake from the oven, spread the peanut butter evenly over the top of the cake. Allow the cake to cool completely in the pan. When it is almost cool, put it in the refrigerator to firm up the peanut butter.

▸ When the cake is cool and the peanut butter is no longer glossy (it will look dull), heat the milk until it is steaming but not boiling. Add the chocolate chips to the hot milk and stir constantly until the chips are completely melted and the mixture is smooth. Carefully spread over the peanut butter and refrigerate. If you like a harder chocolate topping, store the cake in the refrigerator. If you like a softer topping, store at room temperature.

Rootin' Tootin' Raisin Spice Cake

This cake is a great one to take to a special occasion. It tastes delicious and it travels well.

> Makes 15 servings

Preparation time: 5 minutes ▼ **Baking time:** 50 minutes ▼ **Freezes well**

3½ cups unbleached all-purpose flour

2 teaspoons baking soda

2 teaspoons ground cinnamon

½ teaspoon salt

⅓ cup canola oil

1 cup Sucanat or brown sugar

2 teaspoons flax powder

½ cup apple cider, apple juice, or water

2 cups unsweetened applesauce (preferably organic)

¾ cup raisins (preferably organic)

½ cup chopped walnuts (optional)

▶ Preheat the oven to 350°F. Coat a Bundt pan with non-stick cooking spray.

▶ In a large bowl, combine the flour, baking soda, cinnamon, and salt. Using an electric mixer, beat the oil and sweetener until combined. Mix the flax powder with the apple cider in a small bowl. Add to the oil mixture and mix until combined. Beat in the applesauce. On low speed, add the dry ingredients to the oil mixture and beat until just combined. Stir in the raisins and nuts by hand.

▶ Pour the batter into the prepared pan. Bake for 50 minutes, or until a toothpick inserted into the center comes out clean. Allow to cool completely in the pan. Transfer from the pan to a serving plate. If desired, dust with powdered sugar before serving.

PER SERVING: 276 calories, 13 g fat (1 g saturated), 38 g carbohydrate, 3 g dietary fiber, 4 g sugar, 4 g protein, 0 mg cholesterol, 178 mg sodium, 153 mg potassium. Calories from fat: 41 percent.

CHERRY + CHOCOLATE = DELICIOUS CAKE

This delicious moist cherry cake dotted with chocolate chips and topped with tangy cherry topping and a drizzle of chocolate syrup was inspired by the cover of a magazine. All the desserts that I see while I'm waiting in line at the grocery store make me want to create them in a vegan version!

Makes 12 servings

Preparation time: cake, 15 minutes; topping, 10 minutes; chocolate syrup, 5 minutes
Baking time: 30 to 35 minutes ▼ **Assembly:** 10 minutes

¾ cup granulated sweetener

½ cup soft vegan butter spread, preferably tub style, at room temperature. (If using stick butter, soften it in the microwave until it is the consistency of tub butter. Do not melt!)

2 teaspoons cherry extract

2¼ cups unbleached all-purpose flour

2½ teaspoons baking powder

¼ teaspoon salt

1¼ cups vanilla vegan milk

½ cup fresh cherries, pitted and chopped

¾ cup vegan chocolate chips

Cherry Filling, page 265

Vegan Chocolate Syrup, page 267

▶ Preheat the oven to 375°F. Coat an 8-inch round springform pan with nonstick cooking spray.

▶ In a bowl, slowly add the granulated sweetener to the butter and beat until light and fluffy. Add the cherry extract and mix. In another bowl, combine the flour, baking powder, and salt and mix to combine.

▶ Alternately add the flour mixture and the milk to the butter mixture and stir well. Stir in the chopped cherries and chocolate chips.

▶ Pour into the prepared pan and bake for 30 to 35 minutes, or until a toothpick inserted into the center comes out clean. Allow the cake to cool completely in the pan before assembling. While the cake is cooling, make the Cherry Filling and the Vegan Chocolate Syrup.

▶ When the cake is cool, remove the collar of the pan. With a sharp knife, cut the rounded top off the cake and discard (or eat!) it. Replace the collar of the pan. Gently pour the Cherry Filling over the cake.

▶ Refrigerate for at least 2 hours before serving. When the cherries are completely cool, drizzle the Vegan Chocolate Syrup over the cherries in a delicate lattice pattern.

Going Nuts for Banana Bread ♡

*This moist banana bread is so good it can be eaten just as it is—without frosting.
I like to wrap these mini loaves in foil, put festive pieces of fabric tied with twine or
hemp around them, and give them as gifts at Christmas time. I add sprigs of silk
greenery to make an eye-catching gift that is as attractive as it is delicious!*

> Makes 15 servings

Preparation time: 15 minutes ▼ Baking time: 75 minutes ▼ Freezes well

1 cup unbleached all-purpose
flour

1 cup whole wheat flour

1 teaspoon baking soda

½ teaspoon salt

¾ cup pure maple syrup

1½ cups mashed ripe bananas
(about 3 medium-size bananas)

2 teaspoons flax powder

½ cup water

¼ cup canola oil

¼ cup unsweetened applesauce
(preferably organic)

¾ cup chopped pecans (optional)

PER SERVING: 197 calories, 8 g fat
(<1 g saturated), 30 g carbohydrate,
3 g dietary fiber, 10 g sugar, 3 g
protein, 0 mg cholesterol, 94 mg
sodium, 198 mg potassium. Calories
from fat: 37 percent.

▶ Preheat the oven to 350°F. Lightly grease an 8 by 3½ by
2½-inch loaf pan with nonstick cooking spray.

▶ In a medium-size bowl, combine the flours, baking soda,
and salt. In another bowl, combine the maple syrup with
the mashed banana. In a small cup, mix the flax powder
with the ½ cup of water, pour into the banana mixture,
and stir to combine. Add the canola oil, applesauce, and
pecans and mix. Pour the banana mixture into the flour
mixture and stir until just combined.

▶ Pour into the prepared pan. Bake for about 75 minutes,
or until a toothpick inserted into the center comes out
clean. Remove from the oven and allow to cool for 10
minutes in the pan.

▶ Remove the loaf from the pan and let cool completely on
a wire rack.

Variation: Use three 5 by 2½ by 2½-inch mini loaf pans
and bake at 350°F for 45 minutes.

FRUITY PUMPKIN BREAD ♥

This bread is so incredibly moist and delicious that even I find it hard to believe that it's healthy. I like to make this bread to take along to potluck suppers and buffets. And just like the Going Nuts for Banana Bread, page 98, this bread can be eaten for breakfast or dessert and makes a great gift.

> ### Makes 15 servings

Preparation time: 15 minutes ▼ **Baking time:** 85 minutes ▼ **Freezes well**

1½ cups unbleached all-purpose flour

1½ cups whole wheat flour

2 teaspoons ground cinnamon

2 teaspoons baking soda

¼ teaspoon salt

2 cups pure maple syrup

1 (15-ounce) can pure pumpkin puree

½ cup canola oil

½ cup unsweetened applesauce (preferably organic)

4 teaspoons flax powder

¾ cup water

1 large baking apple (such as Macintosh) peeled, cored, and diced

1 cup dried cranberries

▶ Preheat the oven to 350°F. Coat a Bundt pan with non-stick cooking spray.

▶ Combine the flours, cinnamon, baking soda, and salt in a large bowl. Combine the maple syrup, pumpkin, oil, and applesauce in another bowl. In a small bowl, combine the flax powder and the ¾ cup of water. Add to the liquid ingredients and combine.

▶ Add the diced apple and cranberries to the liquids and stir. Slowly add the flour mixture to the liquid ingredients. Mix to just combine.

▶ Pour the batter into the prepared pan. Bake for about 85 minutes, or until a toothpick inserted into the center comes out clean. Allow the cake to cool completely in the pan.

▶ Transfer from the pan to a serving plate.

....

Variation: Use five 5 by 2½ by 2½-inch mini loaf pans and bake at 350°F for 60 minutes.

PER SERVING: 421 calories, 8 g fat (<1 g saturated), 85 g carbohydrate, 7 g dietary fiber, 27 g sugar, 3 g protein, 0 mg cholesterol, 252 mg sodium, 259 mg potassium. Calories from fat: 17 percent.

CUPCAKES
AND MUFFINS

CANDY CANE CUPCAKES

This cupcake brings up images of sucking on a candy cane at holiday time. The cake is lightly sweet and is topped with peppermint cream. If using peppermint candies with red stripes, the frosting will be light pink in color. Wonderfully delicious . . . and a different taste treat!

Makes 20 cupcakes

Preparation time: cupcakes, 15 minutes; frosting, 10 minutes
Baking time: 25 minutes ▼ **Assembly:** 10 minutes

¼ cup soft vegan butter spread, preferably tub style, at room temperature. (If using stick butter, soften it in the microwave until it is the consistency of tub butter. Do not melt!)

1¼ cups pure maple syrup

1 tablespoon vanilla extract

4½ cups unbleached all-purpose flour

1½ tablespoons baking powder

¼ teaspoon salt

2½ cups vegan milk

Pink Peppermint Buttercream Frosting, page 280

PER SERVING: 330 calories, 7.8 g fat (2.3 g saturated), 61.1 g carbohydrate, 1 g dietary fiber, 36.6 g sugar, 3.9 g protein, 0 mg cholesterol, 98 mg sodium. Calories from fat: 12 percent.

▸ Preheat the oven to 350°F. Line twenty cupcake cups.

▸ Place the butter in a large bowl and cream until light and fluffy. Slowly add the maple syrup and beat again. Add the vanilla and continue to mix.

▸ In another bowl, combine the flour, baking powder, and salt. Alternately add the flour mixture and the milk to the butter mixture, stirring after each addition. Stir at least one hundred strokes, until the batter is smooth.

▸ Carefully pour into the prepared cupcake tin(s). Fill each cup two-thirds full of batter. If there are any empty cups in the tin, fill them halfway with water so that the tin doesn't warp during baking. Bake for 25 minutes, or until a toothpick inserted into the center of a cupcake comes out clean. Allow the cupcakes to cool for 10 minutes in the tin(s). Then transfer them to a wire rack and let cool completely before frosting.

▸ While the cupcakes are baking, prepare the Pink Peppermint Frosting. When the cupcakes are ready to frost, pipe the frosting, using a large star tip, onto the top of each cupcake.

PEPPERMINT PATTY CUPCAKES

Who doesn't like a refreshingly sweet peppermint patty—mint . . . chocolate? What a great combination. This cupcake combines a delicious chocolate cake with a wonderful mint frosting. Enjoy!

Makes 16 cupcakes

Preparation time: cupcakes, 15 minutes; frosting, 10 minutes
Baking time: 25 minutes ▼ **Assembly:** 10 minutes

2½ cups unbleached all-purpose flour

⅔ cup unsweetened cocoa powder

1½ teaspoons baking powder

½ teaspoon baking soda

1 teaspoon instant coffee crystals (optional)

¼ teaspoon salt

⅓ cup unsweetened applesauce (preferably organic)

⅓ cup canola oil

1½ cups light brown sugar (firmly packed)

1 teaspoon egg replacer (such as Ener-G)

¼ cup water

1½ cups vegan milk

Pink Peppermint Buttercream Frosting (page 280)

PER SERVING: 405 calories, 11.6 g fat (2.5 g saturated), 74.8 g carbohydrate, 1.8 g dietary fiber, 56.6 g sugar, 3.4 g protein, 0 mg cholesterol, 121 mg sodium. Calories from fat: 18 percent.

▶ Preheat the oven to 350°F. Line sixteen cupcake cups.

▶ Combine the flour, cocoa powder, baking powder, baking soda, coffee crystals, and salt. In another large bowl, combine the applesauce, oil, and brown sugar and mix until well blended. In a small bowl, combine the egg replacer with the ¼ cup of water. Add to the applesauce mixture and beat until smooth.

▶ Alternately add the flour mixture and the milk to the applesauce mixture, stirring after each addition. When combined, stir at least one hundred vigorous strokes, until the batter is smooth.

▶ Carefully pour into the prepared cupcake tin(s). Fill each cup two-thirds full of batter. If there are any empty cups in the tin, fill them halfway with water so that the tin doesn't warp during baking. Bake for 25 to 30 minutes, until a toothpick inserted into the center of a cupcake comes out clean. Allow the cupcakes to cool for 10 minutes in the tin(s). Then transfer them to a wire rack and let cool completely before frosting.

▶ While the cupcakes are baking, prepare the Pink Peppermint Frosting. When the cupcakes are ready to frost, pipe the frosting, using a large star tip, onto the top of each cupcake.

CHOCOLATE PEANUT BUTTER CUPCAKES

With the slightly salty peanut butter taste and the sweetness of chocolate cake, this cupcake will make you think of a peanut butter cup. Yummy!

> **Makes 16 cupcakes**

Preparation time: cupcakes, 15 minutes; frosting, 10 minutes
Baking time: 25 minutes ▼ **Assembly:** 10 minutes

2½ cups unbleached all-purpose flour

⅔ cup unsweetened cocoa powder

1½ teaspoons baking powder

½ teaspoon baking soda

1 teaspoon instant coffee crystals (optional)

¼ teaspoon salt

⅓ cup unsweetened applesauce (preferably organic)

⅓ cup canola oil

1½ cups light brown sugar (firmly packed)

1 teaspoon egg replacer (such as Ener-G)

¼ cup water

1½ cups vegan milk

Peanut Butter Buttercream Frosting, page 282

PER SERVING: 416 calories, 17.3 g fat (3.8 g saturated), 63.3 g carbohydrate, 2.4 g dietary fiber, 44.4 g sugar, 5.8 g protein, 0 mg cholesterol, 165 mg sodium. Calories from fat: 27 percent.

▶ Preheat the oven to 350°F. Line sixteen cupcake cups.

▶ Combine the flour, cocoa powder, baking powder, baking soda, coffee crystals, and salt. In another large bowl, combine the applesauce, oil, and brown sugar and mix until well blended. In a small bowl, combine the egg replacer with the ¼ cup of water. Add to the applesauce mixture and beat until smooth.

▶ Alternately add the flour mixture and the milk to the applesauce mixture, stirring after each addition. When combined, stir at least one hundred vigorous strokes, until the batter is smooth.

▶ Carefully pour into the prepared cupcake tin(s). Fill each cup two-thirds full of batter. If there are any empty cups in the tin, fill them halfway with water so that the tin doesn't warp during baking. Bake for 25 to 30 minutes, until a toothpick inserted into the center of a cupcake comes out clean. Allow the cupcakes to cool for 10 minutes in the tin(s). Then transfer them to a wire rack and let cool completely before frosting.

▶ While the cupcakes are baking, prepare the Peanut Butter Buttercream Frosting. When the cupcakes are ready to frost, pipe the frosting, using a large star tip, onto the top of each cupcake.

VANILLA PEANUT BUTTER CUPCAKES

Lightly sweet vanilla cake smothered with creamy peanut butter frosting create this delectable cupcake that will be enjoyed by both young and old!

Makes 20 cupcakes

Preparation time: cupcakes, 15 minutes; frosting, 10 minutes
Baking time: 25 minutes ▼ **Assembly:** 10 minutes

¾ cup soft vegan butter spread, preferably tub style, at room temperature. (If using stick butter, soften it in the microwave until it is the consistency of tub butter. Do not melt!)

1¼ cups pure maple syrup

1 tablespoon vanilla extract

4½ cups unbleached all-purpose flour

1½ tablespoons baking powder

¼ teaspoon salt

2½ cups vegan milk

Peanut Butter Buttercream Frosting, page 282

PER SERVING: 387 calories, 12.7 g fat (3.3 g saturated), 63 g carbohydrate, 1.5 g dietary fiber, 37.5 g sugar, 6.3 g protein, 0 mg cholesterol, 143 mg sodium. Calories from fat: 20 percent.

▶ Preheat the oven to 350°F. Line twenty cupcake cups.

▶ Place the butter in a large bowl and cream until light and fluffy. Slowly add the maple syrup and beat again. Add the vanilla and continue to mix.

▶ In another bowl, combine the flour, baking powder, and salt. Alternately add the flour mixture and the milk to the butter mixture, stirring after each addition. Stir at least one hundred strokes, until the batter is smooth.

▶ Carefully pour into the prepared cupcake tin(s). Fill each cup two-thirds full of batter. If there are any empty cups in the tin, fill them halfway with water so that the tin doesn't warp during baking. Bake for 25 minutes, or until a toothpick inserted into the center of a cupcake comes out clean. Allow the cupcakes to cool for 10 minutes in the tin(s). Then transfer them to a wire rack and let cool completely before frosting.

▶ While the cupcakes are baking, prepare the Peanut Butter Buttercream Frosting. When the cupcakes are ready to frost, pipe the frosting, using a large star tip, onto the top of each cupcake.

PEANUT BUTTER CREAM CUPCAKES ♥

This cupcake differs from the chocolate peanut butter because it's filled with gooey peanut butter marshmallow cream and topped with a dark chocolate candy coating. Mmmmmm!

> **Makes 16 cupcakes**

Preparation time: cupcakes, 15 minutes; peanut butter cream, 5 minutes
Baking time: 25 minutes ▼ **Assembly:** 15 minutes

2½ cups unbleached all-purpose flour

⅔ cup unsweetened cocoa powder

1½ teaspoons baking powder

½ teaspoon baking soda

1 teaspoon instant coffee crystals

¼ teaspoon salt

⅓ cup unsweetened applesauce (preferably organic)

⅓ cup canola oil

1½ cups light brown sugar (firmly packed)

1 teaspoon egg replacer (such as Ener-G)

¼ cup water

1½ cups vegan milk

Filling:
1½ cups vegan marshmallow cream

¾ cup natural peanut butter

Topping:
3 tablespoons vegan milk

1 cup chocolate chips

▶ Preheat the oven to 350°F. Line sixteen cupcake cups.

▶ Combine the flour, cocoa powder, baking powder, baking soda, coffee crystals, and salt. In another large bowl, combine the applesauce, oil, and brown sugar and mix until well blended. In a small bowl, combine the egg replacer with the ¼ cup of water. Add to the applesauce mixture and beat until smooth.

▶ Alternately add the flour mixture and the milk to the applesauce mixture, stirring after each addition. When combined, stir at least one hundred vigorous strokes, until the batter is smooth.

▶ Carefully pour into the prepared cupcake tin(s). Fill each cup two-thirds full of batter. If there are any empty cups in the tin, fill them halfway with water so that the tin doesn't warp during baking. Bake for 25 to 30 minutes, until a toothpick inserted into the center of a cupcake comes out clean. Allow the cupcakes to cool for 10 minutes in the tin(s). Then transfer them to a wire rack and let cool completely before frosting.

▶ While the cupcakes are baking, make the peanut butter cream. In a small bowl, mix 1¼ cups of the vegan marshmallow cream with the peanut butter (reserve ¼ cup of plain marshmallow cream to use later). Set both aside. Also, prepare the chocolate topping: Heat the milk in a small saucepan over medium heat. Add the chocolate chips and stir until completely melted.

continues

continued

PER SERVING: (not including garnish) 250 calories, 4 g fat (2 g saturated fat), 52 g carbohydrate, 2 g dietary fiber, 33 g sugar, 4 g protein, 0 mg cholesterol, 105 mg sodium. Calories from fat: 6 percent.

▶ To assemble: Core each cupcake, being careful not to cut a hole in the bottom. Cut the top off the piece of cake that you remove to use as a "cork" to top off the cupcake. Fill the hole with peanut butter marshmallow cream. Put the chocolate "cork" back on to cover the hole. Spread the melted chocolate over the top of the cupcakes. Chill to set. You will have some peanut butter marshmallow cream left over after filling the cupcakes. Mix this with the reserved plain marshmallow cream to make a lighter peanut butter whipped topping. Pipe a small dollop of this whipped topping on top of each cupcake.

S'MORES CUPCAKES ♡

Gooey marshmallow, chocolate, and graham crackers . . . these cupcakes evoke memories of the awesome campfire favorite.

> **Makes 16 cupcakes**

Preparation time: cupcakes, 15 minutes; chocolate cream, 10 minutes
Baking time: 25 minutes ▼ **Assembly:** 15 minutes

2½ cups unbleached all-purpose flour

⅔ cups unsweetened cocoa powder

1½ teaspoons baking powder

½ teaspoon baking soda

1 teaspoon instant coffee crystals (optional)

¼ teaspoon salt

⅓ cup unsweetened applesauce (preferably organic)

⅓ cup canola oil

1½ cups brown sugar (firmly packed)

1 teaspoon egg replacer (such as Ener-G)

¼ cup water

1½ cups vegan milk

▶ Preheat the oven to 350°F. Line sixteen cupcake cups.

▶ Combine the flour, cocoa powder, baking powder, baking soda, coffee crystals, and salt. In another large bowl, combine the applesauce, oil, and brown sugar and mix until well blended. In a small bowl, combine the egg replacer with the ¼ cup of water. Add to the applesauce mixture and beat until smooth.

▶ Alternately add the flour mixture and the milk to the applesauce mixture, stirring after each addition. When combined, stir at least one hundred vigorous strokes, until the batter is smooth.

▶ Carefully pour into the prepared cupcake tin(s). Fill each cup two-thirds full of batter. If there are any empty cups in the tin, fill them halfway with water so that the tin doesn't warp during baking. Bake for 25 to 30 minutes, until a toothpick inserted into the center of a cupcake comes out clean. Allow the cupcakes to cool for 10 minutes in the tin(s). Then transfer them to a wire rack and let cool completely before frosting.

continues

continued

Chocolate avocado cream:

2 ripe avocados

5½ tablespoons unsweetened
  cocoa powder

¾ cup powdered sugar

1 teaspoon vanilla extract

2 teaspoons water

To assemble:

1 cup vegan marshmallow cream

24 graham cracker sticks, or 6
  graham crackers broken into
  quarters

1 tablespoon mini vegan
  chocolate chips

PER SERVING: (not including garnish)
253 calories, 9.5 g fat (1.3 g
saturated fat), 41.2 g carbohydrate,
4 g dietary fiber, 20.5 g sugar, 4.3 g
protein, 0 mg cholesterol, 93 mg
sodium. Calories from fat: 15 percent.

▶ While the cupcakes are baking, make the chocolate avocado cream. Wash the avocados. Cut in half. Remove the pits (see Note) and discard them. Peel and discard the skin. Slice the avocados. Put them and the remaining topping ingredients in a food processor. Process until smooth and creamy.

▶ To assemble: Using the large star tip, pipe chocolate avocado cream around the outside of the top of each cupcake. This will provide a "fence" for the marshmallow cream. Place about a tablespoon of marshmallow cream in the center of each cupcake. Sprinkle each cupcake with a few chocolate chips. Poke two graham sticks into the center of each cupcake before serving.

Note: To remove an avocado pit, put the avocado half with the pit on a cutting board. Use a large knife to chop down on the pit (keep your hands out of the way, if you want to keep all ten fingers!). The knife will penetrate the pit just a little. Twist it and the pit should simply twist loose. Presto! Pit is out!

JUST LIKE GRANDMA
USED TO MAKE CUPCAKES

This recipe is for a traditional cupcake—chocolate cake with either vanilla or chocolate icing. It's reminiscent of a simpler time, before gourmet flavored coffee, computers, and hybrid cars!

Makes 16 cupcakes

Preparation time: cupcakes, 15 minutes; frosting, 10 minutes
Baking time: 25 minutes

2½ cups unbleached all-purpose flour

⅔ cup unsweetened cocoa powder

1½ teaspoons baking powder

½ teaspoon baking soda

1 teaspoon instant coffee crystals (optional)

¼ teaspoon salt

⅓ cup unsweetened applesauce (preferably organic)

⅓ cup canola oil

1½ cups light brown sugar (firmly packed)

1 teaspoon egg replacer (such as Ener-G)

¼ cup water

1½ cups vegan milk

Chocolate Buttercream Frosting, page 281, or Vanilla Buttercream Frosting, page 283

▶ Preheat the oven to 350°F. Line 16 cupcake cups (see Note).

▶ Combine the flour, cocoa powder, baking powder, baking soda, coffee crystals, and salt. In another large bowl, combine the applesauce, oil, and brown sugar and mix until well blended. In a small bowl, combine the egg replacer with the ¼ cup of water. Add to the applesauce mixture and beat until smooth.

▶ Alternately add the flour mixture and the milk to the applesauce mixture, stirring after each addition. When combined, stir at least one hundred vigorous strokes, until the batter is smooth.

▶ Carefully pour into the prepared cupcake tin(s). Fill each cup two-thirds full of batter. If there are any empty cups in the tin, fill them halfway with water so that the tin doesn't warp during baking. Bake for 25 to 30 minutes, until a toothpick inserted into the center of a cupcake comes out clean. Allow the cupcakes to cool for 10 minutes in the tin(s). Then transfer them to a wire rack and let cool completely before frosting.

▶ While the cupcakes are baking, prepare the Chocolate or Vanilla Buttercream Frosting. Frost the cooled cupcakes.

PER SERVING: 357 calories, 11.6 g fat (2.5 g saturated), 62.4 g carbohydrate, 1.8 g dietary fiber, 44.2 g sugar, 3.4 g protein, 0 mg cholesterol, 121 mg sodium. Calories from fat: 18 percent.

Note: This cupcake recipe also will make a delicious chocolate cake. Prepare it in the same way as for the cupcakes, but pour it into a greased 8-inch round cake pan and bake at 350°F for 45 to 50 minutes.

MUFFINS

All muffins in this section can also be made as muffin tops. Muffin tops (remember the Seinfeld episode?) can now be made using a special tin so there are no "stumps" to discard. Muffin top pans are available at some kitchen stores and online. A muffin top is larger and flatter than a muffin, sort of a cross between a muffin and a cookie. Either way that you bake them, these muffins are scrumptious!

....

BANANA RASPBERRY MUFFINS

Tasty fruity muffins . . . a great way to start or end your day.

> **Makes 8 muffins or muffin tops**

Preparation time: 10 minutes ▼ **Baking time:** 25 minutes

1 cup oat flour (you may grind
   rolled oats using a food
   processor or blender to equal
   1 cup of oat flour.)

1 cup whole wheat flour

½ cup granulated sweetener

1 teaspoon baking powder

½ teaspoon baking soda

¼ cup water

1 teaspoon egg replacer
   (such as Ener-G)

3 very ripe bananas (see Note),
   fork mashed

¾ cup fresh raspberries, rinsed
   and patted dry

▸ Preheat the oven to 375°F. Line eight muffin cups, or prepare a muffin top pan according to the manufacturer's directions.

▸ Combine the flours, sweetener, baking powder, and baking soda in a bowl. In another bowl, combine the ¼ cup of water with the egg replacer, then stir in the mashed bananas. Add to the flour mixture and stir to combine. Fold in the raspberries.

▸ Carefully pour into the prepared muffin tin(s). Fill each cup two-thirds full of batter. If there are any empty cups in the tin, fill them halfway with water so that the tin doesn't warp during baking. Bake for 20 to 25 minutes, until a toothpick inserted into the center of a muffin comes out clean. Allow the muffins to cool for 10 minutes in the tin(s). Then transfer them to a wire rack and let cool completely.

PER SERVING: 196 calories, 1.5 g fat (0 g saturated), 44.1 g carbohydrate, 3.5 g dietary fiber, 18.4 g sugar, 3.7 g protein, 0 mg cholesterol, 81 mg sodium. Calories from fat: 2 percent.

Note: Very ripe bananas are the ones that your children will look at and say, "Ewwww!" because they're all black and mushy looking. The darker they are, the sweeter they will be. If you only have yellow bananas, or worse yet, yellow with green bananas, wait for a few days to make these muffins so they will taste delicious!

BANANA CRUMB MUFFINS

Yummy banana muffins topped with crunchy crumbs.

> **Makes 8 muffins or muffin tops**

Preparation time: 10 minutes ▼ **Baking time:** 25 minutes

1 cup oat flour (You may grind rolled oats in a food processor or blender to equal 1 cup of oat flour.)

1 cup whole wheat flour

¼ cup granulated sweetener

1 teaspoon baking powder

½ teaspoon baking soda

¼ cup water

1 teaspoon egg replacer (such as Ener-G)

3 very ripe bananas (see Note), fork mashed

Topping:

¼ cup light brown sugar

¼ cup oat flour (or grind rolled oats to a fine flour, as above)

1 tablespoon very cold vegan butter, such as Spectrum or Earth Balance. In this case, stick style works much better than tub style.

▶ Preheat the oven to 375°F. Line eight muffin cups, or prepare a muffin top pan according to the manufacturer's directions.

▶ Combine the flours, sweetener, baking powder, and baking soda in a bowl. In another bowl, combine the ¼ cup of water with the egg replacer, then stir in the mashed bananas. Add to the flour mixture and stir to combine.

▶ In a small bowl, combine the topping ingredients. Use two knives to cut them together. Work until the mixture looks like crumbs.

▶ Carefully pour into the prepared muffin tin(s). Fill each cup two-thirds full of batter. Sprinkle the topping over the muffins. If there are any empty cups in the tin, fill them halfway with water so that the tin doesn't warp during baking. Bake for 20 to 25 minutes, until a toothpick inserted into the center of a muffin comes out clean. Allow the muffins to cool for 10 minutes in the tin(s). Then transfer them to a wire rack and let cool completely.

PER SERVING: 195 calories, 1.7 g fat (0 g saturated), 42.9 g carbohydrate, 3 g dietary fiber, 16.1 g sugar, 4 g protein, 0 mg cholesterol, 82 mg sodium. Calories from fat: 3 percent.

Note: Very ripe bananas are the ones that your children will look at and say, "Ewwww!" because they're all black and mushy looking. The darker they are, the sweeter they will be. If you only have yellow bananas, or worse yet, yellow with green bananas, wait for a few days to make these muffins so they will taste delicious!

ORANGE RASPBERRY MUFFINS ♡

*By now you have probably guessed that I love raspberries. In these muffins I've
teamed up that delicious fruit with citrusy orange. You could, however, substitute
other berries in this muffin. Orange blueberry are good as are orange cranberry
(use dried cranberries if you want them to stay more intact instead of exploding and
"melting" into the muffin).*

> **Makes 9 muffins or muffin tops**

Preparation time: 10 minutes ▼ **Baking time:** 25 minutes

1½ cups oat flour (You may grind
rolled oats using a food
processor or blender to equal
1½ cups of oat flour.)

1½ cups whole wheat flour

1½ cups sugar

1 teaspoon baking powder

¾ teaspoon baking soda

½ cup water

2 teaspoons egg replacer
(such as Ener-G)

½ cup orange juice

⅓ cup canola oil

½ teaspoon orange extract

1 cup raspberries

PER SERVING: 315 calories, 8.9 g fat
(<1 g saturated), 56.7 g
carbohydrate, 2.7 g dietary fiber,
31.6 g sugar, 4 g protein, 0 mg
cholesterol, 97 mg sodium. Calories
from fat: 14 percent.

▶ Preheat the oven to 375°F. Line nine muffin cups, or prepare a muffin top pan according to the manufacturer's
directions.

▶ Combine the flours, sugar, baking powder, and baking
soda in a bowl. In another bowl, combine the water with
the egg replacer. Stir in the orange juice, oil, and orange
extract. Add to the flour mixture and stir to combine.
Fold in the raspberries.

▶ Carefully pour into the prepared muffin tin(s). Fill each
cup two-thirds full of batter. If there are any empty cups
in the tin, fill them halfway with water so that the tin
doesn't warp during baking. Bake for 25 to 30 minutes,
until a toothpick inserted into the center of a muffin
comes out clean. Allow the muffins to cool for 10 minutes in the tin(s). Then transfer them to a wire rack and
let cool completely.

(NOT JUST) FOR KIDS

FRUIT CRÈME POPS

What could be better than fruit salad on a stick on a hot summer day? These Popsicles rock, especially the crème—they are awesome with the tangy fruit!

....

RASPBERRY CRÈME POPS ♡

Raspberry and crème—just right for a hot day.

> Makes 4 servings

Preparation time: puree, 10 minutes; crème, 5 minutes ▼ **Cooling time:** ½ hour
Assembly: 5 minutes ▼ **Freezing time:** at least 8 hours
(The total time from start to ready to eat is 9 hours
but your time actually working on them is 20 minutes!)

Fruit:

2 cups raspberries or blueberries

1 to 2 tablespoons sugar
(depending on the sweetness of
the fruit)

Crème:

3 ounces (¼ [12-ounce] package)
firm silken tofu

¼ teaspoon vanilla extract

1 tablespoon sugar

1 tablespoon water

PER SERVING: 72 calories, 1.3 g fat,
14 g carbohydrate, 4.2 g dietary fiber,
9.2 g sugar, 2.5 g protein, 0 mg
cholesterol, 3 mg sodium. Calories
from fat: 2 percent.

▸ Prepare the fruit: Put the cleaned fruit and the sugar to taste in a saucepan. Bring to a boil. Boil for 5 minutes, until the fruit is soft. (Enough water should be given off by the fruit that you won't have to add any liquid.) Cool the fruit mixture completely.

▸ To make the crème: Put all the ingredients for the crème in a food processor (a small one, if you have it). Blend until smooth and remove from the processor bowl. Rinse and dry the food processor.

▸ When the fruit is cool, put in the food processor and whirl until smooth, then divide among four 3-ounce Popsicle molds (or you may use 3-ounce bathroom cups). Divide the crème among the four Popsicles. Use a knife to swirl the crème into the fruit. Put the tops on the Popsicle molds. If using cups, cover with aluminum foil and poke lollipop sticks in the middle of the foil and through the fruit mixture. The foil will hold the sticks upright until the Popsicles are frozen. Place in the freezer overnight. To unmold, run under hot water for a few seconds and pop out.

PEACH CRÈME POPS ♥

These pops taste just like a frozen peach pie. What a treat!

> **Makes 4 servings**

Preparation time: puree, 10 minutes; crème, 5 minutes ▼ **Cooling time:** ½ hour
Assembly: 5 minutes ▼ **Freezing time:** at least 8 hours
(The total time from start to ready to eat is 9 hours
but your time actually working on them is 20 minutes!)

Fruit:

2 cups peaches, peeled and cubed

1 to 2 tablespoons sugar
(depending on the sweetness
of fruit)

2 tablespoons water

Crème:

3 ounces (¼ [12-ounce] package)
firm silken tofu

¼ teaspoon vanilla extract

1 tablespoon sugar

1 tablespoon water

PER SERVING: 73 calories, 1.1 g fat,
14.8 g carbohydrate, 1.5 g dietary
fiber, 13.6 g sugar, 2.5 g protein,
0 mg cholesterol, 3 mg sodium.
Calories from fat: 2 percent.

▶ Prepare the fruit: Put the prepared fruit and the sugar to taste in a saucepan. Bring to a boil. Boil for 5 minutes, until the fruit is soft. (Enough water should be given off by the fruit that you won't have to add any liquid.) Cool the fruit mixture completely.

▶ To make the crème: Put all the ingredients for the crème in a food processor (a small one, if you have it). Blend until smooth and remove from the processor bowl. Rinse and dry the food processor.

▶ When the fruit is cool, put in the food processor and whirl until smooth, then divide among four 3-ounce Popsicle molds (or you may use 3-ounce bathroom cups). Divide the crème among the four Popsicles. Use a knife to swirl the crème into the fruit. Put the tops on the Popsicle molds. If using cups, cover with aluminum foil and poke lollipop sticks in the middle of the foil and through the fruit mixture. The foil will hold the sticks upright until the Popsicles are frozen. Place in the freezer overnight. To unmold, run under hot water for a few seconds and pop out.

STRAWBERRY CRÈME POPS

What could taste more like summer than strawberries? Delicious mixed with the crème!

> **Makes 4 servings**

Preparation time: puree, 10 minutes; crème, 5 minutes ▼ **Cooling time:** ½ hour
Assembly: 5 minutes ▼ **Freezing time:** at least 8 hours
(The total time from start to ready to eat is 9 hours
but your time actually working on them is 20 minutes!)

Fruit:

2 cups strawberries, rinsed, hulled, and sliced

2 dried pitted dates

¼ cup water (for soaking dates)

Crème:

3 ounces (¼ [12-ounce] package) firm silken tofu

¼ teaspoon vanilla extract

1 tablespoon sugar

1 tablespoon water

PER SERVING: 63 calories, 1.1 g fat, 12.2 g carbohydrate, 2 g dietary fiber, 9.5 g sugar, 2.3 g protein, 0 mg cholesterol, 4 mg sodium. Calories from fat: 2 percent.

▶ Prepare the fruit: Put the strawberries in a food processor. Put the dates and ¼ cup water in a microwave and heat on HIGH until the water steams. Let sit for 1 minute. This will make the dates easier to process with the strawberries. Drain the dates (discard the water) and place in the food processor with the strawberries. Whirl until the mixture is smooth. If using the same food processor, put the strawberry mixture in a pitcher (so it's easier to get into the Popsicle molds) and rinse out the processor bowl.

▶ To make the crème: Put the ingredients for the crème in a food processor (a small one if you have it). Blend until smooth.

▶ Divide the fruit mixture among four 3-ounce Popsicle molds (or you may use 3-ounce bathroom cups). Divide the crème among the four Popsicles. Use a knife to swirl the crème into the fruit. Put the tops on the Popsicle molds. If using cups, cover with aluminum foil and poke lollipop sticks in the middle of the foil and through the fruit mixture. The foil will hold the sticks upright until the Popsicles are frozen. Place in the freezer overnight. To unmold, run under hot water for a few seconds and pop out.

MORE FUN FAVORITES

The following recipes will please the young as well as those young at heart!

....

FRUITY COOKIE PIZZA

Here's a yummy way to get your children to eat more fresh fruit: Put it all on a giant cookie and call it pizza! And the bonus is . . . adults will love it, too!

You may use any combination of toppings for this "pizza," depending on what you like. Be creative!

> **Makes 16 servings**

Preparation time: crust, 10 minutes; toppings, 15 minutes ▼ **Baking time:** 15 minutes
Cooling time: 30 minutes ▼ **Assembly:** 5 minutes

Cookie Crust:

¼ cup water

1 teaspoon egg replacer (such as Ener-G)

⅓ cup soft vegan butter spread, preferably tub style, at room temperature. (If using stick butter, soften it in the microwave until it is the consistency of tub butter. Do not melt!)

¼ cup unsweetened applesauce (preferably organic)

1 cup sugar

1 teaspoon vanilla extract

2½ cups unbleached all-purpose flour

¾ teaspoon baking powder

½ teaspoon baking soda

▶ Preheat the oven to 375°F. In a small bowl, mix the ¼ cup of water and egg replacer. In a separate bowl, cream the butter with the applesauce, sugar, vanilla, and egg replacer mixture. In another bowl, combine the flour, baking powder, and baking soda. Pour the dry ingredients into the creamed mixture and stir. Form into a large ball (add more flour if necessary). Put the ball on floured parchment paper. Roll out into a circle about ¼ inch thick. The circle will be the size of a small pizza. Slide the parchment paper (with its "pizza") onto a cookie sheet. Bake for 15 minutes. As soon as you can handle the crust, use a round template, such as a small pizza pan or large plate, to the cut the crust into a neat circle (this is easier to do when the crust is still warm, because it's softer). Allow the crust to cool completely on a wire rack.

continues

continued

Strawberry sauce:

2½ cups strawberries, washed, hulled, and sliced

3 dried pitted dates soaked in ¼ cup water

Fruit toppings:

½ cup strawberries, washed, hulled, and sliced

⅓ cup unsweetened shredded coconut

⅔ cup fresh pineapple, cut into small cubes

1 banana, sliced

⅓ cup raspberries, washed and patted dry

PER SERVING: 156 calories, 1.1 g fat, 34.4 g carbohydrate, 1.9 g dietary fiber, 17 g sugar, 2.9 g protein, 0 mg cholesterol, 41 mg sodium. Calories from fat: 2 percent.

▶ While the crust is cooling, make the strawberry sauce. Put the strawberries and soaked dates (discard the soaking water) into a food processor. Whirl until smooth.

▶ When the crust has cooled, assemble the pizza: Place the crust on a serving plate. Spread the strawberry sauce on top of the crust so it looks like a pizza. Sprinkle with coconut (as you would pizza cheese). Sprinkle the remaining toppings on the pizza. Serve immediately.

CRISPIE RICE TREATS ♡

Your child (or you!) no longer has to look longingly at the gelatin-based crispie rice treats of yore. These treats are wonderful for a picnic or a child's classroom party and aren't much more work to make than running to the store to buy a bag of pretzels! I have to admit that they're so good that sometimes I don't wait for them to cool into the squares—I eat them with a spoon right from the bowl!

Makes 16 servings

Preparation time: 5 minutes ▼ **Cooling time:** 1 hour

1 cup vegan marshmallow cream (such as Suzanne's Ricemellow Creme)

½ cup natural peanut butter

3½ cups crispy rice cereal (preferably organic)

- ▸ Line an 8-inch square pan with waxed paper.
- ▸ Mix the marshmallow cream and peanut butter together in a microwave-safe bowl. Heat for about 20 seconds in the microwave on HIGH until warm and "soupy." Mix in the cereal. Press into the prepared pan.
- ▸ Refrigerate for 1 hour.
- ▸ Cut into sixteen squares.

PER SERVING: 100 calories, 4.5 g fat, 13 g carbohydrate, 1 g dietary fiber, 5 g sugar, 3 g protein, 0 mg cholesterol, 50 mg sodium. Calories from fat: 7 percent.

Variation: Add 2 tablespoons of unsweetened cocoa powder to the marshmallow mixture before adding the rice cereal. Stir to combine completely. Mix in the rice cereal and stir to coat.

FRUIT WITH
STRAWBERRY CASHEW CRÈME

This is another variation on a plain fruit salad. Here, fruit is folded into creamy strawberry crème. It can be served in dishes, or if you're using it for kids, it can be fun to scoop it into the flat-bottomed cake cones—most of those available are vegan; just be sure to read the labels!

> **Makes 10 servings**

Preparation time: cashew soaking, 12 hours; crème, 10 minutes; fruit, 15 to 20 minutes
Chilling time: 1 hour

Crème:

1 cup raw cashews

2 pitted dried dates

4½ teaspoons water

¼ cup vanilla extract

⅓ cup sliced strawberries

Fruit:

3 cups fruit, washed and cut into bite-size pieces. (I have used peaches, strawberries, bananas, raspberries, and cherries for my salad. Sometimes I just use one kind of fruit.)

▶ To make the crème: Soak the cashews for 12 hours in enough water to cover them. After 12 hours, remove them from the water, place them in a food processor, and discard the water. Microwave the dates on HIGH for 20 seconds in ¼ cup of water to soften (discard water). Add to the processor the 4½ teaspoons of fresh water, and the drained dates, vanilla, and sliced strawberries. Process until very smooth. Refrigerate for 1 hour.

▶ Fold the prepared fruit into chilled strawberry crème. Chill until serving.

▶ To serve, scoop into dishes or flat-bottomed cake ice-cream cones, garnish if desired, and serve immediately.

PER SERVING: 119 calories, 6.5 g fat (1.2 g saturated fat), 11.4 g carbohydrate, 1.5 g dietary fiber, 6.2 g sugar, 2.5 g protein, 0 mg cholesterol, 3 mg sodium. Calories from fat: 10 percent.

DESSERT TAPAS

The word tapas is derived from the Spanish verb tapar, "to cover." Apparently, the tradition of tapas began many years ago as a way to protect cheap wine from fruit flies. A piece of bread and salty meat usually provided a cover for the wine. This cover also activated thirst and thus increased alcohol sales. Well, that was many, many years ago and tapas have changed a great deal. How many times have you gone to a restaurant or a party and said, "Gee, they (the desserts, of course) all look so good, I wish I could try them all!"? Now, with dessert tapas, you can, because they're bite-size desserts.

....

CHOCOLATE RASPBERRY BITES ♡

Delicious chocolate candy shells filled with tart raspberry sauce and topped with creamy chocolate cream. Paradise for your palate! (And a favorite of mine!)

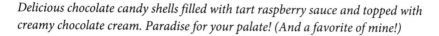

Makes 12 tapas

Preparation time: cordial cups, 15 minutes; raspberry sauce, 15 minutes; chocolate avocado cream, 10 minutes ▼ **Assembly:** 10 minutes

Dessert shells (see Note on page 128):
1⅓ cups vegan chocolate chips

Raspberry sauce:
¾ cup raspberries, cleaned and rinsed

2 tablespoons + 1 teaspoon water

1 teaspoon cornstarch

Chocolate avocado cream:
1 ripe avocado

3 tablespoons unsweetened cocoa powder

6 tablespoons powdered sugar

½ teaspoon vanilla extract

1 teaspoon water

Garnish (optional):
12 raspberries (preferably organic)

12 small mint leaves

PER SERVING: 140 calories, 8.3 g fat (3.8 g saturated fat), 19.1 g carbohydrate, 3.1 g dietary fiber, 14.6 g sugar, 1.4 g protein, 0 mg cholesterol, 4 mg sodium. Calories from fat: 13 percent.

▶ Melt the chocolate chips in a double boiler on the stove or in the microwave. In the microwave, use a MEDIUM-HIGH setting for 1 minute at a time. Stir between each minute. The melting time will vary, depending on the strength of your microwave. If using the microwave, be careful—it is possible to burn chocolate! Oops!

▶ When the chocolate is melted, pour a small amount into each candy mold and use the back of a spoon to spread the chocolate around the entire mold, or use a pastry brush to "paint" the chocolate in the mold. Place the filled molds in the freezer to harden faster. When the chocolate is dull in color (it will be shiny when it's melted or wet), carefully pop out of the molds and set aside.

▶ While the chocolate is hardening, prepare the Raspberry Sauce. Put the raspberries and 1 teaspoon of the water in a small pan and bring to a boil. Boil for about 2 minutes, until the fruit is very liquid. Combine the cornstarch and the remaining 2 tablespoons of water in a small cup. Pour this mixture into the hot fruit and bring back to a boil while stirring constantly. This will thicken the fruit. It will continue to thicken as it cools. Allow to cool completely before spooning into the chocolate cups (because I'm naturally impatient, I put the pan in the freezer—just don't forget it or you'll then have to wait until it thaws!)

continues

continued

▸ While the chocolate cups are hanging out and the raspberry sauce is cooling, make the chocolate avocado cream. Wash the avocado. Cut it in half. Remove the pit (see Note) and discard it. Peel and discard the skin. Slice the avocado. Put it and remaining chocolate avocado cream ingredients in a food processor. Process until smooth and creamy.

▸ Now you're ready to assembly the cups. Divide the raspberry sauce evenly among the twelve chocolate cordial cups. Pipe the chocolate avocado cream (using a large star tip) on top of the sauce. If garnishing, top with a fresh raspberry and a small mint leaf. (I suggest to people that they may want to remove the leaf before eating. It certainly won't harm them, but I don't like the taste of mint mixed in the flavors of raspberry and chocolate.) Store refrigerated. For best results, serve cold as well, such as using an appetizer dish set on ice.

Notes:

- You will need a plastic or silicone mold that makes twelve small candy shells. I used a Wilton candy mold/cordial cups (available at many craft stores, in the candy-making section).
- To remove an avocado pit, put the avocado half with the pit on a cutting board. Use a large knife to chop down on the pit (keep your hands out of the way, if you want to keep all ten fingers!). The knife will penetrate the pit just a little. Twist it and the pit should simply twist loose. Presto! Pit is out!

PEACH SALSA WITH TORTILLA TRIANGLES

Hot, savory, and sweet are flavor contrasts that make an interesting combination. Spicy hot pepper, savory onion, and sweet peaches work together to make this salsa an experience for your mouth!

Makes 14 servings

Preparation time: salsa, 20 minutes; tortillas, 20 minutes

Peach salsa:

2 cups fresh peaches, peeled and cut into small cubes

¼ cup onion, diced small

½ teaspoon grated fresh ginger

2 tablespoons chopped fresh cilantro

1 tablespoon lime juice

½ small hot pepper, diced (see Note)

Tortilla triangles:

1 cup whole wheat flour

1 cup unbleached all-purpose flour

½ to ¾ cup water

Oil, for frying

2 tablespoons sugar

1 teaspoon ground cinnamon

2 tablespoons oil

PER SERVING: 100 calories, 2.2 g fat (0 g saturated fat), 18.2 g carbohydrate, 1 g dietary fiber, 4 g sugar, 2.1 g protein, 0 mg cholesterol, 1 mg sodium. Calories from fat: 3 percent.

Note: The amount of pepper that you use will vary greatly depending on your "heat tolerance" and the type of hot pepper that you use.

▶ Combine all the salsa ingredients in a bowl, mix, and set aside.

▶ Place the flours in a bowl. Add ½ cup of water. Stir until moistened. If still crumbly, slowly add small amounts of water and stir until the mixture forms a ball. Gently knead the ball of dough a few times before dividing it into seven equal pieces. Coat each ball with flour and roll out very thin. Heat a skillet to medium-high heat. Coat with oil. Fry each side of the tortilla for 2 minutes, or until browned.

▶ Mix together the sugar and cinnamon. Brush the top of each tortilla with oil and sprinkle with the cinnamon mixture. Cut each tortilla into six triangles. Place under the broiler until golden brown. Watch the triangles all the time they're under the broiler—it only takes 2 to 3 minutes to brown them and 30 more seconds to burn!

▶ Arrange the triangles around your salsa bowl and serve.

....

Variations:

• You may want to add ⅛ to ¼ teaspoon of ground cayenne pepper to the cinnamon mixture for a spicy touch on the tortilla triangles.

• You may use premade tortillas instead of making your own. Just brush the tops of seven tortillas with oil, sprinkle with the cinnamon mixture, and broil, just as in the last step of the directions. Read the label to be sure there isn't a lot of gunk in the tortillas—stuff that you can't even pronounce!

BANANA CANNOLI ♡

Cannoli are an Italian pastry consisting of a flaky crust wrapped around a creamy, chocolate chip–dotted, sweetened ricotta cheese filling. Sounds yummy . . . but nutritionally a bit scary. I set out to make a healthier, vegan version; what I (okay, my daughter) came up with is the idea for banana cannoli. These cannoli have a banana leather (dehydrated banana) shell filled with a scrumptious chocolate cream. The base of the chocolate cream is avocado; while being high in fat, it is heart healthy because that fat is mostly monounsaturated—which has been proven to actually lower cholesterol. But don't be scared off if I made it sound too healthy—rest assured, this dessert is delicious!

> ### Makes 12 cannoli or 36 appetizer bites

Preparation time: shells, 10 minutes; chocolate avocado cream, 10 minutes
Dehydration time: 11 hours ▼ **Assembly:** 10 minutes ▼ **Freezes well**

Shell:

4 medium-size ripe (yellow with black spots) bananas

¼ teaspoon ground cinnamon

1 teaspoon lemon juice

Chocolate avocado cream:

2 ripe avocados

6 tablespoons unsweetened cocoa powder

¾ cup powdered sugar

1 teaspoon vanilla extract

2 teaspoons water

▶ Put the shell ingredients in a food processor or blender and process until smooth. Spread in a thin layer on a tray in a dehydrator or on parchment paper placed on a baking sheet. Because I don't have a dehydrator, I have to give directions to use a stove. If you do have a dehydrator, follow the manufacturer's directions to dehydrate the banana. Set your oven to its lowest setting (mine is 175°F). Leave the baking sheet in the oven overnight (10 hours). Remove from the oven. While warm, remove from the parchment paper and cut into four equal rectangles (I use kitchen shears for this). Immediately roll around cannoli forms (see Note on page 131). Secure with a band made of aluminum foil (see Note on page 131). Return to the baking sheet and dehydrate for another hour. Allow to cool before removing the foil rings and taking off the cannoli form. Allow to cool completely before filling.

▶ Wash the avocados. Cut in half. Remove the pits (see Note on page 131) and discard them. Peel and discard the skin. Slice the avocados. Put them and the remaining cream ingredients in a food processor. Process until smooth and creamy.

continues

continued

▸ To assemble: Put the chocolate avocado cream in a pastry bag fitted with a large tip. Squeeze into the shells (filling from each side). Cut each shell into three pieces. Chill. When ready to serve, sprinkle with powdered sugar.

▸ If serving on a tapas tray, instead of cutting each shell into three small cannoli, you can cut them into bite-size slices.

Notes:

- Cannoli forms are metal tubes around which you wrap a cannoli shell, or in this case, the fruit leather, so that it forms a tube shape. I found them to be sold in sets of four—available at kitchen stores and at many sites on the Internet.
- Work with the fruit leather when it's warm. It tends to get brittle as it cools. If this happens, return it to the oven to heat it up. Be sure it's warm to roll it onto the form.
- I used foil bands to secure the shells for further dehydrating so that they didn't unwrap. To make a foil band, simply tear a small piece of foil and fold as if making a ring for your finger. Just be sure it's long enough to secure the shell.
- To remove an avocado pit, put the avocado half with the pit on a cutting board. Use a large knife to chop down on the pit (keep your hands out of the way, if you want to keep all ten fingers!). The knife will penetrate the pit just a little. Twist it and the pit should simply twist loose. Presto! Pit is out!

PER SERVING (BASED ON 12 CANNOLI-SIZE SERVINGS): 125 calories, 5.4 g fat (1 g saturated), 20.9 g carbohydrate, 4.1 g dietary fiber, 12.5 g sugar, 1.6 g protein, 0 mg cholesterol, 3 mg sodium. Calories from fat: 49.

LEMON BITES ♡

The avocado cream base may make this look more like a lime bite, but don't be fooled—dig in and you'll find yourself won over by the refreshing taste!

> Makes 18 bites

Preparation time: cake, 10 minutes; lemon cream, 10 minutes; cream cheese, 10 minutes
Baking time: 30 minutes ▼ **Assembly:** 15 minutes

1 cup unbleached all-purpose flour

½ teaspoon baking powder

¼ teaspoon baking soda

2½ tablespoons soft vegan butter spread, preferably tub style, at room temperature. (If using stick butter, soften it in the microwave until it is the consistency of tub butter. Do not melt!)

¼ cup pure maple syrup

⅓ cup lemon juice

2 teaspoons egg replacer (such as Ener-G)

1¾ teaspoons lemon extract

¼ cup plus 2 tablespoons vegan milk

▶ Preheat the oven to 350°F. Grease a mini loaf pan and set aside.

▶ Combine the flour, baking powder, and baking soda in a small bowl. In a large bowl, cream the butter with the maple syrup. In a third, small bowl, mix the lemon juice with the egg replacer, and add the lemon extract. Cream the lemon mixture into the butter mixture. Add the flour alternately with the milk to the butter mixture. Mix well (stir for at least one hundred strokes after the ingredients are combined). Pour into the prepared pan. Bake for 30 minutes, or until a toothpick inserted into the center of the cake comes out clean.

▶ When the cake is done, allow to cool for 10 minutes in the pan, then carefully remove from the pan and let it cool on a rack until completely cool.

continues

continued

Cream cheese topping:

4 ounces (½ [8-ounce] container)
vegan cream cheese

1½ teaspoons powdered sugar

¼ teaspoon vanilla extract

Lemon avocado cream:

1 ripe avocado

¼ cup lemon juice

3 tablespoons powdered sugar

Garnish (optional):

4 thin slices lemon

Small mint leaves

▸ While the cake is baking, make the cream cheese topping. Put the cream cheese, sugar, and vanilla in a food processor. Process until smooth and creamy. Remove from the processor and chill. (If you have a mini processor, use that for this cream because it's such a small amount.)

▸ Next, make the lemon avocado cream. Wash the avocado. Cut in half. Remove the pit (see Note) and discard it. Peel and discard the skin. Slice the avocado. Put it and the remaining cream ingredients in a food processor. Process until smooth and creamy. Chill.

▸ To assemble: Slice the cake into nine slices. Cut each in half so that you have bite-size pieces. Lay on a plate. Evenly divide the lemon cream among the pieces of cake. Put the cream cheese topping into a pastry bag, and using large star tip, pipe a dollop onto the lemon avocado cream. Garnish with thinly sliced lemon twists (see Note) and mint leaves, if desired. Chill until serving.

Notes:

- To remove an avocado pit, put the avocado half with the pit on a cutting board. Use a large knife to chop down on pit (keep your hands out of the way, if you want to keep all ten fingers!). The knife will penetrate the pit just a little. Twist it and the pit should simply twist loose. Presto! Pit is out!
- To make a lemon twist, make a cut from the center of a thin slice of lemon to the outer edge (the radius of the lemon slice). Twist the lemon.

PER SERVING: 78 calories, 3.2 g fat (0 g saturated), 11.5 g carbohydrate, 1 g dietary fiber, 4.5 g sugar, 1 g protein, 0 mg cholesterol, 35 mg sodium. Calories from fat: 5 percent.

STRAWBERRY CHEESECAKE BITES

These dessert tapas are so easy you'll want to make them all the time! They're so delicious they'll disappear like magic.

Makes 18 servings

Preparation time: fruit, 10 minutes; cream, 10 minutes ▼ **Assembly:** 10 minutes

4 ounces (½ [8-ounce] container) vegan cream cheese

1½ teaspoons powdered sugar

¼ teaspoon vanilla extract

9 large strawberries, washed and hulled (see Note)

▶ Put the cream cheese, sugar, and vanilla in a food processor. Process until smooth and creamy. Remove from the processor and chill. (If you have a mini processor, use that for this cream because it's such a small amount.)

▶ Slice the strawberries in half the long way so they look like little "boats."

▶ Put the cream cheese mixture into a pastry bag and pipe a dollop on top of each strawberry. Arrange on a plate and chill until serving.

PER SERVING: 10 calories, <1 g fat (0 g saturated), 1.5 g carbohydrate, 0 g dietary fiber, 1.1 g sugar, <1 g protein, 0 mg cholesterol, 5 mg sodium. Calories from fat: 0 percent.

Note: You may use chunks of pineapple cut into bite-size pieces in place of the strawberries, for pineapple cheesecake bites.

FRUIT SPRING ROLLS
WITH RASPBERRY SAUCE

Easy finger food great for a tapas party or anytime you want something refreshing. These fruit spring rolls were inspired by raw veggie spring rolls that I enjoy. I used the same concept, only filled them with seasonal fruit, rolled them in coconut, and made a raspberry dip as a bonus!

> Makes 12 mini rolls

Preparation time: fruit, 20 minutes; sauce, 10 minutes ▾ **Assembly:** 15 minutes

Raspberry dipping sauce:
¾ cup raspberries (preferably organic)

1 tablespoon sugar

½ teaspoon water

Filling: (use organic fruit if possible)
1 peach

1 pear

½ mango (see Note on page 136)

To assemble:
1 tablespoon snipped fresh mint

⅓ cup unsweetened shredded coconut

6 sheets rice paper (see Note on page 136)

▶ To make the raspberry dipping sauce: Put the raspberries, sugar, and water in a small saucepan. Heat to a boil, stirring constantly. Boil until the berries are soft and mushy (about 3 minutes), stirring constantly the entire time. Put the sauce through a strainer to remove the seeds. Chill.

▶ Wash the fruit. Slice into thin sticks about 2 inches long.

▶ Fill a large skillet about half full with water and heat until warm. Do not boil—you have to stick your fingers into this water! Place separate bowls of the fruit, mint, and coconut by a clean work surface.

▶ Dip a rice paper into the hot water for about 3 seconds. Lay on the work surface. Top with one-sixth of the fruit and sprinkle with a little mint. Wrap tightly and roll in the coconut. Transfer to a plate. Continue until all the rice paper and fruit is used.

▶ Cut each roll in half on the diagonal. Arrange on a serving plate with a dish of dipping sauce in the center of the cut rolls. Serve immediately.

PER SERVING: 50 calories, 5 g fat (0 g saturated), 11 g carbohydrate, 1 g dietary fiber, 5 g sugar, 0 g protein, 0 mg cholesterol, 10 mg sodium. Calories from fat: 2 percent.

> **Hint:** If you don't want to make the raspberry sauce or fresh raspberries aren't available, you may use seedless fruit sweetened raspberry spread. Scoop ¼ cup into a microwave-safe bowl. Heat until warm and smooth when stirred.

continues

continued

Notes:

- Edible rice paper is available at most grocery stores, in the Asian foods aisle. The rice paper packs that I've bought come with about a bizillion sheets of rice paper, so practice heating a few first. The key, I've found, is not to leave the rice paper in the water too long. If you do, the rice paper will become the consistency of a soggy paper towel, cling worse than a tangle of cheap plastic wrap, and be thoroughly annoying. Just stick the rice paper into the water long enough to soften so that you can work with it. It'll probably take a few sheets to get the hang of it.
- Feel free to change the combination of fruit that you use. Base it on what you like and what is freshly available at the time.
- How to peel and slice a mango: Use a sharp knife to peel the mango. Make cuts through the flesh of the mango both horizontally and vertically, so the mango looks as if it has ½-inch squares all over it. Cut these squares off the mango's pit.

BOSTON CREAM PIES

I am devoting an entire section to Boston cream pies because there are just so many possibilities. I started out with the traditional vanilla cake, vanilla pudding, and chocolate icing, but then I started switching cake flavors and pudding flavors and came up with some really tasty treats. Each pie is topped off with the decadent chocolate icing you'd expect on a Boston cream pie, so I have included this recipe at the beginning of this section for easy reference. A helpful hint: You will be much happier with the results if you make a cream pie a day before you plan to serve it and then refrigerate it overnight. This allows the tofu in the filling to set.

....

CHOCOLATE GLAZE TOPPING

Makes 1 cup of glaze (enough for one Boston cream pie)

Preparation time: 10 minutes

1 cup powdered sugar

¼ cup canola oil

½ teaspoon vanilla extract

⅙ cup unsweetened cocoa powder (half of a ⅓-cup measuring cup)

3½ tablespoons arrowroot

½ cup water

▶ Place the powdered sugar, canola oil, vanilla, cocoa powder, and arrowroot in a small saucepan and stir to combine, using a wire whisk for best results. Stir in the ½ cup of water. Bring almost to a boil, stirring constantly. Do not boil. Keep stirring until the mixture starts to thicken. Allow to cool until the mixture is of a good spreading consistency.

PER SERVING: 90 calories, 4.7 g fat (0 g saturated), 12.4 g carbohydrate, 0 g dietary fiber, 9.8 g sugar, 0 g protein, 0 mg cholesterol, 0 mg sodium. Calories from fat: 7 percent.

CHOCOLATE RASPBERRY BOSTON CREAM PIE

This creamy pie combines the slightly sweet, tangy taste of raspberries with wonderful dark chocolate.

> Makes 12 servings

Preparation time: cake, 15 minutes; filling, 10 minutes; glaze, 10 minutes
Baking time: 35 minutes ▼ **Assembly:** 10 minutes

1½ cups unbleached all-purpose flour

⅓ cup unsweetened cocoa powder

1 tablespoon baking powder

3 ounces (¼ [12-ounce] package) firm silken tofu

1 teaspoon vanilla extract

½ cup unsweetened applesauce (preferably organic)

¾ cups water or apple juice

¾ cups pure maple syrup

Chocolate Glaze Topping, page 138

Filling:

1 pound (16 ounces, or 1⅓ [12-ounce] packages) firm silken tofu

1 cup powdered sugar

¼ cup raspberry jam

¼ cup unbleached all-purpose flour, or 2 teaspoons xanthan gum (see Note on page 140)

PER SERVING: 290 calories, 6 g fat (<1 g saturated), 57 g carbohydrate, 2 g dietary fiber, 13 g sugar, 4 g protein, 0 mg cholesterol, 38 mg sodium, 179 mg potassium. Calories from fat: 18 percent.

▶ Preheat the oven to 350°F. Lightly grease an 8-inch round springform pan (see Note on page 140) with nonstick cooking spray.

▶ In a large bowl, combine the flour, cocoa powder, and baking powder and stir with a whisk. In a food processor, puree the tofu until smooth. Add the vanilla and applesauce and blend. Add the water and maple syrup and blend. Slowly add the liquid ingredients to the flour mixture, whisking until combined. Do not overmix. Pour the batter into the prepared pan.

▶ Bake for 35 minutes, or until a toothpick inserted into the center comes out clean. Remove the cake from the oven and allow to cool for 10 minutes in the pan. Remove the collar of the pan and flip the cake onto a wire rack to finish cooling. You will be putting the cake back into the pan, so put the collar back on the pan and set aside. Allow the cake to cool completely before filling and assembling.

▶ While the cake is baking, make the filling. Place all the filling ingredients in a food processor and process until smooth. Refrigerate until ready to use.

continues

continued

▸ When the cake is completely cool, cut the rounded top off the cake, with a sharp, long knife or cake wire. Then cut the cake layer in half horizontally, making two layers. Place the top layer back into the springform pan to become the bottom layer of the cake. Pour the filling over the layer in the pan and smooth out. Place the former bottom layer (which will now be the top) upside down onto the filling, so that the top of the cake has a straight, smooth surface. Press down lightly.

▸ When the cake is assembled, make the Chocolate Glaze Topping. Pour the hot topping over the cake and smooth out evenly. Refrigerate overnight before serving. (This allows the topping to thicken and the filling to set.) Remove the collar of the pan before serving. Store in the refrigerator with the collar on.

Notes:
- Xanthan gum will produce a slightly softer filling, but will not give the mild flour taste that you get if you use the ¼ cup of flour.
- If you do not have a springform pan, this cake works nicely in a 9-inch pie plate.

TRADITIONAL BOSTON CREAM PIE

This was my first official Boston cream pie recipe. It got such a great response that I began to create the same type of dessert in different flavor combinations.

Makes 12 servings

Preparation time: cake, 15 minutes; filling, 10 minutes; glaze, 10 minutes
Baking time: 50 minutes ▼ **Assembly:** 10 minutes

¾ cup soft vegan butter spread, preferably tub style, at room temperature. (If using stick butter, soften it in the microwave until it is the consistency of tub butter. Do not melt!)

1¼ cups pure maple syrup

1 tablespoon vanilla extract

4½ cups unbleached all-purpose flour

1½ tablespoons baking powder

¼ teaspoon salt

2½ cups vegan milk

Chocolate Glaze Topping, page 138

Vanilla filling:

1 pound (16 ounces, or 1⅓ [12-ounce] packages) firm silken tofu

1 cup powdered sugar

¼ cup unbleached all-purpose flour, or 2 teaspoons xanthan gum (see Note on page 142)

2 teaspoons vanilla extract

▶ Preheat the oven to 350°F. Coat a 10-inch round spring-form pan (see Note on page 142) with nonstick cooking spray.

▶ Place the butter in a bowl and cream. Slowly add the maple syrup and beat until light and fluffy. Add the vanilla and mix. In another bowl, combine the flour, baking powder, and salt. Alternately add the flour mixture and the milk to the butter mixture and mix well. Pour into the prepared pan and bake for about 50 minutes, or until a toothpick inserted into the center comes out clean.

▶ Remove the cake from the oven and allow to cool for 10 minutes in the pan. Remove the collar of the pan and flip the cake onto a wire rack to finish cooling. Put the collar back on the pan and set aside. Allow the cake to cool completely before filling and assembling.

▶ To make the filling: While the cake is baking, place the tofu in a food processor and whip until smooth, scraping down the sides several times. Add the sugar, flour, and vanilla and process. Refrigerate until ready to assemble the cake.

PER SERVING: 537 calories, 17 g fat (1 g saturated), 86 g carbohydrate, 2 g dietary fiber, 22 g sugar, 11 g protein, 0 mg cholesterol, 115 mg sodium, 353 mg potassium. Calories from fat: 27 percent.

continues

continued

▶ To assemble: When the cake is completely cool, cut the rounded top off the cake, with a sharp, long knife or cake wire. Then cut the cake layer in half horizontally, making two layers. Place the top layer back into the springform pan to become the bottom layer of the cake. Pour the filling over the layer in the pan and smooth out. Place the former bottom layer (which will now be the top) upside down onto the filling, so that the top of the cake has a straight, smooth surface. Press down lightly.

▶ When the cake is assembled, make the Chocolate Glaze Topping. Pour the hot topping over the cake and smooth out evenly. Refrigerate overnight before serving. (This allows the topping to thicken and the filling to set.) Remove the collar of the pan before serving. Store in the refrigerator with the collar on.

Notes:

- Xanthan gum will produce a slightly softer filling, but will not give the mild flour taste that you may get if you use the flour.
- If you do not have a springform pan, this cake works nicely in a 9-inch pie plate.

PEANUT BUTTER BOSTON CREAM PIE

This combination of gooey peanut butter cream and dark chocolate glaze nestled together with moist yellow cake is sure to get rave reviews from friends and family.

> **Makes 12 servings**

Preparation time: cake, 15 minutes; filling, 10 minutes; glaze, 10 minutes
Baking time: 50 minutes ▼ **Assembly:** 10 minutes

¾ cup soft vegan butter spread, preferably tub style, at room temperature. (If using stick butter, soften it in the microwave until it is the consistency of tub butter. Do not melt!)

1¼ cups pure maple syrup

1 tablespoon vanilla extract

4½ cups unbleached all-purpose flour

1½ tablespoons baking powder

¼ teaspoon salt

2½ cups vegan milk

Chocolate Glaze Topping, page 138

Peanut butter filling:

1 pound (16 ounces, or 1⅓ [12-ounce] packages) firm silken tofu

1 cup powdered sugar

¼ cup unbleached all-purpose flour, or 2 teaspoons xanthan gum (see Note on page 144)

2 teaspoons vanilla extract

¾ cup smooth natural peanut butter

▶ Preheat the oven to 350°F. Coat a 10-inch round spring-form pan (see Note on page 144) with nonstick cooking spray.

▶ Place the butter in a bowl and cream. Slowly add the maple syrup and beat until light and fluffy. Add the vanilla and mix. In another bowl, combine the flour, baking powder, and salt. Alternately add the flour mixture and the milk to the butter mixture and stir well. Pour into the prepared pan and bake for about 50 minutes, or until a toothpick inserted into the center comes out clean.

▶ Remove the cake from the oven and allow it to cool for 10 minutes in the pan. Remove the collar of the pan and flip the cake onto a wire rack to finish cooling. You will be putting the cake back into the pan, so put the collar back on the pan and set aside. Allow the cake to cool completely before filling and assembling.

▶ To make the filling: Place the tofu in a food processor and whip until smooth, scraping down the sides several times. Add the sugar, flour, and vanilla and process. Add the peanut butter and process until smooth. Refrigerate until ready to assemble the cake.

continues

continued

▸ To assemble: When the cake is completely cool, cut the rounded top off the cake, with a sharp, long knife or cake wire. Then cut the cake layer in half horizontally, making two layers. Place the top layer back into the springform pan to become the bottom layer of the cake. Pour the filling over the layer in the pan and smooth out. Place the former bottom layer (which will now be the top) upside down onto the filling, so that the top of the cake has a straight, smooth surface. Press down lightly.

▸ When the cake is assembled, make the Chocolate Glaze Topping. Pour the hot topping over the cake and smooth out evenly. Refrigerate overnight before serving. (This allows the topping to thicken and the filling to set.) Remove the collar of the pan before serving. Store in the refrigerator with the collar on.

PER SERVING: 646 calories, 26 g fat (3 g saturated), 90 g carbohydrate, 3 g dietary fiber, 22 g sugar, 16 g protein, 0 mg cholesterol, 205 mg sodium, 523 mg potassium. Calories from fat: 34 percent.

Notes:

• Xanthan gum will produce a slightly softer filling, but will not give the mild flour taste that you get if you use the ¼ cup of flour.

• If you do not have a springform pan, this cake works nicely in a 9-inch pie plate.

TRIPLE-CHOCOLATE BOSTON CREAM PIE

Beware: This cream pie—made of moist chocolate cake with creamy chocolate filling and topped with a dark chocolate glaze—is for the serious chocolate lover only.

Makes 12 servings

Preparation time: cake, 15 minutes; filling, 10 minutes; glaze, 10 minutes
Baking time: 35 minutes ▼ **Assembly:** 10 minutes

1½ cups unbleached all-purpose flour

⅓ cup unsweetened cocoa powder

1 tablespoon baking powder

3 ounces (¼ [12-ounce] package) firm silken tofu

1 teaspoon vanilla extract

½ cup unsweetened applesauce (preferably organic)

¾ cup water or apple juice

¾ cup pure maple syrup

Chocolate Glaze Topping, page 138

Filling:

1 pound (16 ounces, or 1⅓ [12-ounce] packages) firm silken tofu

1 cup powdered sugar

¼ cup unbleached all-purpose flour, or 2 teaspoons xanthan gum (see Note on page 146)

2 cups vegan chocolate chips

PER SERVING: 466 calories, 17 g fat (6 g saturated), 74 g carbohydrate, 4 g dietary fiber, 14 g sugar, 10 g protein, 0 mg cholesterol, 43 mg sodium, 363 mg potassium. Calories from fat: 31 percent.

▶ Preheat the oven to 350°F. Lightly grease an 8-inch round springform pan (see Note on page 146) with nonstick cooking spray.

▶ In a large bowl, combine the flour, cocoa powder, and baking powder and stir with a whisk. In a food processor, puree the tofu until smooth. Add the vanilla and applesauce and blend. Add the water and maple syrup and blend. Slowly add the liquid ingredients to the flour mixture and whisk until combined. Do not overmix. Pour the batter into the prepared pan.

▶ Bake for 35 minutes, or until a toothpick inserted into the center comes out clean. Remove the cake from the oven and allow to cool for 10 minutes in the pan. Remove the collar of the pan and flip the cake onto a wire rack to finish cooling. You will be putting the cake back into the pan, so put the collar back on the pan and set aside. Allow the cake to cool completely before filling and assembling.

▶ While the cake is baking, make the filling. Place all the filling ingredients except the chocolate chips in a food processor and process until smooth. Melt the chocolate chips in a microwave or double boiler. Pour the melted chips into the filling mixture and process until smooth. Refrigerate until ready to use.

continues

continued

▶ To assemble: When the cake is completely cool, cut the rounded top off the cake, with a sharp, long knife or cake wire. Then cut the cake layer in half horizontally, making two layers. Place the top layer back into the springform pan to become the bottom layer of the cake. Pour the filling over the layer in the pan and smooth out. Place the former bottom layer (which will now be the top) upside down onto the filling, so that the top of the cake has a straight, smooth surface. Press down lightly.

▶ When the cake is assembled, make the Chocolate Glaze Topping. Pour the hot topping over the cake and smooth out evenly. Refrigerate overnight before serving. (This allows the topping to thicken and the filling to set.) Remove the collar of the pan before serving. Store in the refrigerator with the collar on.

Notes:
- Xanthan gum will produce a slightly softer filling, but will not give the mild flour taste that you get if you use the ¼ cup of flour.
- If you do not have a springform pan, this cake works nicely in a 9-inch pie plate.

CHOCOLATE CARAMEL BOSTON CREAM PIE

This gooey combination of chocolate cake, vanilla filling, caramel sauce, nuts, and chocolate glaze topping is the perfect dessert when you're in the mood to splurge.

Makes 12 servings

Preparation time: cake, 15 minutes; filling, 10 minutes; glaze, 10 minutes; caramel sauce, 10 minutes ▼ **Baking time:** 35 minutes ▼ **Assembly:** 10 minutes

1½ cups unbleached all-purpose flour

⅓ cup unsweetened cocoa powder

1 tablespoon baking powder

3 ounces (¼ [12-ounce] package) firm silken tofu

1 teaspoon vanilla extract

½ cup unsweetened applesauce (preferably organic)

¾ cups water or apple juice

¾ cups pure maple syrup

Chocolate Glaze Topping, page 138

¾ cups chopped pecans, for garnish

Filling:

1 pound (16 ounces, or 1⅓ [12-ounce] packages) firm silken tofu

1 cup powdered sugar

1 teaspoon vanilla extract

¼ cup unbleached all-purpose flour, or 2 teaspoons xanthan gum (see Note on page 148)

▶ Preheat the oven to 350°F. Lightly grease an 8-inch round springform pan (see Note on page 148) with non-stick cooking spray.

▶ In a large bowl, combine the flour, cocoa powder, and baking powder and stir with a whisk. In a food processor, puree the tofu until smooth. Add the vanilla and apple-sauce and blend. Add the water and maple syrup and blend. Slowly add the liquid ingredients to the flour mix-ture and whisk until combined. Do not overmix. Pour the batter into the prepared pan.

▶ Bake for 35 minutes, until a toothpick inserted into the center comes out clean. Remove the cake from the oven and allow it to cool for 10 minutes in the pan. Remove the collar of the pan and flip the cake onto a wire rack to fin-ish cooling. You will be putting the cake back into the pan, so put the collar back on the pan and set aside. Allow the cake to cool completely before filling and assembling.

▶ To make the filling: While the cake is baking, place all the filling ingredients in a food processor and process until smooth. Refrigerate until ready to use.

continues

continued

Caramel sauce:

⅓ cup corn syrup or agave nectar

⅓ cup brown sugar

3 tablespoons vanilla vegan milk

2 teaspoons vanilla extract

¼ teaspoon salt

▸ To make the caramel sauce: Place the sweeteners in a small pan and bring to a boil. Simmer until the mixture gets to the soft-ball stage (240°F on a candy thermometer, if you have one). Stir in the milk, vanilla, and salt. Remove from the heat and allow to cool. (The mixture will thicken as it cools.)

▸ To assemble: When the cake is completely cool, cut the rounded top off the cake, with a sharp, long knife or cake wire. Then cut the cake layer in half horizontally, making two layers. Place the top layer back into the springform pan to become the bottom layer of the cake. Pour the filling over the layer in the pan and smooth out. Place the former bottom layer (which will now be the top) upside down onto the filling, so that the top of the cake has a straight, smooth surface. Press down lightly.

▸ When the cake is assembled, make the Chocolate Glaze Topping. Pour the hot topping over the cake and smooth out evenly. Refrigerate for 10 minutes. Carefully drizzle the caramel sauce over the chocolate glaze and sprinkle the nuts over the top of the cake. Refrigerate overnight before serving. (This allows the topping to thicken and the filling to set.) Remove the collar of the pan before serving, but store in the refrigerator with the collar on.

PER SERVING: 460 calories, 14 g fat (2 g saturated), 76 g carbohydrate, 3 g dietary fiber, 15 g sugar, 10 g protein, 0 mg cholesterol, 60 mg sodium, 431 mg potassium. Calories from fat: 27 percent.

Notes:
• Xanthan gum will produce a slightly softer filling, but will not give the mild flour taste that you get if you use the ¼ cup of flour.
• If you do not have a springform pan, this cake works nicely in a 9-inch pie plate.

CHOCOLATE PEANUT BUTTER BOSTON CREAM PIE

Tender chocolate cake filled with creamy peanut butter makes this cake a tasty dessert at any time. It is topped off with a dark chocolate glaze.

Makes 12 servings

Preparation time: cake, 15 minutes; filling, 10 minutes; glaze, 10 minutes
Baking time: 35 minutes ▼ **Assembly:** 10 minutes

1½ cups unbleached all-purpose flour

⅓ cup unsweetened cocoa powder

1 tablespoon baking powder

3 ounces (¼ [12-ounce] package) firm silken tofu

1 teaspoon vanilla extract

½ cup unsweetened applesauce (preferably organic)

¾ cups water or apple juice

¾ cups pure maple syrup

Chocolate Glaze Topping, page 138

Filling:

1 pound (16 ounces, or 1⅓ [12-ounce] packages) firm silken tofu

1 cup powdered sugar

¾ cup smooth natural peanut butter

¼ cup unbleached all-purpose flour, or 2 teaspoons xanthan gum (see Note on page 150)

▸ Preheat the oven to 350°F. Lightly grease an 8-inch round springform pan (see Note on page 150) with non-stick cooking spray.

▸ In a large bowl, combine the flour, cocoa powder, and baking powder and stir with a whisk. In a food processor, puree the tofu until smooth. Add the vanilla and applesauce and blend. Add the water and maple syrup and blend. Slowly add the liquid ingredients to the flour mixture and whisk until combined. Do not overmix. Pour the batter into the prepared pan.

▸ Bake for 35 minutes, or until a toothpick inserted into the center comes out clean. Remove the cake from the oven and allow it to cool for 10 minutes in the pan. Remove the collar of the pan and flip the cake onto a wire rack to finish cooling. You will be putting the cake back into the pan, so put the collar back on the pan and set aside. Allow the cake to cool completely before filling and assembling.

▸ While the cake is baking, make the filling. Place all the filling ingredients in a food processor and process until smooth. Refrigerate until ready to use.

continues

continued

▸ To assemble: When the cake is completely cool, cut the rounded top off the cake, with a sharp, long knife or cake wire. Then cut the cake layer in half horizontally, making two layers. Place the top layer back into the springform pan to become the bottom layer of the cake. Pour the filling over the layer in the pan and smooth out. Place the former bottom layer (which will now be the top) upside down onto the filling, so that the top of the cake has a straight, smooth surface. Press down lightly.

▸ When the cake is assembled, make the Chocolate Glaze Topping. Pour the hot topping over the cake and smooth out evenly. Refrigerate overnight before serving. (This allows the topping to thicken and the filling to set.) Remove the collar of the pan before serving. Store in the refrigerator with the collar on.

PER SERVING: 427 calories, 17 g fat (3 g saturated), 59 g carbohydrate, 3 g dietary fiber, 14 g sugar, 13 g protein, 0 mg cholesterol, 115 mg sodium, 471 mg potassium. Calories from fat: 34 percent.

Notes:
- Xanthan gum will produce a slightly softer filling, but will not give the mild flour taste that you get if you use the ¼ cup of flour.
- If you do not have a springform pan, this cake works nicely in a 9-inch pie plate.

PIES
AND TARTS

WETZEL'S PRETZEL PIE ♥

Impressive to look at and scrumptious to eat, this concoction of vanilla vegan ice cream coupled with chocolate, nuts, and pretzels is truly a fabulous creation! It's like a sundae in a pie pan. I named it after my maiden name, which conveniently rhymes with pretzel.

Makes 12 servings

Preparation time: filling, 5 minutes; crust, 10 minutes; syrup, 5 minutes; freeze, 3 hours

Syrup:

¾ cup unsweetened cocoa powder

1¼ cups pure maple syrup

2 teaspoons vanilla extract

Crust:

2 cups vegan chocolate chips

2 cups crushed salted pretzels, (be sure to check that the pretzels do not contain hydrogenated oils.)

At least 1 dozen whole twist-shaped, salted pretzels (about 3½ inches in diameter), for garnish

Filling:

4 (1-pint) containers nondairy vanilla ice cream (see Note on page 153)

½ cup chopped peanuts

▶ Coat an 8-inch round springform pan with nonstick cooking spray.

▶ To make the syrup: In a small bowl, combine the cocoa powder, maple syrup, and vanilla. Stir with a wire whisk and set aside. In a microwave or double boiler, melt the chocolate chips. Place the crushed pretzels in a small bowl. Pour half of the melted chocolate over the pretzels and toss to cover. Pour into the bottom of the prepared pan. Refrigerate until ready to fill.

▶ To make the crust: Take the whole pretzels and dip them three-quarters of the way into the melted chocolate, starting at the bottom. The two top loops of each pretzel will remain uncovered and will provide you with a clean place for picking them up. Place the chocolate-covered pretzels on a waxed paper–covered cookie sheet. (Be sure to make a few more than you think you will need in case you miscalculate or break some. If you have extras, you can use them whole for a garnish or just eat them!) Place the pretzels in the freezer to harden the chocolate while you work on the rest of the pie.

Note: I like to use Tofutti nondairy frozen dessert for this pie. I find that its consistency works well—and it tastes delicious!

continues

continued

▸ Soften the ice cream. (I use the DEFROST function on my microwave to do this—the ice cream should be the consistency of soft-serve ice cream, not runny.) Spread half of the ice cream (about two containers' worth) over the crushed pretzels in the bottom of the pan. Drizzle half of the chocolate syrup over the ice cream. Sprinkle with ¼ cup of the peanuts.

▸ Spread the rest of the ice cream over the topping. Make the top flat and smooth. Press the chocolate-covered pretzels into the pie at the side of the pan so that when the collar of the pan is removed, the pretzels form the side crust. Part of the pretzel will be showing above the top of the pie, almost like a fence. Pour the rest of the syrup evenly on top. Sprinkle with the remaining peanuts. Freeze for at least 3 hours before serving. Remove the collar of the pan and allow to soften for 10 minutes before serving.

PER SERVING: 460 calories, 19 g fat (5 g saturated), 70 g carbohydrate, 4 g dietary fiber, 35 g sugar, 7 g protein, 0 mg cholesterol, 530 mg sodium. Calories from fat: 36 percent.

Hint: Running the serving knife under hot water before cutting makes the cutting of this pie easier.

I Love Chocolate Cream Pie

This creamy chocolate-filled pie laced with coconut nestled in a chocolate-coconut candy pie shell turns out best if you make it the day before serving so that the filling has a chance to set. It will maintain its shape better when you cut it into slices.

Makes 16 servings

Preparation time: filling, 5 minutes; shell, 10 minutes ▼ **Assembly:** 5 minutes

Pie shell:

½ cup vanilla vegan creamer

2 cups vegan chocolate chips

1½ cups unsweetened shredded coconut

Filling:

1 pound (16 ounces, or 1⅓ [12-ounce] packages) firm silken tofu

1 cup powdered sugar

1 teaspoon coconut extract

2 cups vegan chocolate chips

1 cup unsweetened shredded coconut

Additional coconut, for garnish (optional)

▸ Coat a 9-inch pie plate with nonstick cooking spray. Heat the creamer in a small pan until hot but not boiling. Add the chocolate chips slowly and stir until melted, keeping the heat low. Stir in the coconut. Pour into the prepared pie plate and refrigerate until the shell is hardened.

▸ While the shell is in the refrigerator, prepare the filling. Place the tofu in a food processor and process until smooth, scraping down the sides of the processor as necessary. Add the sugar and coconut extract. Melt the chocolate chips in a microwave or double boiler. Pour the melted chocolate into the tofu mixture and process until combined. Stir in the coconut by hand.

▸ Pour into the prepared pie shell. Sprinkle with additional coconut, if desired.

▸ Refrigerate until ready to serve (overnight if possible, to give the tofu filling time to set).

PER SERVING: 476 calories, 35 g fat (28 g saturated), 43 g carbohydrate, 8 g dietary fiber, <1 g sugar, 6 g protein, 0 mg cholesterol, 43 mg sodium. Calories from fat: 61 percent.

MOM'S APPLE CRISP ♥

Apple crisp has all the good taste of apple pie without the crust. It's wonderful served warm with a scoop of cold nondairy vanilla frozen dessert. The cold vanilla ice cream nicely complements the warm, spicy apples with the crunchy topping.

Makes 12 servings

Preparation time: apples, 20 minutes; apple filling, 10 minutes; topping, 5 minutes
Baking time: 20 minutes

Apples:

15 medium-size baking apples (I like a combination of Macintosh and a more firm apple such as Idared or Rome), peeled, cored, and sliced

¾ cup water

2½ teaspoons ground cinnamon

¼ teaspoon ground cardamom (optional)

2 tablespoons arrowroot

Topping:

½ cup whole wheat flour

½ cup Sucanat or brown sugar

½ cup ground walnuts

3 tablespoons canola oil

▶ Preheat the oven to 350°F. Coat a 9 by 12-inch baking pan with nonstick cooking spray.

▶ Place the apples in a heavy cooking pot. Add ½ cup of the water. Cover and cook until the apples are soft but not mushy. Add the spices and stir to combine. Remove from the heat.

▶ Stir the arrowroot into the remaining ¼ cup of water. Stir the arrowroot mixture into the hot apples. The mixture will thicken from the heat of the apples—do not boil. Pour the apples into the prepared pan.

▶ To make the topping: Place all the topping ingredients in a bowl and stir with a fork to combine. Sprinkle the apples with the topping.

▶ Bake for 20 minutes, or until the crumb topping begins to brown. Serve warm with a scoop of nondairy vanilla ice cream, if desired.

PER SERVING: 280 calories, 7 g fat (<1 g saturated), 58 g carbohydrate, 9 g dietary fiber, <0.1 g sugar, 2 g protein, 0 mg cholesterol, 4.5 mg sodium. Calories from fat: 20 percent.

ALL-AMERICAN
APPLE CRUMB PIE

Is there anything that makes your house smell better than a warm apple pie baking in the oven? This pie is delicious alone or with a scoop of nondairy vanilla frozen dessert on top.

> **Makes 10 servings**

Preparation time: apples, 15 minutes; apple filling, 10 minutes; topping, 5 minutes; crust, 10 minutes
▼ **Baking time:** 20 minutes

Standard Vegan Single Piecrust, page 286

10 medium-size baking apples (I like a combination of Macintosh and a more firm apple, such as Idared or Rome) peeled, cored, and sliced

½ cup water

1½ teaspoons ground cinnamon

½ teaspoon ground cardamom (optional)

1 tablespoon arrowroot

Crumb topping:

½ cup unbleached all-purpose flour

½ cup granulated sweetener

2 tablespoons vegetable shortening (preferably nonhydrogenated, such as Spectrum or Earth Balance)

PER SERVING: 262 calories, 8.4 g fat (1.2 g saturated), 46 g carbohydrate, 4 g dietary fiber, 4 g protein, 0 mg cholesterol, 61 mg sodium. Calories from fat: 13 percent.

▶ Preheat the oven to 400°F. Coat an 8-inch pie plate with nonstick cooking spray.

▶ Prepare the piecrust. Weight the crust with another empty pie plate filled with a little water or pie weights to keep the crust from bubbling or shrinking while it bakes. You can also line the piecrust with aluminum foil and fill the foil with dried beans. Bake the piecrust for 10 minutes, or until the edges begin to brown slightly.

▶ While the crust is baking, make the apple filling. Peel, core, and slice the apples and place in a heavy cooking pot. Add ¼ cup of the water. Cover and cook until the apples are soft but not mushy. Add the spices, stir to combine, and remove from the heat.

▶ Stir the arrowroot into the remaining ¼ cup of water. Stir the arrowroot mixture into the hot apples. The mixture will thicken from the heat of the apples—do not boil. Pour the apples into the prepared crust when it is ready, making sure to remove pie weights before putting the apple filling in the crust.

▶ To make the topping: Place all the topping ingredients in a bowl and cut the shortening into the flour with two knives until the dough forms pieces that are no larger than a pea. Sprinkle the apples with topping. Bake for 10 minutes, or until the crumb topping begins to brown. Serve warm with a scoop of nondairy vanilla ice cream, if desired.

AWARD-WINNING PEACH CRUMB PIE

Fresh peach pie is a scrumptious summer treat. It's a three-step process, but you'll be glad that you made it when you smell the warm, spicy aroma filling your kitchen.

> ### Makes 10 servings

Preparation time: peaches, 15 minutes; peach filling, 10 minutes; topping, 5 minutes; crust, 10 minutes ▾ **Baking time:** 20 minutes

Standard Vegan Single Piecrust, page 286

6 cups sliced medium-size peaches (8 to 10 peaches)

½ cup water

1½ teaspoons ground cinnamon

1 tablespoon arrowroot

Crumb topping:

½ cup unbleached all-purpose flour

½ cup granulated sweetener

2 tablespoons vegetable shortening (preferably nonhydrogenated, such as Spectrum or Earth Balance)

PER SERVING: 230 calories, 13 g fat (1.2 g saturated), 37 g carbohydrate, 2.3 g dietary fiber, 3 g protein, 0 mg cholesterol, 59 mg sodium. Calories from fat: 13 percent.

▶ Preheat the oven to 400°F. Coat an 8-inch pie plate with nonstick cooking spray.

▶ Prepare the piecrust. Weight the crust with another empty pie plate filled with a little water or pie weights to keep the crust from bubbling or shrinking while it bakes. You can also line the piecrust with aluminum foil and fill the foil with dried beans. Bake the piecrust for 10 minutes, or until the edges begin to brown slightly.

▶ While the crust is baking, make the peach filling. Place the peaches in a heavy cooking pot. Add ¼ cup of the water. Cover and cook until the peaches are soft but not mushy. Add the cinnamon to the peaches and stir to combine. Remove from the heat.

▶ Stir the arrowroot into the remaining ¼ cup of water. Stir the arrowroot mixture into the hot peaches. The mixture will thicken from the heat of the peaches—do not boil. Pour the peaches into the prepared crust when it is ready, making sure to remove the pie weights before putting the peach filling in the crust.

▶ To make the topping: Place all the topping ingredients in a bowl and cut the shortening into the flour with two knives until the dough forms pieces no larger than a pea. Sprinkle the peaches with the topping. Bake for 10 minutes, or until the crumb topping begins to brown. Serve warm with a scoop of nondairy vanilla ice cream, if desired.

RAVE REVIEW
RAISIN CRUMB PIE

My father told me that back in his day raisin pie was called "funeral pie" because it was traditional to serve it at family gatherings after a funeral. Back then, fresh fruit wasn't always so readily available, and because raisins are dried, they were something that most people had on hand all the time. If you're looking for something different, this is a good pie to try. Fresh raisin pie is almost impossible to get anymore, vegan or not.

> ### Makes 10 servings

Preparation time: filling, 10 minutes; crust, 10 minutes ▼ **Baking time:** 20 minutes

Standard Vegan Single Piecrust, page 286

3 cups raisins (preferably organic)

1¼ cups water

¾ teaspoon lemon juice

¾ cup pure maple syrup

3 tablespoons arrowroot

Crumb topping:

½ cup unbleached all-purpose flour

½ cup granulated sweetener

2 tablespoons vegetable shortening (preferably nonhydrogenated, such as Spectrum)

PER SERVING: 390 calories, 8 g fat (3 g saturated), 79 g carbohydrate, 2 g dietary fiber, 15 g sugar, 4 g protein, 0 mg cholesterol, 66 mg sodium, potassium 400 mg. Calories from fat: 13 percent.

▶ Preheat the oven to 400°F. Coat an 8-inch pie plate with nonstick cooking spray.

▶ Prepare the piecrust. Weight the crust with another empty pie plate filled with a little water or pie weights to keep the crust from bubbling or shrinking while it bakes. You can also line the piecrust with aluminum foil and fill the foil with dried beans. Bake the piecrust for 10 minutes, or until the edges begin to brown slightly.

▶ While the crust is baking, make the raisin filling. Place the raisins, 1 cup of the water, and the lemon juice in a small pan. Bring to a boil and simmer for 5 minutes. Add the maple syrup, bring back to a boil, and remove from the heat.

▶ Stir the arrowroot into the remaining ¼ cup of water. Stir the arrowroot mixture into the hot raisins. The mixture will thicken from the heat of the raisins—do not boil. Pour the raisins into the prepared crust when it is ready, making sure to remove the pie weights before putting the raisin filling in the crust.

▶ To make the topping: Place all the topping ingredients in a bowl and cut the shortening into the flour with two knives until the dough forms pieces no larger than a pea. Sprinkle the raisins with the topping. Bake for 10 minutes, or until the crumb topping begins to brown. Serve warm with a scoop of nondairy vanilla ice cream, if desired.

FESTIVE APPLE CRANBERRY PIE

This is a slightly different twist on the traditional apple pie—it has a double crust surrounding cinnamon-spiced apples and tangy cranberries.

Makes 10 servings

Preparation time: apples, 15 minutes; apple filling, 10 minutes; topping, 5 minutes; crust, 10 minutes ▼ **Baking time:** 30 minutes

Standard Vegan Double Piecrust, page 287

10 medium-size baking apples (I like a combination of Macintosh and a more firm apple, such as Idared or Rome), peeled, cored, and sliced

¾ cup dried cranberries

½ cup water

1½ teaspoons ground cinnamon

1 tablespoon arrowroot

▶ Preheat the oven to 400°F. Coat an 8-inch pie plate with nonstick cooking spray.

▶ Prepare the piecrust.

▶ Place the apples in a heavy cooking pot. Add the cranberries, then add ¼ cup of the water. Cover and cook until the apples are soft but not mushy and the cranberries are plump but not bursting. Add the cinnamon and stir to combine. Remove from the heat.

▶ Stir the arrowroot into the remaining ¼ cup of water. Stir the arrowroot mixture into the hot apple mixture. The mixture will thicken from the heat of the fruit—do not boil. Pour the apple mixture into the prepared crust.

▶ Remove the top piece of waxed paper from the top crust that you rolled out earlier. Invert onto the pie and remove the other sheet of waxed paper. Press the edges down around the edges of the pie plate. Cut off the edges of the dough from both the upper and lower crusts, to fit pie plate. Crimp together with your fingers. With a sharp knife, make decorative slits in the top of the crust. If desired, brush the crust with vegan milk and sprinkle with sugar.

▶ Bake for 30 minutes, or until the crust begins to brown. Serve warm with a scoop of nondairy vanilla ice cream, if desired.

PER SERVING: 431 calories, 12 g fat (<1 g saturated), 78 g carbohydrate, 7 g dietary fiber, 3 g protein, 0 mg cholesterol, 14 mg sodium. Calories from fat: 23 percent.

WASHINGTON'S CHERRY CRUMB PIE

This luscious cherry crumb pie has all the flavor of the traditional favorite but less fat and calories.

Makes 10 servings

Preparation time: cherries, 15 minutes; cherry filling, 10 minutes; topping, 5 minutes; crust, 10 minutes ▼ **Baking time:** 20 minutes

Standard Vegan Single Piecrust, page 286

4 cups fresh cherries, pitted and halved

1 cup apple juice (or water)

2 tablespoons arrowroot

¼ cup water

Crumb topping:

½ cup unbleached all-purpose flour

½ cup granulated sweetener

2 tablespoons vegetable shortening (preferably nonhydrogenated, such as Spectrum or Earth Balance)

▶ Preheat the oven to 400°F. Coat an 8-inch pie plate with nonstick cooking spray.

▶ Prepare the piecrust. Weight the crust with another empty pie plate filled with a little water or pie weights to keep the crust from bubbling or shrinking while it bakes. You can also line the piecrust with aluminum foil and fill the foil with dried beans. Bake the piecrust for 10 minutes, or until the edges begin to brown slightly.

▶ While the crust is baking, make the filling. Place the cherries in a heavy cooking pot. Add the apple juice. Cover and cook until the cherries are soft, about 8 minutes, and remove from the heat.

▶ Stir the arrowroot into the ¼ cup of water. Stir the arrowroot mixture into the hot cherries. The mixture will thicken from the heat of the cherries—do not boil. Pour the cherries into the prepared crust when it is ready, making sure to remove the pie weights before putting the cherry filling in the crust.

▶ To make the topping: Place all the topping ingredients in bowl and cut the shortening into the flour with two knives until the dough forms pieces no larger than a pea. Sprinkle the cherries with the topping.

▶ Bake for 10 minutes, or until the crumb topping begins to brown. Serve warm with a scoop of nondairy vanilla ice cream, if desired.

PER SERVING: 235 calories, 8 g fat (3 g saturated), 38 g carbohydrate, 2 g dietary fiber, 3 g protein, 0 mg cholesterol, 59 mg sodium, 130 mg potassium. Calories from fat: 13 percent.

Hint: You may want to place a piece of aluminum foil on the oven rack under this pie, as the cherry juice tends to drip out.

NEWFANGLED MINCE PIE

If you liked the taste of mince pie, but thought that you'd never be able to have it again because you are now vegan, I have a compromise for you. This pie mimics the spicy flavor and "meaty" texture of the real thing. And because it's made with TVP (textured vegetable protein), it packs a healthy dose of protein without any added fat. For those of you who are not familiar with TVP, check the Stocking Your Vegan Pantry section on page 19 for a more complete description.

> ### Makes 8 servings

Preparation time: mince filling, 10 minutes; crust, 10 minutes ▼ **Baking time:** 30 minutes

Standard Vegan Double Piecrust, page 287

¾ cup TVP (Grape-Nuts–size granules)

1¼ cups apple cider or apple juice

4 cups baking apples (such as Macintosh or Rome), peeled, cored, and sliced

¾ cup raisins (preferably organic)

1¼ teaspoons ground cinnamon

½ teaspoons ground nutmeg

½ teaspoon ground cloves

½ teaspoon ground allspice (optional)

▶ Preheat the oven to 400°F. Coat an 8-inch pie plate with nonstick cooking spray.

▶ Prepare the piecrust.

▶ Heat ¾ cup of apple cider.

▶ Place the TVP in a small bowl and cover with ¾ cup of the hot cider. Cover and set aside. Place the apples in a heavy cooking pot with the raisins and the remaining ½ cup of apple cider. Cover the pot and cook until the apples are soft. Add the spices and drained TVP and stir to combine. Remove from the heat. Pour the filling into the prepared crust.

▶ Remove the top piece of waxed paper from the top crust that you rolled out earlier and then set it aside. Invert the top crust onto the pie and remove the other sheet of waxed paper. Press the dough down around the edges of the pie plate. Cut off the edges of the dough from both the upper and lower crusts, to fit the pie plate. Crimp together with your fingers. With a sharp knife, make decorative slits in the top of the crust. If desired, brush the crust with vegan milk and sprinkle with sugar.

▶ Bake for 30 minutes, or until the crust begins to brown. Serve warm with a scoop of nondairy vanilla ice cream, if desired.

PER SERVING: 315 calories, 12 g fat (1 g saturated), 47 g carbohydrate, 4 g dietary fiber, 7 g protein, 0 mg cholesterol, 17 mg sodium, 394 mg potassium. Calories from fat: 32 percent.

FALL HARVEST PIE

This pie is a unique blend of foods that are bountiful in the fall—sweet potatoes, apples, and cranberries—whose flavors naturally complement each other.

> **Makes 10 servings**

Preparation time: filling, 15 minutes; crust, 10 minutes; crumbs, 5 minutes
Baking time: 25 minutes

Standard Vegan Single Piecrust, page 286

3 medium-size sweet potatoes, peeled and diced

4 medium-size baking apples (such as Macintosh or Rome), peeled, cored, and sliced

½ cup water

1 cup dried cranberries

½ cup pure maple syrup

1 tablespoon vanilla extract

2 tablespoons arrowroot

⅓ cup chopped walnuts

Crumb topping:

¼ cup canola oil

⅓ cup Sucanat or brown sugar

⅓ cup whole wheat flour

PER SERVING: 534 calories, 17 g fat (1 g saturated), 92 g carbohydrate, 7 g dietary fiber, 10 g sugar, 4 g protein, 0 mg cholesterol, 18 mg sodium, 213 mg potassium. Calories from fat: 26 percent.

▸ Preheat the oven to 400°F. Coat an 8-inch pie plate with nonstick cooking spray.

▸ Prepare the piecrust. Weight the crust with another empty pie plate filled with a little water or pie weights to keep the crust from bubbling or shrinking while it bakes. You can also line the piecrust with aluminum foil and fill the foil with dried beans. Bake the piecrust for 10 minutes, or until the edges begin to brown slightly.

▸ While the crust is baking, make the filling. Place the sweet potatoes in a small pot and cover with water. Cook until soft when pricked with a fork. Drain the sweet potatoes and set aside. Place the apples in the same pot. Add ¼ cup of the water and the cranberries. Cook until the apples begin to soften. Return the sweet potatoes to the pot. Add the maple syrup and vanilla.

▸ In a small cup, mix the remaining ¼ cup of water with the arrowroot. Add to the hot filling mixture and stir until the mixture thickens—do not boil. Remove from the heat and stir in the nuts. Pour the filling into the prepared crust when it is ready, making sure to remove the pie weights before putting the filling in the crust.

▸ To make the topping: Place all the topping ingredients in a bowl and cut the oil into the flour with two knives until the dough forms pieces no larger than a pea. Sprinkle the filling with the topping.

▸ Bake for 15 minutes, or until the crumb topping begins to brown.

STATE FAIR PEAR PIE

This isn't just your average pear pie—you'll love this mouthwatering mixture of pears, apples, cranberries, nuts, and sweet vanilla syrup.

Makes 10 servings

Preparation time: peeling/coring apples and pears, 20 minutes; fruit filling, 10 minutes; crust, 10 minutes ▼ **Baking time:** 30 minutes

Standard Vegan Double Piecrust, page 287

6 pears, peeled, cored, and sliced

4 medium-size baking apples (such as Macintosh), peeled, cored, and sliced

¾ cup dried cranberries

½ cup apple juice or water

¾ cup pure maple syrup

1 tablespoon vanilla extract

2 tablespoons arrowroot

½ cup chopped walnuts

PER SERVING: 419 calories, 16 g fat (1 g saturated), 68 g carbohydrate, 8 g dietary fiber, 32 g sugar, 5 g protein, 0 mg cholesterol, 121 mg sodium, 340 mg potassium. Calories from fat: 23 percent.

▶ Preheat the oven to 400°F. Coat an 8-inch pie plate with nonstick cooking spray.

▶ Prepare the piecrust.

▶ Place the pears and apples in a heavy cooking pot with the cranberries and ¼ cup of the apple juice. Cover and cook until the fruit is soft. Add the maple syrup and vanilla and stir to combine.

▶ In a small cup, combine the remaining ¼ cup of apple juice with the arrowroot. Add to the hot fruit and stir until thickened—do not boil. Remove from the heat. Stir in the walnuts and pour the filling into the prepared crust.

▶ Remove the top piece of waxed paper from the top crust that you rolled out earlier and then set it aside. Invert the top crust onto the pie and remove the other sheet of waxed paper. Press down the dough around the edges of the pie plate. Cut off the edges of the dough from both the upper and lower crusts, to fit the pie plate. Crimp together with your fingers. With a sharp knife, make decorative slits in the top of the crust. If desired, brush the crust with vegan milk and sprinkle with sugar.

▶ Bake for 30 minutes, or until the crust begins to brown. Serve warm with a scoop of nondairy vanilla ice cream, if desired.

CONFETTI FRUIT PIE ♡

This pie doesn't just taste good, it's festive looking with its contrast of golden peaches and bright colorful raspberries.

Makes 10 servings

Preparation time: peaches, 15 minutes; fruit filling, 10 minutes; topping, 5 minutes; crust, 10 minutes ▼ **Baking time:** 25 minutes

Standard Vegan Single Piecrust, page 286

5 medium-size peaches (about 8 peaches), peeled and sliced

1 cup raspberries

½ cup water

1 tablespoon arrowroot

Crumb topping:

½ cup unbleached all-purpose flour

½ cup granulated sweetener

2 tablespoons vegetable shortening (preferably nonhydrogenated, such as Spectrum)

PER SERVING: 235 calories, 8 g fat (3 g saturated), 38 g carbohydrate, 3 g dietary fiber, 3 g protein, 0 mg cholesterol, 6 mg sodium, 209 mg potassium. Calories from fat: 13 percent.

▶ Preheat the oven to 400°F. Coat an 8-inch pie plate with nonstick cooking spray.

▶ Prepare the piecrust. Weight the crust with another empty pie plate filled with a little water or pie weights to keep the crust from bubbling or shrinking while it bakes. You can also line the piecrust with aluminum foil and fill the foil with dried beans. Bake the piecrust for 10 minutes, or until the edges begin to brown slightly.

▶ While the crust is baking, make the peach filling. Place the peaches in a heavy cooking pot with the raspberries. Add ¼ cup of the water. Cover and cook until the fruit is soft but not mushy. Remove from the heat.

▶ Stir the arrowroot into the remaining ¼ cup of water. Stir the arrowroot mixture into the hot peach mixture. The mixture will thicken from the heat of the fruit—do not boil. Pour the fruit mixture into the prepared crust when it is ready, making sure to remove the pie weights before putting the filling in the crust.

▶ To make the topping: Place all the topping ingredients in a bowl and cut the shortening into the flour with two knives until the dough forms pieces no larger than a pea. Sprinkle the peach mixture with the topping.

▶ Bake for 15 minutes, or until the crumb topping begins to brown. Serve warm with a scoop of nondairy vanilla ice cream, if desired.

BEATS SINGIN' THE BLUES PIE

This tasty treat is made with fresh blueberries, and the natural sugar in the fruit makes for a lightly sweetened filling. A dusting of crumbs completes the pie.

Makes 10 servings

Preparation time: washing/sorting blueberries, 5 minutes; fruit filling, 10 minutes; topping, 5 minutes; crust, 10 minutes ▼ **Baking time:** 25 minutes

Standard Vegan Single Piecrust, page 286

6 cups fresh blueberries

½ cup water

1 tablespoon arrowroot

Crumb topping:

½ cup unbleached all-purpose flour

½ cup granulated sweetener

2 tablespoons vegetable shortening (preferably nonhydrogenated, such as Spectrum or Earth Balance)

PER SERVING: 240 calories, 9 g fat (3 g saturated), 40 g carbohydrate, 3 g dietary fiber, 3 g protein, 0 mg cholesterol, 11 mg sodium, 101 mg potassium. Calories from fat: 13 percent.

▶ Preheat the oven to 400°F. Coat an 8-inch pie plate with nonstick cooking spray.

▶ Prepare the piecrust. Weight the crust with another empty pie plate filled with a little water or pie weights to keep the crust from bubbling or shrinking while it bakes. You can also line the piecrust with aluminum foil and fill the foil with dried beans. Bake the piecrust for 10 minutes, or until the edges begin to brown slightly.

▶ While the crust is baking, make the blueberry filling. Place the blueberries in a heavy cooking pot. Add ¼ cup of the water to the fruit. Cover and cook until the fruit is soft and remove from the heat.

▶ Stir the arrowroot into the remaining ¼ cup of water. Stir the arrowroot mixture into the hot blueberries. The mixture will thicken from the heat of the fruit—do not boil. Pour the fruit into the prepared crust when it is ready, making sure to remove the pie weights before putting the filling in the crust.

▶ To make the topping: Place all the topping ingredients in a bowl and cut the shortening into the flour with two knives until the dough forms pieces no larger than a pea. Sprinkle the blueberries with the topping.

▶ Bake for 15 minutes, or until the crumb topping begins to brown. Serve warm with a scoop of nondairy vanilla ice cream, if desired.

FRUIT COBBLER

This is a great dessert to prepare when you're pressed for time. It tastes similar to a pie, but without the work of making a piecrust!

> **Makes 8 servings**

Preparation time: fruit, 20 minutes; crumbs, 5 minutes ▼ **Baking time:** 20 minutes

4 cups fruit (blueberries, raspberries, peaches, cherries—your choice), washed, peeled if necessary, and cut into bite-size pieces if necessary

4 teaspoons sugar

1 cup water

¼ cup cornstarch

Crumb topping:

½ cup unbleached all-purpose flour

½ cup sugar

2 tablespoons cold shortening (preferably unhydrogenated, such as Spectrum or Earth Balance)

PER SERVING: 238 calories, 3.6 g fat (1 g saturated fat), 50.8 g carbohydrate, 1.7 g dietary fiber, 34.2 g sugar, 2.4 g protein, 0 mg cholesterol, 2 mg sodium. Calories from fat: 5 percent.

▶ Preheat the oven to 350°F. Spray eight individual oven-safe dishes or an 8-inch baking dish with nonstick cooking spray.

▶ Put the fruit, sugar, and ½ cup of the water in a saucepan. Bring to a boil. Cook until the fruit is soft.

▶ Mix the cornstarch with the remaining ½ cup of water. Add to the boiling fruit. Stir until the mixture comes to a boil again. It will thicken as it comes to a boil. Remove from the heat.

▶ To make the topping: Combine the flour and sugar. Using two knives, cut the shortening into the flour mixture until it is the consistency of coarse sand.

▶ Put the fruit in the baking dish(es). Sprinkle with the crumbs. Bake for 20 minutes, or until the crumb topping begins to brown. (If you're in a hurry, you can broil the fruit cobbler to brown the crumbs. Set the oven rack to the highest setting. Keep an eye on the cobbler because as soon as you turn your back, it will burn!

FRUIT SPREAD

(Makes 1 cup of fruit sauce)

Preparation time: 20 minutes

2 cups fresh fruit (apples,
  blueberries, raspberries,
  peaches, or cherries), washed,
  peeled if necessary, and cut into
  bite-size pieces if necessary

¼ cup water

2 tablespoons cornstarch

¼ cup water

2 teaspoons sugar (optional)

▶ Put the fruit and ¼ cup of the water into a saucepan and bring to a boil. If adding sugar, add it now. Boil the fruit until it is soft. If using raspberries or blueberries, boil until the berries break open and combine with the water to form a sauce. Remove from the heat.

▶ Combine the cornstarch with the remaining ¼ cup of water. Bring the fruit to a boil again and add the cornstarch. Stirring constantly, bring to a boil once again. The mixture will thicken as it boils and will continue to thicken as it cools. Remove from the heat and allow to cool completely.

Notes:
- You may use the sauce as a topping for fruit ice cream (pages 250–252) or as a spread on toast or crackers.
- In addition, I like to bake it in the middle of My Grandmother's Crumb Cake (page 70). If you do this, after you prepare the pan according to the recipe directions, pour half of the batter into the pan and spread it out. Top with the fruit spread. Put the remaining batter on top of this and sprinkle with crumbs. Don't worry if the batter and/or fruit doesn't completely cover the layer below—it will be fine once it's baked. Bake according to the recipe directions. I especially like blueberries and raspberries in this cake!

PER SERVING: 25 calories, 0.1 g fat (0 g saturated fat), 6.2 g carbohydrate, 0.6 g dietary fiber, 4.1 g sugar, 0.3 g protein, 0 mg cholesterol, 1 mg sodium. Calories from fat: 0 percent.

PUMPKIN PIE

What would your favorite holiday feast be without a traditional pumpkin pie? Here is a veganized version of the classic favorite. You won't even miss the eggs and milk.

> Makes 10 servings

Preparation time: filling, 10 minutes; crust, 10 minutes ▾ **Baking time:** 65 minutes

Standard Vegan Single Piecrust, page 286

1 (15-ounce) can pure pumpkin puree, or 2 cups cooked, pureed fresh pumpkin

1 cup vegan milk

⅓ cup pure maple syrup

2 teaspoons pumpkin pie spice (see Note)

1 tablespoon arrowroot

2 teaspoons flax powder

½ cup water

Ground cinnamon, for garnish

▶ Preheat the oven to 425°F. Coat an 8-inch pie plate with nonstick cooking spray.

▶ Prepare the piecrust. Weight the crust with another empty pie plate filled with a little water or pie weights to keep the crust from bubbling or shrinking while it bakes. You can also line the piecrust with aluminum foil and fill the foil with dried beans. Bake the piecrust for 10 minutes, or until the edges begin to brown slightly. Set the crust aside.

▶ To make the filling: Place all the ingredients except the flax powder and ½ cup of water in a food processor or blender (or even use a hand mixer) and process until smooth. Stir the flax powder into the ½ cup of water. Add to the pumpkin mixture and pulse to combine. Pour into the prepared crust and sprinkle lightly with cinnamon.

▶ Bake for 15 minutes at 425°F. Reduce the heat to 350°F and bake for 50 minutes. The pie will become firm as it cools. Allow the pie to cool for at least 4 hours before serving.

Variation: For something different, try substituting either 2 cups cooked and pureed carrots or sweet potatoes for the pumpkin. The only difference I notice when I do this is in the texture. I actually like the texture of the sweet potato pie better—it's smoother. The carrots make a pie filling with a coarser consistency, more like the pumpkin.

PER SERVING: 188 calories, 6 g fat (<1 g saturated), 31 g carbohydrate, 2 g dietary fiber, 13 g sugar, 3 g protein, 0 mg cholesterol, 121 mg sodium, 191 mg potassium. Calories from fat: 13 percent.

Note: You can substitute 1 teaspoon of ground cinnamon plus ½ teaspoon of ground ginger plus ½ teaspoon of ground cloves for the 2 teaspoons of pumpkin pie spice.

FUNNY CAKE ♡

This is a veganized version of a Pennsylvania German treat that I grew up with. It's a moist yellow cake baked in a flaky piecrust with a layer of gooey chocolate on the bottom. It's a cake, but it looks like a pie—hence the name.

Makes 10 servings

Preparation time: cake, 10 minutes; chocolate sauce, 10 minutes; crust, 10 minutes
Baking time: 35 to 40 minutes

Standard Vegan Single Piecrust, page 286

Chocolate sauce:
1 cup powdered sugar
¼ cup canola oil
½ teaspoon vanilla extract
⅙ cup unsweetened cocoa powder (half of a ⅓-cup measuring cup)
3½ tablespoons arrowroot
½ cup water

Cake:
¼ cup + 1 tablespoon soft vegan butter spread, preferably tub style, at room temperature. (If using stick butter, soften it in the microwave until it is the consistency of tub butter. Do not melt!)
½ cup pure maple syrup
1½ teaspoons vanilla extract
2¼ cups unbleached all-purpose flour
¾ tablespoon baking powder
¼ teaspoon salt
1¼ cups vegan milk

▸ Preheat the oven to 375°F. Coat an 8-inch pie plate with nonstick cooking spray.

▸ Prepare the piecrust.

▸ To make the chocolate sauce: Place the powdered sugar, canola oil, vanilla, cocoa powder, and arrowroot in a small saucepan and stir to combine, using a wire whisk for best results. Stir in the ½ cup of water. Turn on the heat and bring almost to a boil, stirring constantly. Keep stirring until the mixture starts to thicken—do not boil. Remove from the heat and set aside while you prepare the cake.

▸ To make the cake: Place the butter in a bowl and cream. Slowly add the maple syrup and beat until light and fluffy. Add the vanilla and mix. In another bowl, combine the flour, baking powder, and salt. Alternately add the flour mixture and the milk to the butter mixture and stir well.

▸ Pour the chocolate sauce in the prepared crust. Spoon the cake batter onto the chocolate sauce, evenly spacing five mounds around the pie pan. The mixture will spread during baking. Bake for 35 to 40 minutes, or until a toothpick inserted into the cake comes out clean. Allow the cake to cool completely before serving.

PER SERVING: 369 calories, 16 g fat (1.6 g saturated), 60 g carbohydrate, 2 g dietary fiber, 21.7 g sugar, 6 g protein, 0 mg cholesterol, 216 mg sodium, 148 mg potassium. Calories from fat: 19 percent.

ISLAND BREEZES CREAM PIE

This scrumptious, fluffy coconut cream pie conjures up images of tropical paradise in my mind.

Makes 10 servings

Preparation time: filling, 15 minutes; crust, 10 minutes ▼ **Baking time:** 10 minutes

Standard Vegan Single Piecrust,
  page 286

¾ cup water

2 tablespoons agar

32 ounces (2⅔ [12-ounce]
  packages) firm silken tofu

2 cups powdered sugar

4 teaspoons coconut extract

2¼ cups unsweetened shredded
  coconut

▶ Preheat the oven to 400°F. Coat an 8-inch pie plate with nonstick cooking spray.

▶ Prepare the piecrust. Weight the crust with another empty pie plate filled with a little water or pie weights to keep the crust from bubbling or shrinking while it bakes. You can also line the piecrust with aluminum foil and fill the foil with dried beans. Bake the piecrust for 10 minutes, or until the edges begin to brown slightly.

▶ Remove from the oven and set aside. Meanwhile, place the ¾ cup of water in a small pan and bring to a boil. Sprinkle the agar over the water and stir to combine. Simmer for 10 to 15 minutes, or until the agar has completely dissolved.

▶ While the agar is simmering, place the tofu in a food processor. Process until smooth, scraping down the sides as necessary. Add the powdered sugar and coconut extract. Process until combined. Add the agar mixture when it is ready. Process until the mixture is smooth and creamy. Stir in the coconut by hand, reserving ¼ cup for garnish.

▶ Pour into the prepared crust. Sprinkle with the reserved coconut. Refrigerate for at least 8 hours before serving so the filling sets.

Variation: For an interesting coconut flavor, toast the coconut before adding it to the filling and using it for a garnish. To toast coconut, you can spread it out in a thin layer on foil that has been coated with nonstick cooking spray. Broil until it begins to brown. Stir and place under the broiler again. Keep stirring until all the coconut is a light brown color. In the filling, replace the powdered sugar with brown sugar. Keep the rest of the recipe the same.

PER SERVING: 486 calories, 18 g fat (6 g saturated), 67 g carbohydrate, 3 g dietary fiber, 3 g sugar, 16 g protein, 0 mg cholesterol, 82 mg sodium, 778 mg potassium. Calories from fat: 13 percent.

Peppermint Patty Cream Pie

Tofu cream pies are always light and fluffy because the tofu provides a creamy base from which to work. All tofu pies should be made the day before you plan to serve them so they have time to set. This winning combination of chocolate and mint reminds me of a York Peppermint Patty.

> **Makes 10 servings**

Preparation time: filling, 15 minutes; topping, 10 minutes; crust, 10 minutes
Baking time: 10 minutes

Standard Vegan Single Piecrust, page 286

1 pound (16 ounces, or 1⅓ [12-ounce] packages) firm silken tofu

1 cup powdered sugar

2 teaspoons vanilla extract

1½ cups vegan chocolate chips

Topping:

1 pound (16 ounces, or 1⅓ [12-ounce] packages) firm silken tofu

1 cup powdered sugar

¼ cup unbleached all-purpose flour

1½ teaspoons peppermint extract

PER SERVING: 423 calories, 20 g fat (6 g saturated), 50 g carbohydrate, 1.5 g dietary fiber, 3 g sugar, 14 g protein, 0 mg cholesterol, 111 mg sodium, 488 mg potassium. Calories from fat: 24 percent.

▸ Preheat the oven to 400°F. Coat an 8-inch pie plate with nonstick cooking spray.

▸ Prepare the piecrust. Weight the crust with another empty pie plate filled with a little water or pie weights to keep the crust from bubbling or shrinking while it bakes. You can also line the piecrust with aluminum foil and fill the foil with dried beans. Bake the piecrust for 10 minutes, or until the edges begin to brown slightly.

▸ Remove from the oven and set aside. Meanwhile, place the tofu in a food processor and process until smooth, scraping down the sides as necessary. Add the powdered sugar and vanilla. Melt the chocolate chips in a microwave or double boiler. Pour into the tofu mixture and blend until combined. Pour into the prepared crust.

▸ To make the topping: Rinse and dry the food processor. Place the tofu in the processor and process until smooth, scraping down the sides as necessary. Add the powdered sugar, flour, and peppermint extract and mix. Carefully mound onto the chocolate layer.

▸ Refrigerate for at least 8 hours before serving so the filling sets. You may want to refrigerate the topping in a separate container to allow it to set before putting it on the pie. It will be easier to mound onto the filling.

A HINT OF MINT CREAM PIE

This pie was inspired by one of my favorite ice cream flavors—mint chocolate chip. It has all the flavor of that delicious ice cream but none of the startling green color, which is achieved by adding artificial coloring.

Makes 10 servings

Preparation time: filling, 15 minutes; crust, 10 minutes ▼ **Baking time:** 10 minutes

Standard Vegan Single Piecrust, page 286

¾ cup water

2 tablespoons agar

32 ounces (2⅔ [12-ounce] packages) firm silken tofu

2 cups powdered sugar

1 tablespoon peppermint extract

1½ cups vegan chocolate chips

▶ Preheat the oven to 400°F. Coat an 8-inch pie plate with nonstick cooking spray.

▶ Prepare the piecrust. Weight the crust with another empty pie plate filled with a little water or pie weights to keep the crust from bubbling or shrinking while it bakes. You can also line the piecrust with aluminum foil and fill the foil with dried beans. Bake the piecrust for 10 minutes, or until the edges begin to brown slightly.

▶ Remove from the oven and set aside. Meanwhile, place the ¾ cup of water in a small pan and bring to a boil. Sprinkle the agar over the water and stir to combine. Simmer for 15 minutes, or until the agar has completely dissolved.

▶ While the agar is simmering, place the tofu in a food processor. Process until smooth, scraping down the sides as necessary. Add the powdered sugar and peppermint extract. Add the agar mixture when it is ready. Process until the mixture is smooth and creamy. Stir in the chocolate chips by hand. Pour into the prepared crust.

▶ Refrigerate for at least 8 hours before serving so the filling sets.

PER SERVING: 478 calories, 20 g fat (6 g saturated), 62 g carbohydrate, 2 g dietary fiber, 3 g sugar, 16 g protein, 0 mg cholesterol, 22 mg sodium, 504 mg potassium. Calories from fat: 36 percent.

YOU GOT YOUR CHOCOLATE IN MY PEANUT BUTTER CREAM PIE

Fluffy peanut butter cream mounded on a dark chocolate filling will make this a favorite for both chocolate and peanut butter lovers.

> Makes 10 servings

Preparation time: filling, 15 minutes; topping, 10 minutes; crust, 10 minutes
Baking time: 10 minutes

Standard Vegan Single Piecrust, page 286

1 pound (16 ounces, or 1⅓ [12-ounce] packages) firm silken tofu

1 cup powdered sugar

2 teaspoons vanilla extract

1½ cups vegan chocolate chips

Topping:

1 pound (16 ounces, or 1⅓ [12-ounce] packages) firm silken tofu

1 cup powdered sugar

¼ cup unbleached all-purpose flour, or 2 teaspoons xanthan gum (see Note)

1½ teaspoons vanilla extract

¾ cup smooth natural peanut butter

▶ Preheat the oven to 400°F. Coat an 8-inch pie plate with nonstick cooking spray.

▶ Prepare the piecrust. Weight the crust with another empty pie plate filled with a little water or pie weights to keep the crust from bubbling or shrinking while it bakes. You can also line the piecrust with aluminum foil and fill the foil with dried beans. Bake the piecrust for 10 minutes, or until the edges begin to brown slightly.

▶ Remove from the oven and set aside. Meanwhile, place the tofu in a food processor and process until smooth, scraping down the sides as necessary. Add the powdered sugar and vanilla. Melt the chocolate chips in a microwave or double boiler. Pour into the tofu mixture and blend until combined. Pour into the prepared crust.

▶ To make the topping: Rinse and dry the food processor. Place the tofu in the processor and process until smooth, scraping down the sides as necessary. Add the powdered sugar, flour, and vanilla. Add the peanut butter and process until smooth and creamy. Carefully mound onto the chocolate layer.

▶ Refrigerate for at least 8 hours before serving so the filling sets. You may want to refrigerate the topping in a separate container to allow it to set before putting it on the pie. It will be easier to mound onto the filling.

PER SERVING: 482 calories, 20 g fat (6 g saturated), 62 g carbohydrate, 2 g dietary fiber, 3 g sugar, 16 g protein, 0 mg cholesterol, 22 mg sodium, 506 mg potassium. Calories from fat: 36 percent.

Note: Xanthan gum will make a softer topping, but will not give the mild flour taste that you may get when using the flour.

BLACK AND WHITE CREAM PIE

*I named this cream pie Black and White because that's exactly what it is—classic
dark chocolate filling topped with fluffy vanilla cream. Simple and delicious.*

> Makes 10 servings

Preparation time: filling, 15 minutes; topping, 10 minutes; crust, 10 minutes
Baking time: 10 minutes

Standard Vegan Single Piecrust,
page 286

1 pound (16 ounces, or 1⅓
[12-ounce] packages) firm
silken tofu

1 cup powdered sugar

2 teaspoons vanilla extract

1½ cups vegan chocolate chips

Topping:

1 pound (16 ounces, or 1⅓
[12-ounce] packages) firm
silken tofu

1 cup powdered sugar

¼ cup unbleached all-purpose
flour, or 2 teaspoons xanthan
gum (see Note)

1 tablespoon vanilla extract

▶ Preheat the oven to 400°F. Coat an 8-inch pie plate with
nonstick cooking spray.

▶ Prepare the piecrust. Weight the crust with another
empty pie plate filled with a little water or pie weights to
keep the crust from bubbling or shrinking while it bakes.
You can also line the piecrust with aluminum foil and fill
the foil with dried beans. Bake the piecrust for 10 minutes, or until the edges begin to brown slightly.

▶ Remove from the oven and set aside. Meanwhile, place
the tofu in a food processor and process until smooth,
scraping down the sides as necessary. Add the powdered
sugar and vanilla. Melt the chocolate chips in a microwave or double boiler. Pour into the tofu mixture and
blend until combined. Pour into the prepared crust.

▶ To make the topping: Rinse and dry the food processor.
Place the tofu in the processor and process until smooth,
scraping down the sides as necessary. Add the powdered
sugar, flour, and vanilla. Carefully mound onto the chocolate layer.

▶ Refrigerate for at least 8 hours before serving so the filling sets. You may want to refrigerate the topping in a
separate container to allow it to set before putting it on
the pie. It will be easier to mound onto the filling.

PER SERVING: 484 calories, 20 g fat
(6 g saturated), 62 g carbohydrate,
2 g dietary fiber, 3 g sugar, 16 g
protein, 0 mg cholesterol, 23 mg
sodium, 507 mg potassium. Calories
from fat: 36 percent.

Note: Xanthan gum will make a softer topping, but you will not get
the mild flour flavor that you may get if you use the flour.

MONKEY'S CHOICE CREAM PIE

For all you banana lovers out there, this combination of sliced bananas, creamy banana filling, and fluffy vanilla cream topping will be a dream come true!

Makes 10 servings

Preparation time: filling, 15 minutes; topping, 10 minutes; crust, 10 minutes
Baking time: 10 minutes

Standard Vegan Single Piecrust, page 286

½ cup water

1 tablespoon agar

1 pound (16 ounces, or 1⅓ [12-ounce] packages) firm silken tofu

1 cup powdered sugar

½ teaspoon lemon juice

2 teaspoons vanilla extract

1½ cups mashed ripe bananas (about 2 bananas), plus 2 medium-size ripe (yellow) bananas

▸ Preheat the oven to 400°F. Coat an 8-inch pie plate with nonstick cooking spray.

▸ Prepare the piecrust. Weight the crust with another empty pie plate filled with a little water or pie weights to keep the crust from bubbling or shrinking while it bakes. You can also line the piecrust with aluminum foil and fill the foil with dried beans. Bake the piecrust for 10 minutes, or until the edges begin to brown slightly.

▸ Remove from the oven and set aside. Meanwhile, place the ½ cup of water in a small pan and bring to a boil. Sprinkle the agar over the water and stir to combine. Simmer for 10 to 15 minutes, or until the agar has completely dissolved.

▸ While the agar is simmering, place the tofu in a food processor and process until smooth, scraping down the sides as necessary. Add the powdered sugar, lemon juice, and vanilla. Add the mashed bananas and puree until smooth and creamy. Add the agar mixture when it is ready. Process until the mixture is combined.

▸ Slice the remaining bananas and place evenly around the bottom of the prepared piecrust. Pour the filling over the sliced bananas.

continues

continued

Topping:

1 pound (16 ounces, or 1⅓ [12-ounce] packages) firm silken tofu

1 cup powdered sugar

¼ cup unbleached all-purpose flour, or 2 teaspoons xanthan gum (see Note)

1 tablespoon vanilla extract

PER SERVING: 425 calories, 13 g fat (1 g saturated), 62 g carbohydrate, 2 g dietary fiber, 3 g sugar, 16 g protein, 0 mg cholesterol, 31 mg sodium, 754 mg potassium. Calories from fat: 27 percent.

▶ To make the topping: Rinse and dry the food processor. Place the tofu in the processor and process until smooth, scraping down the sides as necessary. Add the powdered sugar, flour, and vanilla and mix. Carefully mound onto the banana layer.

▶ Refrigerate for at least 8 hours before serving so the filling sets. You may want to refrigerate the topping in a separate container to allow it to set before putting it on the pie. It will be easier to mound onto the filling.

Note: Xanthan gum will give a softer topping, but you will not get the mild flour taste that you may have if you use the flour.

THAT'S ONE NUTTY BANANA!

As a child, I used to love slices of banana smeared with peanut butter, and this pie reminds me of that snack.

> Makes 10 servings

Preparation time: filling, 15 minutes; topping, 10 minutes; crust, 10 minutes
Baking time: 10 minutes

Standard Vegan Single Piecrust, page 286

Peanut butter sauce:
¼ cup pure maple syrup
¼ cup smooth natural peanut butter
½ teaspoon vanilla extract
¼ cup water

Filling:
½ cup water
1 tablespoon agar
1 pound (16 ounces, or 1⅓ [12-ounce] packages) firm silken tofu
1 cup powdered sugar
½ teaspoon lemon juice
1 teaspoon vanilla extract
1½ cups mashed ripe (yellow) bananas (about 2 bananas), plus 2 medium-size ripe (yellow) bananas

▶ Preheat the oven to 400°F. Coat an 8-inch pie plate with nonstick cooking spray.

▶ Prepare the piecrust. Weight the crust with another empty pie plate filled with a little water or pie weights to keep the crust from bubbling or shrinking while it bakes. You can also line the piecrust with aluminum foil and fill the foil with dried beans. Bake the piecrust for 10 minutes, or until the edges begin to brown slightly. Remove from the oven and set aside.

▶ To make the sauce: Place all of the sauce ingredients in a small bowl. Mix until combined. Set aside.

▶ To make the filling: Place the ½ cup of water in a small pan and bring to a boil. Sprinkle the agar over the water and stir to combine. Simmer for 10 to 15 minutes, or until the agar has completely dissolved. While the agar is simmering, place the tofu in a food processor and process until smooth, scraping down the sides as necessary. Add the powdered sugar, lemon juice, and vanilla. Add the mashed bananas and puree until smooth and creamy. Add the agar mixture when it is ready and process until the mixture is combined. Slice the remaining bananas and place evenly around the bottom of the prepared piecrust. Drizzle the peanut butter sauce over the sliced bananas (reserving 2 tablespoons of sauce to drizzle on the top of the pie). Then pour the filling over the sliced bananas and smooth it with a spatula. Refrigerate.

continues

continued

Peanut butter topping:

1 pound (16 ounces, or 1⅓ [12-ounce] packages) firm silken tofu

1 cup powdered sugar

¼ cup unbleached all-purpose flour, or 2 teaspoons xanthan gum (see Note)

1½ teaspoons vanilla extract

¾ cup smooth natural peanut butter

PER SERVING: 655 calories, 30 g fat (5 g saturated), 79 g carbohydrate, 4 g dietary fiber, 13 g sugar, 24 g protein, 0 mg cholesterol, 182 mg sodium, 1000 mg potassium. Calories from fat: 38 percent.

▶ To make the peanut butter topping: Rinse and dry the food processor. Place the tofu in the processor and process until smooth, scraping down the sides as necessary. Add the powdered sugar, flour, and vanilla. Add the peanut butter and blend until smooth. Carefully mound onto the filling layer. Drizzle with the reserved peanut butter sauce. Refrigerate for at least 8 hours before serving so the filling sets. You may want to refrigerate the topping in a separate container to allow it to set before putting it on the pie. It will be easier to mound onto the filling.

Note: Xanthan gum will produce a slightly softer topping, but it will not have the mild flour flavor that you may get if you use the flour.

MIDNIGHT MONKEY CREAM PIE

This pie is like a fluffy chocolate-covered banana. Don't be alarmed if the topping turns from a nice creamy white to a faded yellow color—it's because of the banana.

Makes 10 servings

Preparation time: filling, 15 minutes; topping, 10 minutes; crust, 10 minutes
Baking time: 10 minutes

Standard Vegan Single Piecrust, page 286

1 pound (16 ounces, or 1⅓ [12-ounce] packages) firm silken tofu

1 cup powdered sugar

2 teaspoons vanilla extract

1½ cups vegan chocolate chips

2 medium-size ripe (yellow) bananas

Topping:

1 pound (16 ounces, or 1⅓ [12-ounce] packages) firm silken tofu

½ cup powdered sugar

1½ cups mashed very ripe bananas (about 2 bananas)

¼ cup unbleached all-purpose flour, or 2 teaspoons xanthan gum (see Note)

½ teaspoon lemon juice

1 teaspoon vanilla extract

▶ Preheat the oven to 400°F. Coat an 8-inch pie plate with nonstick cooking spray.

▶ Prepare the piecrust. Weight the crust with another empty pie plate filled with a little water or pie weights to keep the crust from bubbling or shrinking while it bakes. You can also line the piecrust with aluminum foil and fill the foil with dried beans. Bake the piecrust for 10 minutes, or until the edges begin to brown slightly.

▶ Remove from the oven and set aside. Meanwhile, place the tofu in a food processor and process until smooth, scraping down the sides as necessary. Add the powdered sugar and vanilla. Melt the chocolate chips in a microwave or double boiler. Pour into the tofu mixture and blend until combined.

▶ Slice the bananas and arrange evenly around the bottom of the prepared piecrust. Pour the filling into the prepared crust on top of the sliced bananas.

▶ To make the topping: Rinse and dry the food processor. Place the tofu in the processor and process until smooth, scraping down the sides as necessary. Add the powdered sugar, mashed banana, flour, lemon juice, and vanilla. Carefully mound onto the chocolate layer.

▶ Refrigerate for at least 8 hours before serving so the filling sets. You may want to refrigerate the topping in a separate container to allow it to set before putting it on the pie. It will be easier to mound onto the filling.

PER SERVING: 511 calories, 21 g fat (6 g saturated), 70 g carbohydrate, 4 g dietary fiber, 3 g sugar, 16 g protein, 0 mg cholesterol, 23 mg sodium, 733 mg potassium. Calories from fat: 34 percent.

Note: Xanthan gum will produce a slightly softer topping, but it will not have the mild flour flavor that you may have if you use the flour.

BERRY CHIP CREAM PIE 💞

Creamy raspberry filling and dark chocolate chips make this a mouthwatering blend worthy of any dinner party.

> **Makes 10 servings**

Preparation time: filling, 15 minutes; crust, 10 minutes ▼ **Baking time:** 10 minutes

Standard Vegan Single Piecrust, page 286

¾ cup water

2 tablespoons agar

32 ounces (2⅔ [12-ounce] packages) firm silken tofu

2 cups powdered sugar

1 teaspoon vanilla extract

½ cup raspberry jam, or ¾ cup fresh raspberries

1½ cups vegan chocolate chips

PER SERVING: 533 calories, 20 g fat (6 g saturated), 77 g carbohydrate, 4 g dietary fiber, 3 g sugar, 17 g protein, 0 mg cholesterol, 43 mg sodium, 740 mg potassium. Calories from fat: 33 percent.

▶ Preheat the oven to 400°F. Coat an 8-inch pie plate with nonstick cooking spray.

▶ Prepare the piecrust. Weight the crust with another empty pie plate filled with a little water or pie weights to keep the crust from bubbling or shrinking while it bakes. You can also line the piecrust with aluminum foil and fill the foil with dried beans. Bake the piecrust for 10 minutes, or until the edges begin to brown slightly.

▶ Remove from the oven and set aside. Meanwhile, place the ¾ cup of water in a small pan and bring to a boil. Sprinkle the agar over the water and stir to combine. Simmer for 10 to 15 minutes, or until the agar has completely dissolved.

▶ While the agar is simmering, place the tofu in a food processor and process until smooth, scraping down the sides as necessary. Add the powdered sugar, vanilla, and raspberry jam. Add the agar mixture when it is ready. Process until the mixture is smooth and creamy. Stir in the chocolate chips by hand and pour into the prepared crust.

▶ Refrigerate for at least 8 hours before serving so the filling sets.

PUCKER-UP CREAM PIE

This old-time classic—tangy lemon filling topped with fluffy vanilla cream—will definitely make your taste buds tingle.

> Makes 10 servings

Preparation time: filling, 15 minutes; topping, 10 minutes; crust, 10 minutes
Baking time: 10 minutes

Standard Vegan Single Piecrust, page 286

½ cup lemon juice

1 tablespoon agar

1 pound (16 ounces, or 1⅓ [12-ounce] packages) firm silken tofu

1 cup powdered sugar

1 tablespoon lemon extract

¼ teaspoon turmeric (for color only)

Topping:

1 pound (16 ounces, 1⅓ [12-ounce] packages) firm silken tofu

1 cup powdered sugar

¼ cup unbleached all-purpose flour, or 2 teaspoons xanthan gum (see Note)

1 tablespoon vanilla extract

▶ Preheat the oven to 400°F. Coat an 8-inch pie plate with nonstick cooking spray.

▶ Prepare the piecrust. Weight the crust with another empty pie plate filled with a little water or pie weights to keep the crust from bubbling or shrinking while it bakes. You can also line the piecrust with aluminum foil and fill the foil with dried beans. Bake the piecrust for 10 minutes, or until the edges begin to brown slightly.

▶ Remove from the oven and set aside. Meanwhile, place the lemon juice in a small pan and bring to a boil. Sprinkle the agar over the juice and stir to combine. Simmer for 10 to 15 minutes, or until the agar has completely dissolved. While the agar is simmering, place the tofu in a food processor. Process until smooth, scraping down the sides as necessary. Add the powdered sugar, lemon extract, and turmeric. Add the agar mixture when it is ready. Process until the mixture is smooth and creamy. Pour into the prepared crust.

▶ To make the topping: Rinse and dry the food processor. Place the tofu in the processor and process until smooth, scraping down the sides as necessary. Add the powdered sugar, flour, and vanilla. Carefully mound onto the lemon layer.

▶ Refrigerate for at least 8 hours before serving so the filling sets.

▶ You may want to refrigerate the topping in a separate container to allow it to set before putting it on the pie. It will be easier to mound onto the filling.

Note: Xanthan will produce a slightly softer topping, but it will not have the mild flour flavor that you may have if you use the flour.

PER SERVING: 395 calories, 13 g fat (1 g saturated), 55 g carbohydrate, 1 g dietary fiber, 3 g sugar, 15 g protein, 0 mg cholesterol, 30 mg sodium, 634 mg potassium. Calories from fat: 29 percent.

CLOUDS OF STRAWBERRY PIE

My son, a strawberry lover, asked if I could make strawberry cream pie—so how could I refuse? I created this pie for him as well as to make the most of fresh strawberries in June (although jam or frozen strawberries may be used as well). The light whipped topping adds just the right touch.

> **Makes 10 servings**

Preparation time: filling, 15 minutes; topping, 10 minutes; crust, 10 minutes
Baking time: 10 minutes

Standard Vegan Single Piecrust, page 286

½ cup water

1 tablespoon agar

1 pound (16 ounces, or 1⅓ [12-ounce] packages) firm silken tofu

1 cup powdered sugar

¼ cup strawberry jam, or ¾ cup fresh or frozen strawberries

1 teaspoon vanilla extract

2 to 3 fresh whole strawberries, sliced for garnish (optional)

4 to 5 fresh mint leaves, for garnish (optional)

▶ Coat an 8-inch pie plate with nonstick cooking spray. Preheat the oven to 400°F.

▶ Prepare the piecrust. Weight the crust with another empty pie plate filled with a little water or pie weights to keep the crust from bubbling or shrinking while it bakes. You can also line the piecrust with aluminum foil and fill the foil with dried beans. Bake the piecrust for 10 minutes, or until the edges begin to brown slightly.

▶ Remove from the oven and set aside. Meanwhile, Place the ½ cup of water in a small pan and bring to a boil. Sprinkle the agar over the water and stir to combine. Simmer for 10 to 15 minutes, or until the agar has completely dissolved. While the agar is simmering, place the tofu in a food processor. Process until smooth, scraping down the sides as necessary. Add the powdered sugar, strawberry jam, and vanilla. Add the agar mixture when it is ready. Process until the mixture is smooth and creamy. Pour into the prepared crust.

continues

continued

Topping:

1 pound (16 ounces, or 1⅓ [12-ounce] packages) firm silken tofu

1 cup powdered sugar

¼ cup unbleached all-purpose flour, or 2 teaspoons xanthan gum (see Note)

1 tablespoon vanilla extract

PER SERVING: 396 calories, 13 g fat (1 g saturated), 55 g carbohydrate, 2 g dietary fiber, 3 g sugar, 15 g protein, 0 mg cholesterol, 30 mg sodium, 638 mg potassium. Calories from fat: 29 percent.

▶ To make the topping: Rinse and dry the food processor. Place the tofu in the processor and process until smooth, scraping down the sides as necessary. Add the powdered sugar, flour, and vanilla. Carefully mound onto the strawberry layer. Garnish with sliced fresh strawberries and mint leaves, if desired.

▶ Refrigerate at least 8 hours before serving so the filling may set. You may want to refrigerate the topping in a separate container to allow it to set before putting it on the pie. It will be easier to mound onto the filling.

Note: Xanthan gum will produce a slightly softer topping, but it will not have the mild flour flavor that you may have if you use the flour.

STRAWBERRY SURPRISE CREAM PIE ♡

This is one of my favorite cream pies, even though it contains no chocolate. I always liked strawberry cake topped with coconut icing, so I started to think that maybe I could add just a bit of coconut to the strawberry base that I use for the Clouds of Strawberry Pie. I tried it, made a few other adjustments, and the Strawberry Surprise Cream Pie was born!

Makes 10 servings

Preparation time: filling, 15 minutes; crust, 10 minutes ▼ **Baking time:** 10 minutes

Standard Vegan Single Piecrust, page 286

¾ cup water

2 tablespoons agar

32 ounces (2⅔ [12-ounce] packages) firm silken tofu

2 cups powdered sugar

½ cup strawberry jam, or 1½ cups fresh or frozen strawberries

1 teaspoon coconut extract

1 cup unsweetened shredded coconut

2 to 3 whole strawberries, sliced for garnish (optional)

4 to 5 fresh mint leaves, for garnish (optional)

▸ Preheat the oven to 400°F. Coat an 8-inch pie plate with nonstick cooking spray.

▸ Prepare the piecrust. Weight the crust with another empty pie plate filled with a little water or pie weights to keep the crust from bubbling or shrinking while it bakes. You can also line the piecrust with aluminum foil and fill the foil with dried beans. Bake the piecrust for 10 minutes, or until the edges begin to brown slightly.

▸ Remove from the oven and set aside. Meanwhile, place the ¾ cup of water in a small pan and bring to a boil. Sprinkle the agar over the water and stir to combine. Simmer for 10 to 15 minutes, or until the agar has completely dissolved.

▸ While the agar is simmering, place the tofu in a food processor. Process until smooth, scraping down the sides as necessary. Add the powdered sugar, strawberry jam, and coconut extract. Add the agar mixture when it is ready. Process until the mixture is smooth and creamy. Stir in ¾ cup of the coconut by hand, reserving ¼ cup to sprinkle on top of the pie. Pour the filling into the prepared crust. Garnish with the coconut, sliced fresh strawberries, and mint leaves, if desired.

▸ Refrigerate for at least 8 hours before serving so the filling sets.

PER SERVING: 449 calories, 15 g fat (3 g saturated), 65 g carbohydrate, 3 g dietary fiber, 4 g sugar, 16 g protein, 0 mg cholesterol, 59 mg sodium, 787 mg potassium. Calories from fat: 30 percent.

Variation: Substitute fresh peaches for the strawberries, for a scrumptious coconut peach pie.

Piña Colada Cream Pie

If you enjoy a frosty piña colada on a hot summer day, then you'll love this creamy tropical pineapple and coconut concoction.

> **Makes 10 servings**

Preparation time: filling, 15 minutes; crust, 10 minutes ▼ **Baking time:** 10 minutes

Standard Vegan Single Piecrust, page 286

¾ cup pineapple juice

2 tablespoons agar

32 ounces (2⅔ [12-ounce] packages) firm silken tofu

2 cups powdered sugar

¾ cup crushed pineapple

1 teaspoon coconut extract

1 cup unsweetened shredded coconut

4–5 fresh mint leaves, for garnish (optional)

PER SERVING: 464 calories, 15 g fat (3 g saturated), 69 g carbohydrate, 3 g dietary fiber, 4 g sugar, 16 g protein, 0 mg cholesterol, 60 mg sodium, 798 mg potassium. Calories from fat: 29 percent.

▸ Preheat the oven to 400°F. Coat an 8-inch pie plate with nonstick cooking spray.

▸ Prepare the piecrust. Weight the crust with another empty pie plate filled with a little water or pie weights to keep the crust from bubbling or shrinking while it bakes. You can also line the piecrust with aluminum foil and fill the foil with dried beans. Bake the piecrust for 10 minutes, or until the edges begin to brown slightly.

▸ Remove from the oven and set aside. Meanwhile, place the juice in a small pan and bring to a boil. Sprinkle the agar over the juice and stir to combine. Simmer for 10 to 15 minutes, or until the agar has completely dissolved. While the agar is simmering, place the tofu in a food processor. Process until smooth, scraping down the sides as necessary. Add the powdered sugar, ½ cup of the crushed pineapple, and the coconut extract. Add the agar mixture when it is ready. Process until the mixture is smooth and creamy. Stir in ¾ cup of the coconut by hand (reserving ¼ cup to sprinkle on top of the pie). Stir in the remaining ¼ cup of crushed pineapple by hand.

▸ Pour into the prepared crust. Garnish with additional shredded coconut and mint leaves, if desired.

▸ Refrigerate for at least 8 hours before serving so the filling sets.

Patriotic Cream Pie

I have always loved the taste of blueberry crumb pie so I got to wondering if blueberries would taste good in a cream pie. I tried it and loved it. This pie is similar to the Clouds of Strawberry Cream Pie, page 182, except it calls for blueberries instead of strawberries.

Makes 10 servings

Preparation time: filling, 15 minutes; topping, 10 minutes; crust, 10 minutes
Baking time: 10 minutes

Standard Vegan Single Piecrust,
  page 286

½ cup water or juice

1 tablespoon agar

1 pound (16 ounces, or 1⅓
  [12-ounce] packages) firm
  silken tofu

1 cup powdered sugar

¾ cup fresh or frozen blueberries

1 teaspoon vanilla extract

4 to 5 fresh mint leaves, for
  garnish (optional)

▶ Coat an 8-inch pie plate with nonstick cooking spray. Preheat the oven to 400°F.

▶ Prepare the piecrust. Weight the crust with another empty pie plate filled with a little water or pie weights to keep the crust from bubbling or shrinking while it bakes. You can also line the piecrust with aluminum foil and fill the foil with dried beans. Bake the piecrust for 10 minutes, or until the edges begin to brown slightly.

▶ Remove from the oven and set aside. Meanwhile, place the ½ cup of water in a small pan and bring to a boil. Sprinkle the agar over the water and stir to combine. Simmer for 10 to 15 minutes, or until the agar has completely dissolved. While the agar is simmering, place the tofu in a food processor. Process until smooth, scraping down the sides as necessary. Add the powdered sugar, ½ cup of the fruit, and the vanilla. Add the agar mixture when it is ready. Process until the mixture is smooth and creamy. Pour into the prepared crust.

continues

continued

Topping:

1 pound (16 ounces, or 1⅓ [12-ounce] packages) firm silken tofu

1 cup powdered sugar

¼ cup unbleached all-purpose flour, or 2 teaspoons xanthan gum (see Note)

1 tablespoon vanilla extract

PER SERVING: 349 calories, 7 g fat (1 g saturated), 55 g carbohydrate, 2 g dietary fiber, 3 g sugar, 15 g protein, 0 mg cholesterol, 31 mg sodium, 626 mg potassium. Calories from fat: 19 percent.

▶ To make the topping: Rinse and dry the food processor. Place the tofu in the processor and process until smooth, scraping down the sides as necessary. Add the powdered sugar, flour, and vanilla. Carefully mound onto the blueberry layer. Garnish with the remaining ¼ cup of blueberries and mint leaves, if desired.

▶ Refrigerate for at least 8 hours before serving so the filling sets. You may want to refrigerate the topping in a separate container to allow it to set before putting it on the pie. It will be easier to mound onto the filling.

Note: Xanthan gum will produce a slightly softer topping, but it will not have the mild flour flavor that you may have if you use the flour.

JUST PEEKIN' PIE

One of my favorite preveganism treats was pecan pie. I worked for a long time trying to duplicate that same texture and taste with vegan ingredients, and Just Peekin' Pie is the result. It's very similar to its high-fat nonveganized "cousin" in taste, but of course it's much healthier!

$$\text{Makes 10 servings}$$

Preparation time: filling, 15 minutes; crust, 10 minutes ▼ **Baking time:** 10 minutes

Standard Vegan Single Piecrust, page 286

1 cup pure maple syrup

¼ teaspoon salt

½ cup brown sugar

2 tablespoons vegan butter spread

1½ cups water

1 tablespoon vanilla extract

¼ cup arrowroot

2 cups whole, shelled pecans

PER SERVING: 471 calories, 29 g fat (2 g saturated), 52 g carbohydrate, 2 g dietary fiber, 21 g sugar, 3 g protein, 0 mg cholesterol, 25 mg sodium, 193 mg potassium. Calories from fat: 53 percent.

▶ Preheat the oven to 400°F. Coat an 8-inch pie plate with nonstick cooking spray.

▶ Prepare the piecrust. Weight the crust with another empty pie plate filled with a little water or pie weights to keep the crust from bubbling or shrinking while it bakes. You can also line the piecrust with aluminum foil and fill the foil with dried beans. Bake the piecrust for 10 minutes, or until the edges begin to brown slightly.

▶ Remove from the oven and set aside. Meanwhile, bring the maple syrup, salt, brown sugar, butter, 1 cup of the water, and vanilla to a boil in a small pan. Combine arrowroot and ½ cup of the water in a small bowl. Pour into the hot sugar mixture. Stir until thickened—do not allow the mixture to boil after arrowroot has been added.

▶ Put the nuts in the bottom of the prepared piecrust. Pour the sugar mixture over the nuts. Place in the refrigerator to thicken.

▶ Refrigerate for at least 8 hours before serving so the filling sets.

APPLE DUMPLINGS

I grew up in a Pennsylvania German household, and one of my favorite dishes as a child was apple dumplings, which are pieces of apple covered with sugar and ground cinnamon and wrapped in flaky dough. My mother used to make them for dinner, so it was like eating pie for dinner! Try them in a bowl covered with milk. They're also delicious served warm with a glass of cold vegan milk or a scoop of nondairy vanilla ice cream.

Makes 4 servings

Preparation time: prepping apples, 10 minutes; crust, 10 minutes
Baking time: 20 minutes ▼ **Assembly:** 15 minutes

Crust:

1¼ cups unbleached all-purpose flour

¼ teaspoon salt

¼ cup canola oil, or coconut oil if desired

½ cup + 2 tablespoons cold water or apple juice

Filling:

2 medium-size baking apples, such as Macintosh, cut in half, peeled, and cored

1 teaspoon ground cinnamon

1 teaspoon granulated sweetener

1 teaspoon vegan butter spread (preferably unhydrogenated, such as Spectrum or Earth Balance) (optional)

PER SERVING: 308 calories, 14 g fat (1 g saturated), 42 g carbohydrate, 3 g dietary fiber, <1 g sugar, 4 g protein, 0 mg cholesterol, 15 mg sodium, 124 mg potassium. Calories from fat: 40 percent.

▸ Preheat the oven to 400°F. Coat an 8-inch pie plate with nonstick cooking spray.

▸ To make the crust: Put the flour and salt a in small bowl. Add the canola oil. Stir into the flour until the dough forms pieces no larger than a pea. (If using the coconut oil, which is solid at room temperature like vegetable shortening, cut the oil into the flour with two knives until the dough forms pieces no larger than a pea). Add the water. Stir just until the mixture forms a ball (add more water if necessary). Refrigerate for 10 minutes. Place the ball of dough on a piece of floured waxed paper. Place another piece of waxed paper on top of the ball of dough and push down to flatten. Using a rolling pin, roll the dough as thinly as possible between the two sheets of waxed paper. Remove the top sheet of paper carefully and cut the dough into quarters.

▸ To make the filling: Place one apple half on each quarter of dough, cut side down. Sprinkle each apple half with ¼ teaspoon of cinnamon and ¼ teaspoon of granulated sweetener. Place ¼ teaspoon of butter spread on each apple half, if desired.

▸ Draw up the sides of the dough and press closed to completely seal each apple half in dough. Place in the prepared pan.

▸ Bake for 15 to 20 minutes, or until golden brown.

TANTALIZING TRUFFLE PIE ♡

Here's another wonderfully creamy chocolate and peanut butter concoction. This was the first vegan dessert recipe that I created!

Makes 12 servings

Preparation time: crust, 10 minutes; filling, 10 minutes; topping: 10 minutes
Chilling time: at least 8 hours

Crust:

½ cup pure maple syrup

¼ cup canola oil

½ cup natural peanut butter

1 teaspoon vanilla extract

1 cup unbleached all-purpose flour

Filling:

24 ounces (2 [12-ounce] packages) firm silken tofu

¼ cup smooth natural peanut butter

¾ cup powdered sugar

1 teaspoon vanilla extract

1¼ cups vegan chocolate chips

Peanut butter topping:

6 ounces (½ [12-ounce] package) firm silken tofu

½ cup powdered sugar

1 teaspoon vanilla extract

½ cup smooth natural peanut butter

2 tablespoons unbleached all-purpose flour

▶ Preheat the oven to 375°F. Coat a 9-inch round springform pan with nonstick cooking spray.

▶ To make the crust: In a food processor or small bowl, combine all the crust ingredients and mix thoroughly. Press into the bottom of the prepared springform pan. Prick with a fork and bake for 10 minutes. Remove from the oven and set aside.

▶ To make the filling: Place the tofu in a food processor and process until smooth, scraping down the sides as necessary. Add the peanut butter, sugar, and vanilla and blend. Melt the chocolate chips in a microwave or double boiler. Add to the tofu mixture and blend. Pour onto the prepared crust.

▶ To make the peanut butter topping: Rinse and dry the food processor. Place the tofu in the processor and process until smooth, scraping down the sides as necessary. Add the sugar, vanilla, peanut butter, and flour. Pipe the peanut butter topping in a lattice design, using a plain round decorating tip, and use a star tip to pipe a decorative border around outside edge of the pie.

▶ Refrigerate for at least 8 hours or overnight before serving.

PER SERVING: 527 calories, 29 g fat (7 g saturated), 53 g carbohydrate, 3 g dietary fiber, 11 g sugar, 19 g protein, 0 mg cholesterol, 139 mg sodium, 599 mg potassium. Calories from fat: 47 percent.

Hint: Refrigerate the peanut butter topping overnight before piping onto the pie.

Tarts

A fruit tart is a light, refreshing dessert that looks spectacular. The following tarts are made with a crisp crust that is baked in an 11-inch tart pan with a removable bottom. Each has a small amount of tofu cream on the bottom not only to add a creamy flavor, but also to help hold the fruit in place to truly showcase it. Sliced fruit is arranged on top of the cream and brushed with a thin glaze of warm jam to give it a professional look. I have suggested several combinations, but feel free to vary the kinds of fruit depending on your personal taste and the availability of quality fresh fruit. Have fun and create beautiful, delicious masterpieces! You'll be surprised at how simple it is.

....

THE QUEEN OF TARTS

...spy tart is filled with strawberry cream and topped with a stunning array of ...easonal fruit. It looks spectacular, tastes delicious, and is simple to make.

Makes 12 servings

Preparation time: filling, 5 minutes; fruit, 30 minutes; crust, 10 minutes
Baking time: 20 minutes ▼ **Assembly:** 15 minutes

Tart Crust, page 288

18 ounces (1½ [12-ounce] packages) firm silken tofu

1 cup powdered sugar

1 teaspoon vanilla extract

¼ cup strawberry jam, or ¾ cup fresh or frozen strawberries

2 tablespoons unbleached all-purpose flour

Fruit:

1 cup fresh strawberries

3 kiwifruit

1 cup fresh raspberries or blueberries

Glaze:

½ cup plum or seedless raspberry preserves

PER SERVING: 229 calories, 8 g fat (<1 g saturated), 33 g carbohydrate, 4 g dietary fiber, 2 g sugar, 8 g protein, 0 mg cholesterol, 8 mg sodium, 396 mg potassium. Calories from fat: 31 percent.

▶ Preheat the oven to 375°F. Coat an 11-inch tart pan (with a removable bottom) with nonstick cooking spray. Prepare the tart crust.

▶ While the pie shell is cooling, prepare the filling. Place the tofu in a food processor and blend until smooth, scraping down the sides as necessary. Add the other filling ingredients and blend until smooth. Set aside.

▶ To prepare fruit: Hull the strawberries and cut into slices the long way, then set aside. Peel the kiwifruit and slice, making several triangular cuts evenly spaced along the surface, holding each kiwifruit the long way. When you then slice the kiwifruit into rounds, the slices will have petal-shaped edges. Set aside. Wash the berries and set aside.

▶ When the crust has cooled, spread the filling in it. Arrange the prepared fruit so that all the filling is covered. Warm the preserves on LOW in a microwave and use a pastry brush to brush them over the tops of the fruit to glaze it.

▶ Refrigerate until serving.

TANGY TASTY TART

This tangy treat—tart lemon cream and artfully arrayed glazed fresh fruit—is a wonderful dessert to serve at a dinner party because it looks so beautiful.

Makes 12 servings

Preparation time: filling, 5 minutes; fruit, 30 minutes; crust, 10 minutes
Baking time: 20 minutes ▼ **Assembly:** 15 minutes

Tart Crust, page 288

18 ounces (1½ [12-ounce] packages) firm silken tofu

1 cup powdered sugar

1 tablespoon lemon extract

¼ teaspoon turmeric (for color only)

2 tablespoons unbleached all-purpose flour

Fruit:

4 kiwifruit

1 cup fresh blueberries

1 cup fresh raspberries

Glaze:

½ cup plum or seedless raspberry preserves

▶ Preheat the oven to 375°F. Coat an 11-inch tart pan (with a removable bottom) with nonstick cooking spray.

▶ Prepare the tart crust.

▶ While the pie shell is cooling, prepare the filling. Place the tofu in a food processor and blend until smooth, scraping down the sides as necessary. Add the other filling ingredients and blend until smooth. Set aside.

▶ To prepare the fruit: Peel the kiwifruit and slice, making several triangular cuts evenly spaced along the surface, holding each kiwifruit the long way. When you slice the kiwifruit into rounds, the slices will have petal-shaped edges. Set aside. Wash the berries and set aside.

▶ When the crust has cooled, spread the filling in it. Arrange the prepared fruit so that all the filling is covered. Warm the preserves and use a pastry brush to brush them over the tops of the fruit to glaze it.

▶ Refrigerate until serving.

PER SERVING: 265 calories, 8 g fat (<1 g saturated), 43 g carbohydrate, 4 g dietary fiber, 2 g sugar, 8 g protein, 0 mg cholesterol, 14 mg sodium, 404 mg potassium. Calories from fat: 27 percent.

FRUITY ARTISTRY

ɔeats the simple yet elegant combination of seasonal glazed fresh fruit ɫ in vanilla cream.

> **Makes 12 servings**

Preparation time: filling, 5 minutes; fruit, 30 minutes; crust, 10 minutes
Baking time: 20 minutes ▼ **Assembly:** 15 minutes

Tart Crust, page 288

18 ounces (1½ [12-ounce] packages) firm silken tofu

1 cup powdered sugar

1 tablespoon vanilla extract

2 tablespoons unbleached all-purpose flour

Fruit:

3 kiwifruit

1 cup fresh strawberries

1 cup fresh cherries

½ cup fresh blueberries

Glaze:

½ cup plum or seedless raspberry preserves

PER SERVING: 268 calories, 8 g fat (<1 g saturated), 43 g carbohydrate, 4 g dietary fiber, 2 g sugar, 8 g protein, 0 mg cholesterol, 14 mg sodium, 408 mg potassium. Calories from fat: 27 percent.

▸ Preheat the oven to 375°F. Coat an 11-inch tart pan (with a removable bottom) with nonstick cooking spray.

▸ Prepare the tart crust.

▸ While the pie shell is cooling, prepare the filling. Place the tofu in a food processor and blend until smooth, scraping down the sides as necessary. Add the other filling ingredients and blend until smooth. Set aside.

▸ To prepare the fruit: Peel the kiwifruit and slice, making several triangular cuts evenly spaced along the surface, holding each kiwifruit the long way. When you slice the kiwifruit into rounds, the slices will have petal-shaped edges. Set aside. Hull the strawberries and slice the long way, then set aside. Pit and halve the cherries, wash the berries, and set aside.

▸ When the crust has cooled, spread the filling in it. Arrange the prepared fruit so that all the filling is covered. Warm the preserves and use a pastry brush to brush them over the tops of the fruit to glaze it.

▸ Refrigerate until serving.

A TASTE OF THE TROPICS

This fruit tart is my personal favorite because I adore the taste of coconut. I can't think of anything better than fresh tropical fruit arranged over a sweet coconut cream (except maybe for chocolate!).

Makes 12 servings

Preparation time: filling, 5 minutes; fruit, 30 minutes; crust, 10 minutes
Baking time: 20 minutes ▼ **Assembly:** 15 minutes

Tart Crust, page 288

18 ounces (1½ [12-ounce] packages) firm silken tofu

1 cup powdered sugar

2 teaspoons coconut extract

1 cup unsweetened shredded coconut

Fruit:

3 kiwifruit

1 cup chunked fresh pineapple

1 cup sliced fresh papaya

Glaze:

½ cup plum or seedless raspberry preserves

PER SERVING: 230 calories, 5 g fat (2 g saturated), 41 g carbohydrate, 4 g dietary fiber, 2 g sugar, 8 g protein, 0 mg cholesterol, 14 mg sodium, 409 mg potassium. Calories from fat: 19 percent.

▶ Preheat the oven to 375°F. Coat an 11-inch tart pan (with a removable bottom) with nonstick cooking spray.

▶ Prepare the tart crust.

▶ While the pie shell is cooling, prepare the filling. Place the tofu in a food processor and blend until smooth, scraping down the sides as necessary. Add the other filling ingredients except the coconut and blend until smooth. Stir in the coconut by hand, reserving 2 tablespoons for garnish, if desired. Set aside.

▶ To prepare the fruit: Peel the kiwifruit and slice, making several triangular cuts evenly spaced along the surface, holding each kiwifruit the long way. When you slice the kiwifruit into rounds, the slices will have petal-shaped edges. Set aside. Peel and core the pineapple (or better yet, buy a fresh pineapple that is already cored and peeled), cut into chunks, and set aside. Peel and slice the papaya, cutting into strips with diagonally cut edges, and set aside.

▶ When the crust has cooled, spread the filling in it. Arrange the prepared fruit so that all the filling is covered. Warm the preserves and use a pastry brush to brush them over the tops of the fruit to glaze it. Sprinkle with the reserved shredded coconut, if desired.

▶ Refrigerate until serving.

I'm Nuts for Peanut Butter Tart

This doubly "peanutty" dessert—with peanut butter filling placed in a peanut butter crust—is both spectacular looking and tasty. If you like the taste of peanut butter cookies, you'll love this tart.

Makes 16 servings

Preparation time: filling, 5 minutes; icing, 5 minutes; crust, 10 minutes
Baking time: 20 minutes ▼ **Assembly:** 10 minutes

Crust:

1½ cups whole wheat pastry flour

¼ cup granulated sweetener

¼ cup canola oil

¼ cup smooth natural peanut butter

1 tablespoon pure maple syrup

3 tablespoons water

▶ Preheat the oven to 375°F. Coat an 11-inch tart pan (with a removable bottom) with nonstick cooking spray.

▶ To make the crust: In a small bowl, stir the flour, granulated sweetener, and oil until it resembles coarse crumbs. Cut in the peanut butter with two knives. Slowly stir in the 2 tablespoons of water until the mixture forms a ball in the bowl. Sprinkle flour on a piece of waxed paper. Put the ball of dough onto the floured waxed paper and roll in the flour to coat. Put another piece of waxed paper on top of the ball of dough. Roll out the dough between the two pieces of waxed paper until very thin. Remove the top piece of waxed paper. Flip the dough onto the prepared tart pan. Press the dough around the bottom and up the sides of the pan. Cut to fit at the top. Place pie weights (see Suggested Kitchen Equipment on page 21) in the bottom of the pan and bake for 15 minutes. Combine the maple syrup and the remaining tablespoon of water in a small bowl. After 15 minutes, remove the crust from the oven and brush the maple syrup mixture over it, then bake for 5 more minutes to glaze.

▶ Remove from the oven and allow to cool in the pan for 10 minutes. Remove from the pan and let cool completely before assembling.

continues

continued

Filling:

½ cup water

1 tablespoon agar

18 ounces (1½ [12-ounce] packages) firm silken tofu

1 cup smooth natural peanut butter

¾ cup brown sugar

Peanut butter ornamental icing:

6 ounces (½ [12-ounce] package) firm silken tofu

½ cup smooth natural peanut butter

½ cup powdered sugar

1 teaspoon vanilla extract

2 tablespoons unbleached all-purpose flour

PER SERVING: 362 calories, 19 g fat (3 g saturated), 37 g carbohydrate, 3 g dietary fiber, 2 g sugar, 14 g protein, 0 mg cholesterol, 130 mg sodium, 544 mg potassium. Calories from fat: 45 percent.

▶ To make the filling: While the pie shell is cooling, put the ½ cup of water in a small pan and bring to a boil. Sprinkle the agar on top of the water and stir to combine. Simmer until the agar is completely dissolved, 10 to 15 minutes. Place the tofu in a food processor and blend until smooth, scraping down the sides as necessary. Add the other ingredients including the agar mixture and blend until smooth. Set aside.

▶ To make the peanut butter ornamental icing: Place the tofu in a food processor and blend until smooth, scraping down the sides as necessary. Add the peanut butter and process until smooth. Add the other ingredients and blend until smooth.

▶ When the crust has cooled, spread the filling in it. Pipe the ornamental icing in a shell design around the circumference of the pie.

▶ Refrigerate until serving.

CHEESECAKES

Cheesecakes are so delicious that I couldn't see living without an occasional cheesecake splurge for the rest of my life just because I chose to be vegan. With the many new nondairy ingredients that are becoming available, it's easy to make a delicious vegan cheesecake.

. . . .

CARAMEL APPLE STREUSEL CHEESECAKE

This is actually two luscious desserts in one—a yummy cinnamon swirl cheesecake and a delicious apple crumb pie drizzled with caramel sauce. It has several parts, but don't be put off—it is well worth the effort!

> Makes 16 servings

Preparation time: crust, 10 minutes; filling, 5 minutes; cinnamon filling, 5 minutes; apple topping, 15 minutes (including prepping apples); streusel topping, 5 minutes; caramel topping, 10 minutes
Baking time: 1 hour, 30 minutes ▼ **Cooling time:** 1 hour in the oven with the heat off and door closed ▼ **Chilling time:** at least 8 hours to chill

Crust:

1¼ cups whole wheat flour

½ cup pure maple syrup

¼ cup canola oil

½ teaspoon baking soda

1 tablespoon molasses

½ cup vegan butter spread (preferably unhydrogenated, such as Spectrum)

Pinch of salt

Filling:

1 (12-ounce) package firm silken tofu

4 (8-ounce) containers vegan cream cheese (such as Tofutti, which has no casein)

1 cup granulated sweetener

1 teaspoon vanilla extract

⅓ cup unbleached all-purpose flour

Cinnamon filling:

1 cup reserved filling

1 tablespoon Sucanat or brown sugar

2½ teaspoons ground cinnamon

▶ Preheat the oven to 375°F. Coat a 9-inch round springform pan with nonstick cooking spray.

▶ To make the crust: Combine all the crust ingredients in a food processor or small bowl and mix thoroughly. Press into the bottom of the prepared springform pan. Prick with a fork and bake for 10 minutes. Remove from the oven, reduce the oven heat to 350°F, and set the crust aside.

▶ To make the filling: Combine all the filling ingredients in a food processor and process until smooth and creamy. Remove 1 cup of the filling mixture and stir the Sucanat and cinnamon into it. Pour half of the plain filling onto the crust. Drop spoonfuls of the cinnamon filling onto the plain filling. Pour the remaining plain filling mixture on top. Lightly swirl the filling with a knife—do not completely mix. Place the cheesecake on the middle rack in the oven. Place a shallow pan filled with water on the lower rack of the oven. Bake the cheesecake for 1 hour.

continues

continued

Apple topping:

6 medium-size baking apples (such as Macintosh or Rome), peeled, cored, and sliced

½ cup water

1½ teaspoons ground cinnamon

1 tablespoon arrowroot

Streusel topping:

1 cup unbleached all-purpose flour

¼ cup granulated sweetener

⅓ cup Sucanat or brown sugar

¼ cup canola oil

Caramel topping:

⅓ cup corn syrup or agave nectar

⅓ cup brown sugar

3 tablespoons vegan milk

2 teaspoons vanilla extract

¼ teaspoon salt

PER SERVING: 541 calories, 26 g fat (4 g saturated), 72 g carbohydrate, 4 g dietary fiber, 8 g sugar, 8 g protein, 0 mg cholesterol, 352 mg sodium, 344 mg potassium. Calories from fat: 18 percent.

▶ To make the apple topping: While the cheesecake is baking, place the apples in a pan with ¼ cup of the water. Bring to a boil and simmer until the apples are soft but still hold their shape. Add the cinnamon and stir. In a small bowl, mix the arrowroot and remaining ¼ cup of water and add to the apple mixture. Heat and stir just until the mixture thickens—do not boil. Set aside.

▶ To make the streusel topping: In another bowl, combine all the streusel ingredients. (The mixture should form crumbs.) Remove the cheesecake from the oven after it has baked for 1 hour. Top with the apples and sprinkle with the streusel topping. (Be careful because the cheesecake will be soft.) Return the cheesecake to the oven and bake for another 20 minutes, or until the crumb topping is lightly browned. Turn off the heat and allow the cheesecake to remain in the oven without opening the door for another hour. Remove from the oven and allow to cool completely.

▶ To make the caramel topping: Just prior to serving, place the corn syrup and brown sugar in a small pan and bring to a boil. Simmer until the mixture reaches soft-ball stage (240°F on a candy thermometer). Remove from the heat and stir in the milk, vanilla, and salt. Allow to cool to room temperature before drizzling over the cake.

▶ To serve: Refrigerate the cake for at least 8 hours before serving. Remove the collar from the springform pan before serving and drizzle the room-temperature caramel sauce over the cheesecake or directly onto each slice.

New York–Style Cheesecake ♡

Cheesecake is so delicious, there's no reason you can't enjoy it as a vegan. This recipe captures all the good taste of a New York–style cheesecake without using dairy products or eggs. Try it. I think you'll be pleasantly surprised.

> **Makes 16 servings**

Preparation time: crust, 10 minutes; filling, 10 minutes; topping, 5 minutes
Baking time: 1 hour, 10 minutes ▼ **Cooling time:** 1 hour in the oven
with the heat off and door closed ▼ **Chilling time:** at least 8 hours

Crust:
½ cup pure maple syrup

¼ cup canola oil

1¾ cups whole wheat flour

½ teaspoon vanilla extract

Filling:
4 (8-ounce) containers vegan cream cheese (such as Tofutti, which has no casein)

1 (12-ounce) package firm silken tofu

1 cup granulated sweetener

⅓ cup unbleached all-purpose flour

1 teaspoon vanilla extract

Topping:
6 ounces (½ [12-ounce] package) firm silken tofu

1 tablespoon canola oil

1½ teaspoons lemon juice

¼ teaspoon salt

¾ cup granulated sweetener

¾ teaspoon vanilla extract

PER SERVING: 389 calories, 19 g fat (4 g saturated), 44 g carbohydrate, <1 g dietary fiber, 7 g sugar, 9 g protein, 0 mg cholesterol, 327 mg sodium, 101 mg potassium. Calories from fat: 11 percent.

▶ Preheat the oven to 375°F. Coat a 9-inch round spring-form pan with nonstick cooking spray.

▶ To make the crust: In a food processor or small bowl, combine all the crust ingredients and mix thoroughly. Press into the bottom of the prepared springform pan. Prick with a fork and bake for 10 minutes. Remove from the oven, reduce the oven heat to 350°F, and set the crust aside.

▶ To make the filling: Combine the cream cheese and tofu in a food processor and process until smooth, scraping down the sides as necessary. Add the granulated sweetener and blend until creamy. Add the flour and vanilla, blend, and pour into the prepared crust. Place on the top rack of the oven. Place a shallow pan filled with water on the lower rack of the oven and bake for 50 minutes.

▶ To make the topping: Rinse and dry the food processor. While the cheesecake is baking, place the tofu in the processor and process until smooth, scraping down the sides as necessary. Add the other ingredients and process to blend.

▶ After 50 minutes, pull the cheesecake out of the oven and carefully spread with the topping. Return to the oven and bake for an additional 10 minutes. Turn off the heat and leave the cheesecake in the oven for an additional hour. Remove from the oven and allow to cool completely.

▶ Refrigerate for at least 8 hours or overnight before serving.

THREE CHEERS FOR CHERRY CHEESECAKE ♡

Cheesecake with cherries on top is a classic dessert that I just had to veganize. I developed a basic cheesecake, topped it with fresh cherries, and it turned out beautifully. Fresh cherries really do make all the difference.

Makes 16 servings

Preparation time: crust, 10 minutes; filling, 10 minutes; topping, 10 minutes
Baking time: 60 minutes ▼ **Cooling time:** 1 hour in the oven with the heat off and door closed
Chilling time: at least 8 hours

Crust:
½ cup pure maple syrup
¼ cup canola oil
1¾ cups whole wheat flour
½ teaspoon vanilla extract

Filling:
4 (8-ounce) containers vegan cream cheese (such as Tofutti, which has no casein)
1 (12-ounce) package firm silken tofu
1 cup granulated sweetener
⅓ cup unbleached all-purpose flour
1 teaspoon vanilla extract

Topping:
2 cups fresh cherries, halved and pitted
1 cup apple juice
1 tablespoon arrowroot

PER SERVING: 321 calories, 18 g fat (4 g saturated), 37 g carbohydrate, 2 g dietary fiber, 6 g sugar, 4 g protein, 0 mg cholesterol, 243 mg sodium, 127 mg potassium. Calories from fat: 10 percent.

▸ Preheat the oven to 375°F. Coat a 9-inch round spring-form pan with nonstick cooking spray.

▸ To make the crust: In a food processor or small bowl, combine all the crust ingredients and mix thoroughly. Press into the bottom of the prepared springform pan. Prick with a fork and bake for 10 minutes. Remove from the oven, reduce the oven heat to 350°F, and set the crust aside.

▸ To make the filling: Combine the cream cheese and tofu in a food processor and process until smooth, scraping down the sides as necessary. Add the granulated sweetener and blend until creamy. Add the flour and vanilla, blend, and pour into the prepared crust. Place on the top rack of the oven. Place a shallow pan filled with water on the lower rack of the oven and bake for 60 minutes. Then turn off the heat and leave the cheesecake in the oven for an additional hour.

▸ To make the topping: While the cheesecake is cooling, place the cherries in a small pan with ½ cup of the juice. Bring to a boil and simmer until the cherries are soft. In a small bowl, combine the arrowroot and remaining ½ cup of juice. Add to the hot cherries and stir until thickened—do not boil. (The mixture will thicken more as it cools.) Set aside.

▸ Remove the cheesecake from the oven and carefully spread with the cherry topping. Allow to cool completely. Refrigerate for at least 8 hours or overnight before serving.

SWIRLED RASPBERRY CHEESECAKE

This unique creation consists of raspberry sauce swirled through creamy cheesecake and topped with tangy sweet raspberries—I think you'll really enjoy this deliciously different taste.

Makes 16 servings

Preparation time: crust, 10 minutes; filling, 10 minutes; topping, 10 minutes
Baking time: 60 minutes ▼ **Cooling time:** 1 hour in the oven with the heat off and door closed
Chilling time: at least 8 hours

Crust:
½ cup pure maple syrup
¼ cup canola oil
1¾ cups whole wheat flour
½ teaspoon vanilla extract

Raspberry topping:
1 (12-ounce) package frozen raspberries, or 2 cups fresh raspberries
¼ cup water
⅓ cup granulated sweetener
1 tablespoon arrowroot
2 tablespoons water

Filling:
4 (8-ounce) containers vegan cream cheese (such as Tofutti, which has no casein)
1 (12-ounce) package firm silken tofu
1 cup granulated sweetener
⅓ cup unbleached all-purpose flour
1 teaspoon vanilla extract

PER SERVING: 354 calories, 19 g fat (4 g saturated), 42 g carbohydrate, 1 g dietary fiber, 6 g sugar, 5 g protein, 0 mg cholesterol, 244 mg sodium, 87 mg potassium. Calories from fat: 11 percent.

▶ Preheat the oven to 375°F. Coat a 9-inch round springform pan with nonstick cooking spray.

▶ To make the crust: In a food processor or small bowl, combine all the crust ingredients and mix thoroughly. Press into the bottom of the prepared springform pan. Prick with a fork and bake for 10 minutes. Remove from the oven, reduce the oven heat to 350°F, and set the crust aside.

▶ To make the topping: Bring first three ingredients to a boil in a medium-size saucepan. (If using fresh raspberries, simmer until the berries are soft.) Dissolve the arrowroot in the 2 tablespoons of water and add to the hot raspberry mixture. Heat until just thickened—do not boil. (The mixture will thicken more as it cools.) Set aside.

▶ To make the filling: Combine the cream cheese and tofu in a food processor and process until smooth, scraping down the sides as necessary. Add the granulated sweetener and blend until creamy. Add the flour and vanilla and blend. Pour half the filling into the prepared crust. Spoon ½ cup of the raspberry sauce over the filling. Pour the rest of the filling in the pan and swirl with a knife—be careful not to mix completely. Place on the top rack of the oven. Place a shallow pan filled with water on the lower rack of the oven and bake for 60 minutes.

▶ After 50 minutes, turn off the heat, pull out the cheesecake, and carefully spread with the raspberry topping. Return the cheesecake to the oven and allow it to remain there for an additional hour.

▶ Remove from the oven and allow to cool completely. Refrigerate for at least 8 hours or overnight before serving.

I Dream of Lemon Cream Cheesecake

Tangy lemon cheesecake is a refreshing treat anytime. This dessert looks impressive if garnished with a mound of fresh blueberries and twists of lemon.

Makes 16 servings

Preparation time: crust, 10 minutes; filling, 10 minutes
Baking time: 60 minutes ▼ **Cooling time:** 1 hour in the oven with the heat off and door closed
Chilling time: at least 8 hours

Crust:

½ cup pure maple syrup

¼ cup canola oil

1¾ cups whole wheat flour

½ teaspoon vanilla extract

Filling:

4 (8-ounce) containers vegan cream cheese (such as Tofutti, which has no casein)

1 (12-ounce) package firm silken tofu

1 cup granulated sweetener

½ cup lemon juice

⅓ cup unbleached all-purpose flour

1 tablespoon lemon extract

½ teaspoon turmeric (for color only)

Topping:

6 ounces (½ [12-ounce] package) firm silken tofu

1 tablespoon canola oil

1½ teaspoons lemon juice

¼ teaspoon salt

¾ cup granulated sweetener

¾ teaspoon lemon extract

- Preheat the oven to 375°F. Coat a 9-inch round springform pan with nonstick cooking spray.

- To make the crust: In a food processor or small bowl, combine all the crust ingredients and mix thoroughly. Press into the bottom of the prepared springform pan. Prick with a fork and bake for 10 minutes. Remove from the oven, reduce the oven heat to 350°F, and set the crust aside.

- To make the filling: Combine the cream cheese and tofu in a food processor and process until smooth, scraping down the sides as necessary. Add the granulated sweetener and blend until creamy. Add the remaining ingredients, blend, and pour into the prepared crust.

- Place on the top rack of the oven. Place a shallow pan filled with water on the lower rack of the oven and bake for 50 minutes. While the cheesecake is baking, make the topping by placing all the topping ingredients in a food processor and processing to combine. Set aside.

- After 50 minutes, pull the cheesecake out of the oven and spread evenly with the topping. Return it to the oven and bake for 10 more minutes. Then turn off the heat and leave the cheesecake in there for an additional hour. Remove from the oven and allow to cool completely.

continues

continued

Garnish (optional):

2 lemons, sliced as thinly as
   possible into half-moons

1 cup fresh blueberries, washed
   and dried

▸ To garnish: Remove the collar of the pan. (Slide a sharp knife around the inside of the pan so the cheesecake does not stick to it as you remove the collar.) Firmly press the lemon slices onto the side of the cheesecake with the flat, cut edge lining up along the bottom of the cheesecake and the rounded edge near the top of the cheesecake, and reserving several for later use. Clean off the collar of the pan and put it back on the cheesecake. Refrigerate for at least 8 hours or overnight before serving.

▸ Just before serving, mound the blueberries on top of the cheesecake. Make a slit along the radius of several lemon slices. Twist the lemon slices and place randomly on top of the blueberries. Sprinkle with a little sugar, if desired.

MINTY CHOCOLATE CHIP CHEESECAKE

My oldest daughter can't get enough of mint chocolate chip ice cream, and I was inspired by that flavor to create this cheesecake. I guarantee you're going to love this mint-flavored cheesecake full of vegan chocolate chips in a chocolate cookie crust.

Makes 16 servings

Preparation time: crust, 10 minutes; filling, 10 minutes; topping, 5 minutes ▼ **Baking time:** 1 hour
Cooling time: 1 hour in the oven with the heat off and door closed
Chilling time: at least 8 hours

Crust:
½ cup pure maple syrup
¼ cup canola oil
½ cup unsweetened cocoa powder
1¼ cups whole wheat flour
½ teaspoon vanilla extract

Filling:
4 (8-ounce) containers vegan cream cheese (such as Tofutti, which has no casein)
1 (12-ounce) package firm silken tofu
1 cup granulated sweetener
⅓ cup unbleached all-purpose flour
3 tablespoons peppermint extract
1 cup vegan chocolate chips

▶ Preheat the oven to 375°F. Coat a 9-inch round springform pan with nonstick cooking spray.

▶ To make the crust: In a food processor or small bowl, combine all the crust ingredients and mix thoroughly. Press into the bottom of the prepared springform pan. Prick with a fork and bake for 10 minutes. Remove from the oven, reduce the oven heat to 350°F, and set the crust aside.

▶ To make the filling: Combine the cream cheese and tofu in a food processor and process until smooth, scraping down the sides as necessary. Add the granulated sweetener and blend until creamy. Add the flour and peppermint extract and blend. Stir in the chocolate chips by hand. Place on the top rack of the oven. Place a shallow pan filled with water on the lower rack of the oven and bake for 50 minutes.

continues

continued

Mint topping:

6 ounces (½ [12-ounce] package)
  firm silken tofu

1 tablespoon canola oil

1½ teaspoons lemon juice

¼ teaspoon salt

¾ cup sugar

¾ teaspoon peppermint extract

PER SERVING: 358 calories, 22 g fat
(6 g saturated), 38 g carbohydrate,
3 g dietary fiber, 6 g sugar, 6 g
protein, 0 mg cholesterol, 246 mg
sodium, 128 mg potassium. Calories
from fat: 18 percent.

▶ To make the mint topping: While the cheesecake is baking, combine all the topping ingredients in a food processor and process. Set aside. After the cheesecake has baked for 50 minutes, pull it out and spread evenly with the topping. Return to the oven and bake for 10 more minutes.

▶ Turn off the heat, leaving the cheesecake in the oven for an additional hour. Remove from the oven and allow to cool completely. Refrigerate for at least 8 hours or overnight before serving.

PUMPKIN PIE CHEESECAKE

I make this cheesecake every year for dessert on Thanksgiving Day. The delightful combination of pumpkin and spices tastes just like the holidays to me.

Makes 16 servings

Preparation time: crust, 10 minutes; filling, 10 minutes; topping, 5 minutes ▼ **Baking time:** 1 hour
Cooling time: 1 hour in the oven with the heat off and door closed
Chilling time: at least 8 hours

Crust:

¼ cup vegetable shortening
(preferably nonhydrogenated,
such as Spectrum)

¼ cup brown sugar

1 tablespoon unsweetened
applesauce (preferably organic)

¼ cup molasses

2 teaspoons fresh ginger, or
¾ teaspoon ground

1½ teaspoons white vinegar

½ cup + 2 tablespoons unbleached
all-purpose flour

½ cup + 2 tablespoons whole
wheat flour

½ teaspoon baking soda

¼ teaspoon salt

¼ teaspoon ground cinnamon

¼ teaspoon ground cloves

▶ Preheat the oven to 375°F. Coat a 9-inch round spring-form pan with nonstick cooking spray.

▶ To make the crust: Cream the shortening and sugar together in a large bowl. Add the applesauce, molasses, fresh ginger, and vinegar and beat until combined. Sift together the dry ingredients, including the spices, add to the shortening mixture, and stir to combine. Press into the bottom of the prepared springform pan. Prick with a fork and bake for 10 minutes. Remove from the oven, reduce the oven heat to 350°F, and set the crust aside.

continues

continued

Filling:

4 (8-ounce) containers vegan
  cream cheese (such as Tofutti,
  which has no casein)

1 (12-ounce) package firm
  silken tofu

1 cup granulated sweetener

1 cup cooked, pureed fresh
  pumpkin, or ¾ cup canned
  pure puree

⅓ cup unbleached all-purpose
  flour

½ teaspoon ground cinnamon

1 teaspoon pumpkin pie spice

1 teaspoon vanilla extract

Topping:

6 ounces (½ [12-ounce] package)
  firm silken tofu

1 tablespoon canola oil

1½ teaspoons lemon juice

¼ teaspoon salt

¾ cup granulated sweetener

¾ teaspoon vanilla extract

¼ cup cooked, pureed fresh
  pumpkin or canned pure
  pumpkin puree

½ teaspoon ground cinnamon

PER SERVING: 394 calories, 21 g fat
(5 g saturated), 44 g carbohydrate,
2 g dietary fiber, 1 g sugar, 8 g
protein, 0 mg cholesterol, 318 mg
sodium, 323 mg potassium. Calories
from fat: 15 percent.

▸ To make the filling: Combine the cream cheese and tofu in a food processor and process until smooth, scraping down the sides as necessary. Add the granulated sweetener and blend until creamy. Add the remaining ingredients, blend, and pour into the prepared crust. Place on the top rack of the oven. Place a shallow pan filled with water on the lower rack of the oven and bake for 50 minutes.

▸ To make the topping: Rinse and dry the food processor. While the cheesecake is baking, place the tofu in the processor and process until smooth, scraping down the sides as necessary. Add the other ingredients and process to blend. After 50 minutes, pull the cheesecake out of the oven and carefully spread with the topping.

▸ Return to the oven and bake for an additional 10 minutes. Turn off the heat and leave the cheesecake in there for an additional hour. Remove from the oven and allow to cool completely. Refrigerate for at least 8 hours or overnight before serving.

INSIDE-OUT
PEANUT BUTTER CUP CHEESECAKE

*Here's another cheesecake that combines the flavors of chocolate and peanut butter.
Unlike the Peanut Butter Cup Cheesecake, page 214, which has peanut butter–
flavored filling and a chocolate topping that mimics a peanut butter cup, this
cheesecake takes the peanut butter cup idea and turns it inside out, using chocolate
filling and a peanut butter topping. You're going to love this switch!*

Makes 16 servings

Preparation time: crust, 10 minutes; filling, 10 minutes; topping, 10 minutes ▼ **Baking time:** 1 hour
Cooling time: 1 hour in the oven with the heat off and door closed
Chilling time: at least 8 hours

Crust:
½ cup pure maple syrup

¼ cup canola oil

½ cup natural peanut butter

1 cup unbleached all-purpose
flour

1 teaspoon vanilla extract

Filling:
4 (8-ounce) containers vegan
cream cheese (such as Tofutti,
which has no casein)

1 (12-ounce) package firm
silken tofu

½ cup smooth natural peanut
butter

1 cup granulated sweetener

⅓ cup unbleached all-purpose
flour

1 teaspoon vanilla extract

2 cups vegan chocolate chips

▶ Preheat the oven to 375°F. Coat a 9-inch round springform pan with nonstick cooking spray.

▶ To make the crust: In a food processor or small bowl,
combine all the crust ingredients and mix thoroughly.
Press into the bottom of the prepared springform pan.
Prick with a fork and bake for 10 minutes. Remove from
the oven, reduce the oven heat to 350°F, and set the crust
aside.

▶ To make the filling: Rinse and dry the food processor.
Combine the cream cheese and tofu in the processor and
mix until smooth, scraping down the sides as necessary.
Add the peanut butter and granulated sweetener and
blend until creamy. Add the flour and vanilla and blend.
Melt the chocolate chips in a microwave or double boiler.
Add to the cream cheese mixture, blend, and pour into
the prepared pan. Place on the top rack of the oven. Place
a shallow pan filled with water on the lower rack of the
oven and bake for 50 minutes.

continues

continued

Peanut butter topping:

6 ounces (½ [12-ounce] package) firm silken tofu

1 tablespoon canola oil

1½ teaspoons lemon juice

¼ teaspoon salt

¾ cup sugar

¼ cup smooth natural peanut butter

PER SERVING: 534 calories, 38 g fat (10 g saturated), 40 g carbohydrate, 3 g dietary fiber, 7 g sugar, 13 g protein, 0 mg cholesterol, 347 mg sodium, 347 mg potassium. Calories from fat: 37 percent.

▸ To make the peanut butter topping: Rinse and dry the food processor. While the cheesecake is baking, combine all the topping ingredients in the processor and process. Set aside. After the cheesecake has baked for 50 minutes, pull it out and spread evenly with the topping.

▸ Return to the oven and bake for 10 more minutes. Turn off the heat and leave the cheesecake in there for an additional hour. Remove from the oven and cool completely. Refrigerate for at least 8 hours or overnight before serving.

PEANUT BUTTER CUP CHEESECAKE

This cheesecake tastes just like a gooey Reese's Peanut Butter Cup.

Makes 16 servings

Preparation time: crust, 10 minutes; filling, 10 minutes; topping, 10 minutes
Baking time: 60 minutes ▼ **Cooling time:** 1 hour in the oven with the heat off and door closed
Chilling time: at least 8 hours

Crust:

½ cup pure maple syrup

¼ cup canola oil

½ cup natural peanut butter

1 teaspoon vanilla extract

1 cup unbleached all-purpose flour

Filling:

4 (8-ounce) containers vegan cream cheese (such as Tofutti, which has no casein)

1 (12-ounce) package firm silken tofu

1 cup smooth natural peanut butter

1 cup granulated sweetener

⅓ cup unbleached all-purpose flour

1 teaspoon vanilla extract

Chocolate topping:

½ cup unsweetened cocoa powder

½ cup pure maple syrup

1 teaspoon vanilla extract

PER SERVING: 416 calories, 31 g fat (7 g saturated), 30 g carbohydrate, 3 g dietary fiber, 12 g sugar, 10 g protein, 0 mg cholesterol, 357 mg sodium, 255 mg potassium. Calories from fat: 33 percent.

▶ Preheat the oven to 375°F. Coat a 9-inch round springform pan with nonstick cooking spray.

▶ To make the crust: In a food processor or small bowl, combine all the crust ingredients and mix thoroughly. Press into the bottom of the prepared springform pan. Prick with a fork and bake for 10 minutes. Remove from the oven, reduce the oven heat to 350°F, and set the crust aside.

▶ To make the filling: Rinse and dry the food processor. Combine the cream cheese and tofu in the processor and process until smooth, scraping down the sides as necessary. Add the peanut butter and process until combined. Add the granulated sweetener and blend until creamy. Add the flour and vanilla, blend, and pour into the prepared pan. Place on the top rack of the oven. Place a shallow pan filled with water on the lower rack of the oven and bake for 60 minutes.

▶ After 60 minutes, turn off the heat and leave the cheesecake in there for an additional hour. Remove from the oven and allow to cool completely.

▶ To make the chocolate topping: While the cheesecake is cooling, combine all the topping ingredients in a small bowl and stir until smooth. Spread evenly on top of the cheesecake before refrigerating. (If the topping is too thick, heat for about 10 seconds in the microwave.) Refrigerate for at least 8 hours or overnight before serving.

COCONUT DREAM CHEESECAKE

I love the taste of coconut, and I wanted to see if it would work when combined with a creamy cheesecake filling. Did it ever!

> Makes 16 servings

Preparation time: crust, 10 minutes; filling, 10 minutes; topping, 5 minutes ▼ **Baking time:** 1 hour
Cooling time: 1 hour in the oven with the heat off and door closed
Chilling time: at least 8 hours

Crust:

¾ cup unsweetened shredded coconut

½ cup unbleached all-purpose flour

½ cup pure maple syrup

⅛ cup canola oil

Filling:

4 (8-ounce) containers vegan cream cheese (such as Tofutti, which has no casein)

1 (12-ounce) package firm silken tofu

1 cup granulated sweetener

⅓ cup unbleached all-purpose flour

1 tablespoon coconut extract

1 cup unsweetened shredded coconut

Topping:

6 ounces (½ [12-ounce] package) firm silken tofu

1 tablespoon canola oil

1½ teaspoons lemon juice

¼ teaspoon salt

¾ cup granulated sweetener

¾ teaspoon vanilla extract

▶ Preheat the oven to 375°F. Coat a 9-inch round springform pan with nonstick cooking spray.

▶ To make the crust: In a small bowl, combine all the crust ingredients and mix thoroughly. Press into the bottom of the prepared springform pan and bake for 15 minutes. Remove from the oven, reduce the oven heat to 350°F, and set the crust aside.

▶ To make the filling: Combine the cream cheese and tofu in a food processor and mix until smooth, scraping down the sides as necessary. Add the granulated sweetener and blend until creamy. Add the flour and coconut extract and blend. Stir in coconut by hand, and then pour the filling into the prepared crust. Place on the top rack of the oven. Place a shallow pan filled with water on the lower rack of the oven and bake for 50 minutes.

▶ To make the topping: Rinse and dry the food processor. While the cheesecake is baking, place the tofu in the processor and process until smooth, scraping down the sides as necessary. Add the other ingredients and process to blend. After 50 minutes, pull the cheesecake out of the oven and carefully spread with the topping. Return to the oven and bake for an additional 10 minutes.

▶ Turn off the heat and leave the cheesecake in there for an additional hour. Remove from the oven and allow to cool completely. Refrigerate for at least 8 hours or overnight before serving.

PER SERVING: 376 calories, 21 g fat (6 g saturated), 39 g carbohydrate, <1 g dietary fiber, 7 g sugar, 7 g protein, 0 mg cholesterol, 252 mg sodium, 216 mg potassium. Calories from fat: 16 percent.

TROPICAL CHOCOLATE CHIP CHEESECAKE

One day I was eating a chocolate-covered coconut cream egg (vegan, of course) and it occurred to me that this would make a wonderful cheesecake flavor! I have to say that this is my all-time favorite cheesecake.

> **Makes 16 servings**

Preparation time: crust, 10 minutes; filling, 10 minutes; topping, 5 minutes
Baking time: 60 minutes ▼ **Cooling time:** 1 hour in the oven with the heat off and door closed
Chilling time: at least 8 hours

Crust:
¾ cup unsweetened shredded coconut
½ cup unbleached all-purpose flour
½ cup pure maple syrup
⅛ cup canola oil

Filling:
4 (8-ounce) containers vegan cream cheese (such as Tofutti, which has no casein)
1 (12-ounce) package firm silken tofu
1 cup granulated sweetener
⅓ cup unbleached all-purpose flour
1 tablespoon coconut extract
1 cup unsweetened shredded coconut
1 cup vegan chocolate chips

Chocolate topping:
½ cup unsweetened cocoa powder
½ cup pure maple syrup
1 teaspoon vanilla extract

▶ Preheat the oven to 375°F. Coat a 9-inch round spring-form pan with nonstick cooking spray.

▶ To make the crust: In a small bowl, combine all the crust ingredients and mix thoroughly. Press into the bottom of the prepared springform pan and bake for 15 minutes. Remove from the oven, reduce the oven heat to 350°F, and set the crust aside.

▶ To make the filling: Combine the cream cheese and tofu in a food processor and mix until smooth, scraping down the sides as necessary. Add the granulated sweetener and blend until creamy. Add the flour and coconut extract and blend. Stir in the coconut and chocolate chips by hand and pour the filling into the prepared crust. Place on the top rack of the oven. Place a shallow pan filled with water on the lower rack of the oven and bake for 60 minutes. Turn off the heat and leave the cheesecake in there for an additional hour. Remove from the oven.

▶ To make the chocolate topping: Combine all the topping ingredients in a bowl. Using a wire whisk, mix until creamy. Gently pour the chocolate topping over the cheesecake. Spread evenly. (If the chocolate is too thick to spread, microwave for about 10 seconds.) Refrigerate for at least 8 hours or overnight before serving.

PER SERVING: 395 calories, 23 g fat (8 g saturated), 43 g carbohydrate, 2 g dietary fiber, 13 g sugar, 7 g protein, 0 mg cholesterol, 249 mg sodium, 219 mg potassium. Calories from fat: 19 percent.

PEANUT BUTTER CHOCOLATE CHIP CHEESECAKE

Here's another twist on the chocolate and peanut butter combination. This one is lighter on the chocolate with just a spattering of chocolate chips dotting the rich peanut butter filling. If you like, you could use the chocolate topping from the Peanut Butter Cup Cheesecake, page 214, or the peanut butter topping from the Inside-Out Peanut Butter Cup Cheesecake, page 212, to add a little extra something.

> Makes 16 servings

Preparation time: crust, 10 minutes; filling, 10 minutes ▾ **Baking time:** 50 minutes
Cooling time: 1 hour in the oven with the heat off and door closed
Chilling time: at least 8 hours

Crust:

¼ cup pure maple syrup

⅛ cup canola oil

¼ cup natural peanut butter

½ teaspoon vanilla extract

½ cup + 2 tablespoons unbleached all-purpose flour

Filling:

4 (8-ounce) containers vegan cream cheese (such as Tofutti, which has no casein)

1 (12-ounce) package firm silken tofu

1 cup smooth natural peanut butter

1 cup granulated sweetener

⅓ cup unbleached all-purpose flour

1 teaspoon vanilla extract

¾ cup vegan chocolate chips

PER SERVING: 437 calories, 30 g fat (7 g saturated), 34 g carbohydrate, 2 g dietary fiber, 4 g sugar, 11 g protein, 0 mg cholesterol, 340 mg sodium, 281 mg potassium. Calories from fat: 31 percent.

▶ Preheat the oven to 375°F. Coat a 9-inch round springform pan with nonstick cooking spray.

▶ To make the crust: In a food processor or small bowl, combine all the crust ingredients and mix thoroughly. Press into the bottom of the prepared springform pan, prick with a fork, and bake for 10 minutes. Remove from the oven, reduce the oven heat to 350°F, and set the crust aside.

▶ To make the filling: Rinse and dry the food processor. Combine the cream cheese and tofu in the processor and mix until smooth, scraping down the sides as necessary. Add the peanut butter and process until combined. Add the granulated sweetener and blend until creamy. Add the flour and vanilla and blend. Stir in the chocolate chips by hand and pour the filling into the prepared pan. Place on the top rack of the oven. Place a shallow pan filled with water on the lower rack of the oven and bake for 50 minutes.

▶ Turn off the heat and leave the cheesecake in there for an additional hour. Remove from the oven and allow to cool completely. Refrigerate for at least 8 hours or overnight before serving.

BLACK FOREST CHEESECAKE

If you like chocolate cheesecake, you've got to try this luscious combination of rich chocolate filling and creamy cherry topping. It can also be made with a raspberry topping if you prefer. Both fruits blend wonderfully with chocolate! You might also want to try the Chocolate-Covered Cherry Cheesecake, page 220, which also combines the tastes of chocolate and cherry, but more closely resembles a chocolate-covered cherry.

Makes 16 servings

Preparation time: crust, 10 minutes; filling, 10 minutes; topping, 10 minutes
Baking time: 60 minutes ▼ Cooling time: 1 hour in the oven with the heat off and door closed
Chilling time: at least 8 hours

Crust:
½ cup pure maple syrup
¼ cup canola oil
½ cup unsweetened cocoa powder
1¼ cups whole wheat flour
½ teaspoon vanilla extract

Filling:
3 (8-ounce) containers vegan cream cheese (such as Tofutti, which has no casein)
18 ounces (1½ packages) firm silken tofu
1 cup granulated sweetener
⅓ cup unbleached all-purpose flour
1 teaspoon vanilla extract
2 cups vegan chocolate chips

▶ Preheat the oven to 375°F. Coat a 9-inch round spring-form pan with nonstick cooking spray.

▶ To make the crust: In a food processor or small bowl, combine all the crust ingredients and mix thoroughly. Press into the bottom of the prepared springform pan. Prick with a fork and bake for 10 minutes. Remove from the oven, reduce the oven heat to 350°F, and set the crust aside.

▶ To make the filling: Rinse and dry the food processor. Combine the cream cheese and tofu in the processor and mix until smooth, scraping down the sides as necessary. Add the granulated sweetener and blend until creamy. Add the flour and vanilla and blend. Melt the chocolate chips in a microwave or double boiler. Pour into the cream cheese mixture and blend. Pour into the prepared crust. Place on the top rack of the oven. Place a shallow pan filled with water on the lower rack of the oven and bake for 60 minutes.

continues

continued

Topping:

2 cups fresh cherries, halved and pitted

1 cup apple juice

1 tablespoon arrowroot

▸ To make the topping: While cheesecake is baking, place the cherries in a small pan with ½ cup of the juice. Bring to a boil and simmer until the cherries are soft. In a small bowl, combine the arrowroot and the remaining ½ cup of juice. Add to the hot cherries and stir until thickened—do not boil. (The mixture will thicken more as it cools.) Set aside.

▸ After 60 minutes, turn off the heat and leave the cheesecake in there for an additional hour. Remove from the oven and carefully spread with the cherry topping. Allow to cool completely. Refrigerate for at least 8 hours or overnight before serving.

....

Variation: Use a raspberry topping instead of cherry.

Raspberry topping:

1 (12-ounce) package frozen raspberries, or 2 cups fresh raspberries

¼ cup + 2 tablespoons water

⅓ cup granulated sweetener

1 tablespoon arrowroot

▸ Bring the raspberries, ¼ cup of the water, and the sweetener to a boil in a medium-size saucepan. (If using fresh raspberries, simmer until the berries are soft.) Dissolve the arrowroot in the remaining 2 tablespoons of water and add to the hot raspberry mixture. Heat until just thickened—do not boil. (The mixture will thicken more as it cools.)

PER SERVING (CHEESECAKE WITH CHERRY TOPPING): 431 calories, 24 g fat (7 g saturated), 51 g carbohydrate, 4 g dietary fiber, 7 g sugar, 9 g protein, 0 mg cholesterol, 190 mg sodium, 323 mg potassium. Calories from fat: 25 percent.

PER SERVING (CHEESECAKE WITH RASPBERRY TOPPING): 446 calories, 24 g fat (7 g saturated), 55 g carbohydrate, 4 g dietary fiber, 7 g sugar, 9 g protein, 0 mg cholesterol, 190 mg sodium, 297 mg potassium. Calories from fat: 24 percent.

CHOCOLATE-COVERED
CHERRY CHEESECAKE

This cheesecake was inspired by my love for a good dark chocolate–covered cherry. I think this cheesecake comes pretty close.

> **Makes 16 servings**

Preparation time: crust, 10 minutes; filling, 10 minutes; topping, 10 minutes; cherries, 10 minutes
Baking time: 60 minutes ▼ **Cooling time:** 1 hour in the oven with the heat off and door closed
Chilling time: at least 8 hours

Crust:

½ cup pure maple syrup

¼ cup canola oil

½ cup unsweetened cocoa powder

1¼ cups whole wheat flour

½ teaspoon vanilla extract

Filling:

4 (8-ounce) containers vegan cream cheese (such as Tofutti, which has no casein)

1 (12-ounce) package firm silken tofu

1 cup granulated sweetener

⅓ cup unbleached all-purpose flour

1½ tablespoons cherry extract (optional)

1½ cups fresh cherries, pitted and chopped

▶ Preheat the oven to 375°F. Coat a 9-inch round spring-form pan with nonstick cooking spray.

▶ To make the crust: In a food processor or small bowl, combine all the crust ingredients and mix thoroughly. Press into the bottom of the prepared springform pan, prick with a fork, and bake for 10 minutes. Remove from the oven, reduce the oven heat to 350°F, and set the crust aside.

▶ To make the filling: Rinse and dry the food processor. Combine the cream cheese and tofu in the processor and mix until smooth, scraping down the sides as necessary. Add the granulated sweetener and blend until creamy. Add the flour and cherry extract and blend. Add ¼ cup of the chopped cherries to the food processor and process. Stir the remaining 1¼ cups of cherries into the filling mixture by hand. Pour into the prepared pan and place on the top rack of the oven. Place a shallow pan filled with water on the lower rack of the oven and bake for 60 minutes. Turn off the heat and leave the cheesecake in there an additional hour. Remove from the oven and allow to cool completely.

continues

continued

Chocolate topping:

½ cup unsweetened cocoa powder

½ cup pure maple syrup

1 teaspoon vanilla extract

Garnish (optional):

16 whole fresh cherries with
   stems, pitted

½ cup vegan chocolate chips

PER SERVING: 375 calories, 20 g fat
(4 g saturated), 43 g carbohydrate,
3 g dietary fiber, 13 g sugar, 7 g
protein, 0 mg cholesterol, 248 mg
sodium, 309 mg potassium. Calories
from fat: 14 percent.

▸ To make the chocolate topping: While the cheesecake is
cooling, combine all topping ingredients in a small bowl
and stir until smooth. Spread evenly on top of the cheesecake before refrigerating. If the topping is too thick, microwave for about 10 seconds. Refrigerate at least 8 hours
or overnight before serving.

▸ To garnish: Trim cherry stems to a length of about ½ inch.
Melt the chocolate chips in a microwave or double boiler.
Dip each cherry halfway into the chocolate and place on a
waxed paper– or parchment-lined pan. Put the pan of
cherries in the freezer to harden for 10 minutes. Arrange
evenly around the circumference of the cheesecake.

CHOCOLATE TUXEDO CHEESECAKE

This cheesecake consists of a chocolate cookie crust with creamy chocolate filling and a light vanilla topping—almost like an Oreo cookie!

> **Makes 16 servings**

Preparation time: crust, 10 minutes; filling, 10 minutes; topping, 10 minutes
Baking time: 60 minutes ▼ **Cooling time:** 1 hour in the oven with the heat off and door closed
Chilling time: at least 8 hours

Crust:
½ cup pure maple syrup
¼ cup canola oil
½ cup unsweetened cocoa powder
1¼ cups whole wheat flour
½ teaspoon vanilla extract

Filling:
3 (8-ounce) containers vegan cream cheese (such as Tofutti, which has no casein)
18 ounces (1½ packages) firm silken tofu
1 cup granulated sweetener
⅓ cup unbleached all-purpose flour
1 teaspoon vanilla extract
2 cups vegan chocolate chips

Topping:
6 ounces (½ [12-ounce] package) firm silken tofu
1 tablespoon canola oil
1½ teaspoons lemon juice
¼ teaspoon salt
¾ cup granulated sweetener
¾ teaspoon vanilla extract

PER SERVING: 474 calories, 25 g fat (7 g saturated), 57 g carbohydrate, 3 g dietary fiber, 8 g sugar, 10 g protein, 0 mg cholesterol, 195 mg sodium, 330 mg potassium. Calories from fat: 26 percent.

▶ Preheat the oven to 375°F. Coat a 9-inch round springform pan with nonstick cooking spray.

▶ To make the crust: In a food processor or small bowl, combine all the crust ingredients and mix thoroughly. Press into the bottom of the prepared springform pan. Prick with a fork and bake for 10 minutes. Remove from the oven, reduce the oven heat to 350°F, and set the crust aside.

▶ To make the filling: Rinse and dry the food processor. Combine the cream cheese and tofu in the processor and mix until smooth, scraping down the sides as necessary. Add the granulated sweetener and blend until creamy. Add the flour and vanilla and blend. Melt the chocolate chips in a microwave or double boiler. Pour into the cream cheese mixture and blend. Pour into the prepared crust. Place on the top rack of the oven. Place a shallow pan filled with water on the lower rack of the oven and bake for 50 minutes.

▶ To make the topping: Rinse and dry the food processor. While the cheesecake is baking, place the tofu in the processor and process until smooth, scraping down the sides as necessary. Add the other topping ingredients and process to blend. Set aside.

▶ After 50 minutes, pull the cheesecake out of the oven and carefully spread with the topping. Return it to the oven and bake for an additional 10 minutes. Turn off the heat and leave the cheesecake in there for an additional hour. Remove from the oven and allow it to cool completely. Refrigerate for at least 8 hours or overnight before serving.

PUDDINGS

Tofu puddings are easy and delicious. Unlike traditional puddings, no cook-ing or thickening is involved. The tofu gives the pudding a nice creamy tex-ture. If you want to get creative, you can layer several of the following pudding recipes to make a parfait. For example, you can layer chocolate and peanut butter or chocolate and coconut. Lemon, orange, and coconut make a nice tropical parfait and look pretty garnished with fresh citrus fruit, sprin-kled coconut, and mint leaves. Use your imagination! I usually serve pudding in inexpensive small wine goblets for a festive look.

....

CHOCOLATE LOVER'S PUDDING

This is a treat that I like to make when I'm craving chocolate. It's very versatile and may be used as a dessert on its own, a pie filling, or a topping for a cake.

Makes 8 servings

Preparation time: 5 minutes

1 pound (16 ounces, or 1⅓ [12-ounce] packages) firm silken tofu

1 cup powdered sugar

2 teaspoons vanilla extract

2 cups vegan chocolate chips

¼ cup finely ground vegan chocolate chips, for garnish (optional)

▶ Place the tofu in a food processor and mix until smooth, scraping down the sides as necessary. Add the powdered sugar and vanilla.

▶ Melt the chocolate chips in a microwave or double boiler. Pour the melted chocolate into the tofu mixture and process until combined.

▶ Pour into serving dishes. Sprinkle with finely ground chocolate chips, if desired. Refrigerate until ready to serve.

Variation: Add ¾ cup of vegan chocolate chips or ½ cup of coarsely chopped peanuts to the pudding, for an interesting dessert.

PER SERVING: 297 calories, 14 g fat (8 g saturated), 43 g carbohydrate, 3 g dietary fiber, <1 g sugar, 5 g protein, 0 mg cholesterol, 9 mg sodium, 70 mg potassium. Calories from fat: 39 percent.

Guiltless Pudding

This pudding is a healthier version of Chocolate Lover's Pudding, page 225, because I use stevia to sweeten it. (See Stocking Your Vegan Pantry on page 18 for more information on stevia). The raisins are optional, but keep in mind that they will add some extra sweetness to the pudding. This dessert is also a good source of potassium and iron.

Makes 8 servings

Preparation time: 5 minutes

24 ounces (2 [12-ounce] packages) firm or extra-firm silken tofu

¼ cup carob powder

1 teaspoon stevia

¼ cup raisins (optional, preferably organic)

▸ Place the tofu in a food processor and process until smooth, scraping down the sides as necessary.

▸ Add the carob and stevia to the tofu mixture and process until combined. Stir in the raisins by hand.

▸ Pour into serving dishes and refrigerate until ready to serve.

PER SERVING: 37 calories, <1 g fat (<1 g saturated), 7 g carbohydrate, 1 g dietary fiber, <1 g sugar, 2 g protein, 0 mg cholesterol, 3 mg sodium, 114 mg potassium. Calories from fat: 20 percent.

PEANUT BUTTER AND NO JELLY PUDDING

Smooth, creamy peanut butter pudding makes for a quick, easy, and delicious treat any time.

> Makes 8 servings

Preparation time: 5 minutes

1 pound (16 ounces, or 1⅓ [12-ounce] packages) firm silken tofu

1 cup powdered sugar

2 teaspoons vanilla extract

¾ cup smooth natural peanut butter

¼ cup finely ground peanuts, for garnish (optional)

▶ Place the tofu in a food processor and process until smooth, scraping down the sides as necessary. Add the powdered sugar, vanilla, and peanut butter.

▶ Pour into serving dishes and sprinkle with finely ground peanuts, if desired.

▶ Refrigerate until ready to serve.

....

Variation: Add ¾ cup of vegan chocolate chips to the pudding, for an interesting twist.

PER SERVING: 239 calories, 14 g fat (3 g saturated), 21 g carbohydrate, 2 g dietary fiber, <1 g sugar, 10 g protein, 0 mg cholesterol, 117 mg sodium, 231 mg potassium. Calories from fat: 50 percent.

Bahama Mama Pudding

Coconut pudding is creamy and tropical tasting and is wonderful served alone or with chocolate chips added. Being a chocoholic myself, I always add the chocolate chips!

Makes 8 servings

Preparation time: 5 minutes

1 pound (16 ounces, or 1⅓ [12-ounce] packages) firm silken tofu

1 cup powdered sugar

2 teaspoons coconut extract

¾ cup unsweetened shredded coconut

Fresh mint leaves, for garnish (optional)

▸ Place the tofu in a food processor and process until smooth, scraping down the sides as necessary. Add the powdered sugar and coconut extract. Stir in the coconut by hand.

▸ Pour into serving dishes. Refrigerate until ready to serve.

▸ Garnish with fresh mint leaves, if desired.

Variation: Add ½ cup of vegan chocolate chips to the pudding after it has been processed in the food processor. Stir it into the pudding along with the coconut.

PER SERVING: 113 calories, 4 g fat (2 g saturated), 17 g carbohydrate, <1 g dietary fiber, <1 g sugar, 4 g protein, 0 mg cholesterol, 6 mg sodium, 84 mg potassium. Calories from fat: 28 percent.

THE BERRY BEST PUDDING

Raspberry pudding is light and fruity and, in my opinion, provides a simple and elegant end to a delicious meal.

Makes 8 servings

Preparation time: 5 minutes

1 pound (16 ounces, or 1⅓ [12-ounce] packages) firm silken tofu

1 cup powdered sugar

¼ cup raspberry jam

Fresh raspberries and mint leaves, for garnish (optional)

▸ Place the tofu in a food processor and process until smooth, scraping down the sides as necessary. Add the powdered sugar and jam.

▸ Pour into serving dishes and refrigerate until ready to serve.

▸ Garnish with fresh raspberries and mint leaves, if desired.

PER SERVING: 117 calories, 2 g fat (<1 g saturated), 22 g carbohydrate, <1 g dietary fiber, <1 g sugar, 4 g protein, 0 mg cholesterol, 9 mg sodium, 76 mg potassium. Calories from fat: 15 percent.

CREAMY RICE PUDDING

Smooth rice pudding is always a crowd-pleaser, and this recipe is a great way to use up any leftover rice you may have from last night's stir-fry!

Makes 8 servings

Preparation time: pudding, 5 minutes; rice, 45 minutes

¾ cup apple juice or water

½ cup raisins (preferably organic)

1 pound (16 ounces, or 1⅓ [12-ounce] packages) firm silken tofu

¾ cup pure maple syrup

2 teaspoons vanilla extract

1½ teaspoons ground cinnamon

2 cups cooked brown rice (I like short-grain brown rice or brown basmati), or 2 cups cooked quinoa (see Note)

► Place the apple juice in a small pan and bring to a boil. Add the raisins, cover, and simmer for 5 minutes. Remove from the heat and allow to soak until you are ready to add them to the pudding.

► Place the tofu in a food processor and process until smooth, scraping down the sides as necessary. Add the maple syrup, vanilla, and cinnamon and process until smooth. Pour into a bowl. Add the cooked rice and raisins. (Discard the apple juice in which the raisins were soaking.) Stir to combine. Sprinkle with more cinnamon.

► Refrigerate until cold.

....

Variation: Substitute brandy for apple juice when soaking the raisins, for a festive alternative.

PER SERVING: 197 calories, 3 g fat (<1 g saturated), 40 g carbohydrate, 2 g dietary fiber, 19 g sugar, 5 g protein, 0 mg cholesterol, 11 mg sodium, 221 mg potassium. Calories from fat: 11 percent.

Note: To cook the rice, put 1 cup of rice and 2 cups of water in a saucepan and bring to a boil. Lower the heat, cover, and simmer for 45 minutes. To cook the quinoa, put 1 cup of quinoa and 2 cups of water in a saucepan and cook for 12 minutes. Let steam for 10 minutes).

Orange Chocolate Chip Pudding

I like to combine flavors that are unusual, such as tangy orange and bittersweet chocolate. If you like the taste of this pudding, you should definitely try the Orange You Glad It Has Chocolate Chips Cake, page 89.

Makes 8 servings

Preparation time: 5 minutes

1 pound (16 ounces, or 1⅓ [12-ounce] packages) firm silken tofu

1 cup powdered sugar

2 teaspoons orange extract

1½ cups vegan chocolate chips

4 thin slices orange and mint leaves, for garnish (optional)

▶ Place the tofu in a food processor and process until smooth, scraping down the sides as necessary. Add the powdered sugar and orange extract and blend. Stir in the chocolate chips by hand.

▶ Pour into serving dishes and refrigerate until ready to serve.

▶ Garnish with fresh orange slices and mint leaves, if desired.

PER SERVING: 246 calories, 12 g fat (6 g saturated), 36 g carbohydrate, 2 g dietary fiber, <1 g sugar, 5 g protein, 0 mg cholesterol, 8 mg sodium, 70 mg potassium. Calories from fat: 37 percent.

TANGY LEMON PUDDING

This pudding works well as a light dessert, or it may be used as a pie filling or topping for a cake.

Makes 8 servings

Preparation time: 5 minutes

1 pound (16 ounces, or 1⅓ [12-ounce] packages) firm silken tofu

1 cup powdered sugar

2 teaspoons lemon extract

¼ teaspoon turmeric (for color only)

4 thin slices lemon and mint leaves, for garnish (optional)

▸ Place the tofu in a food processor and process until smooth, scraping down the sides as necessary. Add the powdered sugar, lemon extract, and turmeric and blend.

▸ Pour into serving dishes and refrigerate until ready to serve.

▸ Garnish with fresh lemon slices and mint leaves, if desired.

PER SERVING: 96 calories, 2 g fat (<1 g saturated), 16 carbohydrate, <1 g dietary fiber, <1 g sugar, 4 g protein, 0 mg cholesterol, 5 mg sodium, 70 mg potassium. Calories from fat: 18 percent.

STRAWBERRY FIELDS PUDDING

This simple but tasty strawberry pudding can be used on its own as a dessert, layered with other flavors to make a parfait, put in a pie shell, or mounded onto a cake.

Makes 8 servings

Preparation time: 5 minutes

1 pound (16 ounces, or 1⅓ [12-ounce] packages) firm silken tofu

1 cup powdered sugar

¼ cup strawberry jam, or ¾ cup fresh or frozen strawberries

Fresh strawberries and mint leaves, for garnish (optional)

▸ Place the tofu in a food processor and process until smooth, scraping down the sides as necessary. Add the powdered sugar and jam.

▸ Pour into serving dishes and refrigerate until ready to serve.

▸ Garnish with fresh strawberries and mint leaves, if desired.

PER SERVING: 97 calories, 2 g fat (<1 g saturated), 17 g carbohydrate, <1 g dietary fiber, <1 g sugar, 4 g protein, 0 mg cholesterol, 5 mg sodium, 92 mg potassium. Calories from fat: 18 percent.

DOUGHNUTS, CANDY, AND ICE CREAM

The following three recipes are variations on a doughnut recipe called fasnachts. Fasnachts are traditionally made in Pennsylvania German households on Fat Tuesday, the day before Ash Wednesday, which is the start of the season of Lent leading up to Easter. The idea is to eat as much delicious (albeit fattening) food as you can before Lent begins, when foods become more restricted for a few weeks. Fasnachts are pieces of potato dough deep-fried to a golden brown. They are traditionally eaten plain or with molasses. I like to dust them with powdered sugar so they are more like glazed and powdered doughnuts.

....

FASNACHTS ♡

Preparation time: 30 minutes ▼ **Rising times:** 20 minutes, 1 hour, 45 minutes
Frying time: 1 to 2 hours, depending on the size of the pan that you use

3 (0.75-ounce) packages dry yeast

1 cup lukewarm water

4 cups vegan milk

2 cups plain mashed potatoes
(no vegan milk added)
(see Note)

1 cup canola oil

1 cup granulated sweetener

17 to 18 cups unbleached
all-purpose flour

2 teaspoons flax powder

½ cup water

1 teaspoon salt

1 pound powdered sugar
(optional)

vegetable oil for frying
(enough to fill the pan you
will be using ¾ full)

▶ Dissolve the yeast in the cup of lukewarm water. Allow to sit for about 5 minutes. Meanwhile, heat the milk until almost boiling, but don't boil. Pour into a very large bowl and mix with the mashed potatoes, canola oil, and granulated sweetener. Allow to cool to lukewarm (or you will kill the yeast when you add it).

▶ Add the yeast mixture and 6 cups of the flour. Stir to combine. Allow the mixture to stand for 20 minutes—it will look foamy on top.

▶ In a small bowl, mix the flax powder with the ½ cup of water. Add to the flour mixture and stir to combine. Add the salt and 10 cups of the flour. Add the last cup or two of flour slowly. The dough should be firm enough to stir, yet soft—it will stiffen as you knead. You want tender, flaky doughnuts, not tough ones! When you can no longer stir the dough, turn it out onto a floured work surface and knead until satiny. If the dough is too sticky to work with, add more flour. Coat a large mixing bowl with nonstick cooking spray and place the dough in the bowl. Cover and allow to rise in a warm place until doubled in bulk (at least 1 hour).

PER SERVING: 133 calories, 3 g fat (<1 g saturated), 24 g carbohydrate, <1 g dietary fiber, 3 g protein, 0 mg cholesterol, 4 mg sodium, 47 mg potassium. Calories from fat: 19 percent.

Note: You may cook the potatoes and mash them. The number of potatoes it will take to make 2 cups of mashed will vary, depending on the size of the potato—five medium-size potatoes will probably be enough. I usually use potato flakes because I find that they make a lighter doughnut and they're easier to make. If you choose to use potato flakes, you will need four-cup servings of the potatoes. I use 1⅓ cups of water mixed with ½ cup of vegan milk. I heat the liquid and add 1½ cups of potato flakes. Check the back of the box of the potato flakes that you use, for further direction.

continues

continued

▸ To make the fasnachts: Line cookie sheets with waxed paper or parchment (there is less sticking with parchment). Roll out the dough (in small batches) to about ½-inch thickness. Cut the dough with a sharp knife or pizza cutter into 2 by 1-inch rectangles. Place the rectangles of dough on the prepared cookie sheets. With a sharp knife, cut an X in the center of each piece of dough. This will prevent the center from being too thick and not cooking through entirely. Cover and allow to rise until not quite doubled in size, about 45 minutes. (I find that by the time I am finished cutting all the doughnuts, the first ones are ready to fry.)

▸ Heat the vegetable oil to 375°F. You can either use a pan with a cooking thermometer clipped on the side, or a wok. I find that my electric wok works well for this. It has its own thermostat and a wide area in which to cook the doughnuts. When the oil is at the proper temperature, carefully drop in some of the rectangles of dough. (Don't overcrowd the oil.) The doughnuts will float. When the bottoms are golden brown, turn over.

▸ Remove from the oil with a slotted spoon when both sides are golden brown. Drain on paper towels or cut-up brown paper bags, with the inside of the bag facing up. (To make cleanup easier, I always place aluminum foil beneath the brown paper bags.)

▸ Allow to cool until the doughnuts can be handled, before coating with powdered sugar (if desired): Put the powdered sugar in a plastic or paper bag. Drop three or four doughnuts into the bag. Shake carefully to cover with the sugar. Remove from the bag and let cool completely. The consistency of the powdered sugar covering is directly related to the temperature of the doughnuts at the time of the coating. If you want more of a glaze, coat them when they are warmer. If you want more of a powdered sugar covering, allow them to cool almost completely before coating.

Variation: You may place some of the dough in a greased 8-inch baking dish. Punch holes in the dough (not all the way through). Sprinkle with sugar, maple syrup, and/or vegan butter, if desired. Bake at 400°F until the top is golden brown, 15 to 20 minutes. This will make one breakfast cake.

JELLY-FILLED DOUGHNUTS

Nothing compares to a freshly baked doughnut. If you love jelly doughnuts and have never made them—here's your chance. You will be glad you did, and you'll never want to buy another doughnut again! These treats take a lot of work, but they are worth it.

Makes about 3 dozen doughnuts

Preparation time: 30 minutes ▼ **Rising times:** 20 minutes, 1 hour, 45 minutes
Frying time: 1 hour, depending on the size of the pan that you use

1 (0.75-ounce) package dry yeast

⅓ cup lukewarm water

1⅓ cups vegan milk

½ cup plain mashed potatoes (no vegan milk added) (see Note)

⅓ cup canola oil

⅓ cup granulated sweetener

5 cups unbleached all-purpose flour

1 teaspoon flax powder

¼ cup water

⅓ teaspoon salt

1 (16-ounce) jar jelly or seedless jam, such as raspberry

3 cups powdered sugar (optional)

vegetable oil for frying (enough to fill the pan you will be using ¾ full)

▶ Dissolve the yeast in the cup of lukewarm water. Allow to sit for about 5 minutes. Meanwhile, heat the milk until almost boiling, but don't boil. Pour into a very large bowl and mix with the mashed potatoes, canola oil, and granulated sweetener. Allow to cool to lukewarm (or you will kill the yeast when you add it).

▶ Add the yeast mixture and 1 cup of flour. Stir to combine. Allow the mixture to stand for 20 minutes.

▶ In a small bowl, mix the flax powder with the ¼ cup of water. Add to the flour mixture and stir to combine. Add the salt and 3 more cups of flour. Add the last cup of flour slowly. The dough should be firm enough to stir, yet soft—it will stiffen as you knead. You want tender, flaky doughnuts, not tough ones! When you can no longer stir the dough, turn it out onto a floured work surface and knead until satiny. Coat a large mixing bowl with nonstick cooking spray and place the dough in the bowl. Cover and allow to rise in a warm place until doubled in bulk (at least 1 hour).

PER SERVING: 168 calories, 2 g fat (<1 g saturated), 34 g carbohydrate, <1 g dietary fiber, 2 g protein, 0 mg cholesterol, 9 mg sodium, 49 mg potassium. Calories from fat: 13 percent.

Note: You may cook the potatoes and mash them. The number of potatoes it will take to make ½ cup of mashed will vary, depending on the size of the potato—two medium-size potatoes will probably be enough. I usually use potato flakes because I find that they make a lighter doughnut and they're easier to make. If you choose to use potato flakes, you'll need one ½-cup serving of the potatoes. I use ⅓ cup of water mixed with 2 tablespoons of vegan milk. I heat the liquid and add ¼ cup + 2 tablespoons of potato flakes. Check the back of the box of the potato flakes that you use, for further directions.

continues

continued

▸ To make the doughnuts: Line cookie sheets with waxed paper or parchment (there is less sticking with parchment). Roll out the dough (in small batches) to about ½-inch thickness. Cut with a 2-inch round cutter (or a glass with a 2-inch diameter). Place circles of dough on the prepared cookie sheets. Cover and allow to rise until not quite doubled in size, about 45 minutes. (I find that by the time I am finished cutting all the doughnuts, the first ones are ready to fry.)

▸ Heat the vegetable oil to 375°F. You can either use a pan with a cooking thermometer clipped on the side, or a wok. I find that my electric wok works well for this. It has its own thermostat and a wide area in which to cook the doughnuts. When the oil is at the proper temperature, carefully drop in some circles of dough. (Don't overcrowd the oil.) The doughnuts will float. When the bottoms are golden brown, turn over.

▸ Remove from the oil with a slotted spoon when both sides are golden brown. Drain on paper towels or cut-up brown paper bags, with the inside of the bag facing up. (To make cleanup easier, I always place aluminum foil under the brown bags.) Allow to cool enough so that you can handle them.

▸ Push the handle of a wooden spoon about 2½ to 3 inches into the side of each doughnut to make a hole. Be careful not to push it all the way through the doughnut. Put the jelly into a pastry bag fitted with large round tip (or use a resealable plastic bag; snip 1 corner). Squeeze about 2 teaspoons of jelly into the hole in each doughnut. Dust the doughnuts with powdered sugar.

BOSTON CREAM–FILLED DOUGHNUTS

These delicious tender doughnuts are filled with creamy vanilla filling and topped with dark chocolate. Yum!

> **Makes about 3 dozen doughnuts**

Preparation time: 30 minutes ▼ **Rising times:** 20 minutes, 1 hour, 45 minutes
Frying time: 1 hour depending, on the size of the pan that you use

Doughnuts:

1 (0.75-ounce) package dry yeast

⅓ cup lukewarm water

1⅓ cups vegan milk

½ cup plain mashed potatoes (no vegan added) (see Note)

⅓ cup canola oil

⅓ cup granulated sweetener

5 cups unbleached all-purpose flour

1 teaspoon flax powder

¼ cup water

⅓ teaspoon salt

Vanilla filling:

1 pound (16 ounces, or 1⅓ [12-ounce] packages) firm silken tofu

1 cup powdered sugar

¼ cup unbleached all-purpose flour

2 teaspoons vanilla extract

vegetable oil for frying (enough to fill the pan you will be using ¾ full)

▶ Dissolve the yeast in 1 cup of lukewarm water. Allow to sit for about 5 minutes. Meanwhile, heat the milk until almost boiling, but don't boil. Pour into a very large bowl and mix with the mashed potatoes, canola oil, and granulated sweetener. Allow to cool to lukewarm (or you will kill the yeast when you add it). Add the yeast mixture and 1 cup of flour. Stir to combine. Allow mixture to stand for 20 minutes.

▶ In a small bowl, mix the flax powder with the ¼ cup of water. Add to the flour mixture and stir to combine. Add the salt and 3 more cups of flour. Add the last cup of flour slowly. The dough should be firm enough to stir, yet soft— it will stiffen as you knead. You want tender, flaky doughnuts, not tough ones! When you can no longer stir the dough, turn it out onto a floured counter and knead until satiny. Coat a large mixing bowl with nonstick cooking spray and place the dough in the bowl. Cover and allow to rise in a warm place until doubled in bulk (at least 1 hour).

▶ To make the filling: While the dough is rising, place the tofu in a food processor. Whip until smooth, scraping down the sides several times. Add the sugar, flour, and vanilla and process. Refrigerate until ready to use.

Note: You may cook the potatoes and mash them. The number of potatoes it will take to make ½ cup of mashed will vary, depending on the size of the potato—two medium-size potatoes will probably be enough. I usually use potato flakes because I find that they make a lighter doughnut and they're easier to make. If you choose to use potato flakes, you'll need one ½-cup serving of the potatoes. I use ⅓ cup of water mixed with 2 tablespoons of vegan milk. I heat the liquid and add ¼ cup + 2 tablespoons of potato flakes. Check the back of the box of the potato flakes that you use, for further directions.

continues

continued

▶ To make the doughnuts: Line cookie sheets with waxed or parchment paper (there is less sticking with parchment). Roll out the dough (in small batches) to about ½-inch thickness. Cut with a 2-inch round cutter (or a glass with a 2-inch diameter). Place the circles of dough on lined trays. Cover and allow to rise until not quite doubled in size, about 45 minutes. (I find that by the time I am finished cutting all the doughnuts, the first ones are ready to fry.)

▶ Heat the vegetable oil to 375°F. You can either use a pan with a cooking thermometer clipped on the side, or a wok. I find that my electric wok works well for this. It has its own thermostat and a wide area in which to cook the doughnuts. When the oil is at the proper temperature, carefully drop in some circles of dough. (Don't overcrowd the oil.) The doughnuts will float. When the bottoms are golden brown, turn over.

▶ Remove from the oil with a slotted spoon when both sides are golden brown. Drain on paper towels or cut-up brown paper bags with the inside of the bag facing up. (To make cleanup easier, I always place aluminum foil beneath the brown bags.) Allow to cool.

▶ Push the handle of a wooden spoon about 2½ to 3 inches into the side of each doughnut to make a hole. Be careful not to push it all the way through the doughnut. Put the cream into a pastry bag fitted with large round tip (or use a resealable plastic bag; snip one corner). Squeeze about 2 teaspoons of cream into the hole in each doughnut and then refrigerate.

▶ To make the chocolate topping: Place the powdered sugar, canola oil, vanilla, cocoa powder, and arrowroot in a small saucepan and stir to combine, using a wire whisk for best results. Stir in the ½ cup of water. Bring almost to a boil, stirring constantly. Do not boil. Keep stirring until the mixture starts to thicken. Allow to cool until the mixture is of a good spreading consistency. Pour 1 to 2 tablespoons of chocolate topping over each doughnut and refrigerate. (The topping will thicken as it cools.)

Chocolate glaze topping:

1 cup powdered sugar

¼ cup canola oil

½ teaspoon vanilla extract

⅙ cup unsweetened cocoa powder (half of a ⅓-cup measuring cup)

3½ tablespoons arrowroot

½ cup water

PER SERVING: 152 calories, 5 g fat (<1 g saturated), 23 g carbohydrate, <1 g dietary fiber, <1 g sugar, 4 g protein, 0 mg cholesterol, 6 mg sodium, 110 mg potassium. Calories from fat: 29 percent.

PEANUT BUTTER BALLS ♡

Who can resist creamy peanut butter covered in dark chocolate? These are truly delicious candies—my kids can vouch for that!

> **Makes 3 dozen**

Preparation time: 20 minutes ▼ **Freezing time:** 15 minutes ▼ **Coating:** 15 minutes

1 cup smooth natural peanut butter

½ cup pure pumpkin puree

½ cup powdered sugar

1 (10-ounce) bag vegan chocolate chips

½ cup chopped peanuts (optional)

PER SERVING: 100 calories, 7 g fat (2 g saturated), 9 g carbohydrate, 1 g dietary fiber, 3 g protein, 0 mg cholesterol, 43 mg sodium, 68 mg potassium. Calories from fat: 58 percent.

▶ Mix the peanut butter and pumpkin together. Add the powdered sugar. (You may want to use a food processor to mix the filling.) Roll the filling into ¾-inch balls. Place on a waxed paper– or parchment-lined tray. Place in the freezer for 15 minutes so the filling is hard and easier to coat with the warm chocolate.

▶ Line a cookie sheet with waxed paper or parchment. Melt the chocolate chips in a microwave or double boiler until smooth and creamy. (If using a double boiler, keep the water in the double boiler over low heat so that the chocolate remains hot and thin.) Pierce each ball of filling with a toothpick to use as a handle. Dip each ball of filling in the chocolate and place on the prepared cookie sheet.

▶ If desired, sprinkle with chopped peanuts. Refrigerate to harden the chocolate.

▶ Store the candy in the refrigerator in an airtight container.

COCONUT CREAM EGGS ♡

Here's my vegan version of the traditional candy coconut cream eggs.

> Makes 4 dozen

Preparation time: 20 minutes ▼ **Chilling time:** 10 minutes
Freezing time: 15 minutes ▼ **Coating:** 15 minutes

12 ounces (1 package) firm
silken tofu

4 ounces (½ [8-ounce] container)
vegan cream cheese

1⅓ cups prepared mashed
potatoes (see Note)

2 cups powdered sugar

1 teaspoon coconut extract

3 cups unsweetened shredded
coconut

4 cups vegan chocolate chips

▶ Place the tofu in a food processor and process until smooth, scraping down the sides as necessary. Add the cream cheese and process until smooth. Add the mashed potatoes, powdered sugar, and coconut extract and process until smooth. Stir in the coconut by hand, mixing well. Chill the filling for 10 minutes so that it is easier to handle.

▶ Line a cookie sheet with waxed paper or parchment. Roll or spoon the filling into small log- or egg-shaped pieces about ¾ by ½ inch (the filling may still be soft). Place the logs of filling on the prepared cookie sheet. Freeze for 15 minutes, or until the filling is easy to handle.

▶ Melt the chocolate chips in a microwave or double boiler until smooth and creamy. (If using a double boiler, keep the water in the double boiler over low heat so that the chocolate remains hot and thin.) Pierce each log of filling with a toothpick to use as a handle. Dip the filling log in the chocolate. Place on the prepared cookie sheet. Refrigerate to harden the chocolate.

▶ Store the candy in the refrigerator in an airtight container.

PER SERVING: 123 calories, 6 g fat (4 g saturated), 17 g carbohydrate, 1 g dietary fiber, <1 g sugar, 2 g protein, 0 mg cholesterol, 13 mg sodium, 83 mg potassium. Calories from fat: 37 percent.

Note: You may peel, boil, and mash the potatoes. The number of potatoes needed will vary depending on size—three or four medium-size potatoes will probably be enough. I use instant potato flakes because I think they are much easier and make a lighter filling. I use ¾ cup of water mixed with ⅓ cup of vegan milk. I heat the liquid and add ¾ cup of potato flakes. This makes two servings, which is equal to 1⅓ cups of potatoes. Check on the back of the box of the potato flakes that you use, for further directions.

MELT-IN-YOUR-MOUTH FUDGE

Upon becoming a vegan, were you afraid that your days of enjoying a luscious, creamy piece of sinfully rich fudge were over? Well, have I got good news for you! This vegan fudge recipe is sure to satisfy even the most savage sweet tooth.

> **Makes 6 to 7 dozen pieces of fudge**

Preparation time: 5 minutes

1 (8-ounce) container vegan
cream cheese

4 cups powdered sugar

1 cup vegan chocolate chips

1 teaspoon vanilla extract

PER SERVING: 45 calories, 1 g fat
(<1 g saturated), 8 g carbohydrate,
<1 g dietary fiber, <1 g protein,
0 mg cholesterol, 14 mg sodium,
<1 mg potassium. Calories from fat:
12 percent.

▸ Place the cream cheese in a food processor and blend until smooth. Add the powdered sugar and vanilla. Melt the chocolate chips in a microwave or double boiler. Pour into the cream cheese mixture and process until blended.

▸ Line an 8-inch square pan with waxed paper, leaving the paper extended to form handles. Pour the fudge into the prepared pan. Refrigerate until firm.

▸ Pull the waxed paper out of the pan. Cut the fudge into bite-size pieces.

▸ Store the fudge in the refrigerator in an airtight container.

RAISIN AND PEANUT CLUSTERS

This candy—peanuts and raisins nestled in rich, dark chocolate—can be made in a snap and tastes fantastic.

> ### Makes 2 dozen

Preparation time: 5 minutes ▼ **Forming into mounds:** 10 minutes

2½ cups vegan chocolate chips

1 cup whole roasted peanuts, salted

1 cup raisins (preferably organic)

PER SERVING: 137 calories, 8 g fat (3 g saturated), 17 g carbohydrate, 2 g dietary fiber, 2 g protein, 0 mg cholesterol, 3 mg sodium, 85 mg potassium. Calories from fat: 49 percent.

▶ Line a cookie sheet with waxed paper or parchment. Melt the chocolate in a microwave or double boiler. Mix in the peanuts and raisins. Drop by teaspoonfuls onto the prepared cookie sheet.

▶ Refrigerate until hard. Store in the refrigerator in an airtight container.

CHOCOLATE COCONUT NESTS

This delicious candy can be used as a basket or nest to hold other small candy or it can be eaten alone—take your pick.

> **Makes 1 dozen**

Preparation time: 5 minutes ▼ **Forming into mounds:** 10 minutes

2 cups vegan chocolate chips

1½ cups shredded coconut

½ teaspoon coconut extract

PER SERVING: 158 calories, 11 g fat
(7 g saturated), 19 g carbohydrate,
2 g dietary fiber, 1 g protein, 0 mg
cholesterol, 4 mg sodium, 19 mg
potassium. Calories from fat: 54
percent.

▶ Line a cookie sheet with waxed paper or parchment. Melt the chocolate chips in a microwave or double boiler. Mix in the coconut and coconut extract. Drop by tablespoonfuls onto the prepared cookie sheet.

▶ Press a knuckle into the center of each candy to make an indentation. Refrigerate until hard. Store in the refrigerator in an airtight container.

Variation: You can fill these nests with vegan jelly beans or vegan candy-coated chocolates, if desired.

ICE CREAM

I call these next few desserts ice cream because they look like creamy soft-serve ice cream, and they taste delicious. But, there's absolutely no cream in them. You're actually eating a fruit salad, but your brain and taste buds will be telling you that you're having ice cream! I've included a few of my favorites, but feel free to experiment with different types of fruit. Just be sure to include the banana—that's the secret to the creamy texture!

....

MEXICAN CHOCOLATE
ICE CREAM

An interesting blend of sweetness with a touch of spice is the hallmark of this different dessert.

Makes 2 servings

Freezing time: 24 hours, prior to making this recipe ▼ **Preparation time:** 5 minutes

½ avocado, sliced and frozen

1 banana, cut into bite-size
  chunks and frozen

1 teaspoon ground cinnamon

1 tablespoon unsweetened
  cocoa powder

1 tablespoon pure maple syrup

¼ teaspoon ground red pepper
  (see Note)

¼ cup water

▶ Put all the ingredients in a food processor or blender such as a Vita-Mix. Process until smooth, scraping down the sides as necessary. Scoop out and serve immediately.

PER SERVING: 169 calories, 8 g fat (1.4 g saturated), 27 g carbohydrate, 6.4 g dietary fiber, 13.6 g sugar, 2.2 g protein, 0 mg cholesterol, 7 mg sodium. Calories from fat: 12 percent.

Note: You may adjust the amount of red pepper according to your "hotness level." You should be able to feel the hotness in your mouth as an aftertaste. The heat shouldn't overpower the other flavors.

PEACHES 'N' CREAM
ICE CREAM

This is a refreshing fruit dessert that is light and just right on a hot summer day.

Freezing time: 24 hours, prior to making this recipe ▼ **Preparation time:** 5 minutes

½ cup peaches, pitted, peeled, cubed, and frozen

1 banana, cut into bite-size chunks and frozen

⅛ teaspoon vanilla extract (optional)

¼ cup water

▶ Put all the ingredients in a food processor or blender such as a Vita-Mix. Process until smooth, scraping down the sides as necessary. Scoop out and serve immediately.

PER SERVING: 70 calories, 0.3 g fat, 17.6 g carbohydrate, 2.2 g dietary fiber, 10.8 g sugar, 1 g protein, 0 mg cholesterol, 2 mg sodium. Calories from fat: 0 percent.

CHOCOLATE CHERRY ICE CREAM ♡♡

This is one of my favorite desserts. It's so healthy, I feel funny calling it dessert, but it looks like chocolate soft-serve ice cream and tastes great! I eat it almost every night!

> **Makes 2 servings**

Freezing time: 24 hours, prior to making this recipe ▼ **Preparation time:** 5 minutes

1 banana, cut into bite-size chunks and frozen

12 red cherries, pitted and frozen

2 tablespoons unsweetened cocoa powder

¼ cup water

▶ Put all the ingredients in a food processor or blender such as a Vita-Mix. Process until smooth, scraping down the sides as necessary. Scoop out and serve immediately.

PER SERVING: 81 calories, 1 g fat, 20.5 g carbohydrate, 3.8 g dietary fiber, 10.9 g sugar, 2 g protein, 0 mg cholesterol, 3 mg sodium. Calories from fat: 2 percent.

Note: I top this dessert with 2 tablespoons of mini vegan chocolate chips for some added crunch! I believe that you can never have too much chocolate!

PINEAPPLE COCONUT ICE CREAM

This ice cream is very refreshing. The pineapple adds just the right amount of sweetness.

Makes 2 servings

Freezing time: 24 hours, prior to making this recipe ▼ **Preparation time:** 5 minutes

1 banana, cut into bite-size chunks and frozen

½ cup pineapple, cubed and frozen

¼ teaspoon coconut extract (optional)

¼ cup water

¼ cup unsweetened shredded coconut

▶ Put all the ingredients except the coconut in a food processor or blender such as a Vita-Mix. Process until smooth, scraping down the sides as necessary. Scoop into serving bowls, sprinkle with coconut, and serve immediately.

PER SERVING: 109 calories, 3.6 g fat, 20.2 g carbohydrate, 3 g dietary fiber, 11.7 g sugar, 1.2 g protein, 0 mg cholesterol, 4 mg sodium. Calories from fat: 6 percent.

BEVERAGES AND
SMOOTHIES

Ain't No Chocolate Here Smoothie

This healthy creation tastes so rich that it can just as easily be served as a sinful-tasting snack or dessert as it can be for breakfast. The carob is not as chocolaty as real chocolate, but it has more calcium and no caffeine. You may choose to substitute cocoa powder for the carob (use the same amount of cocoa as you would carob) for a real chocolate shake taste. The banana in this smoothie does not add much banana flavor, but it does add sweetness and a smooth texture.

Serves 1

Preparation time: 5 minutes

1 cup crushed ice

1 cup vegan milk

1 ripe banana (yellow, not too green and not overripe), broken into several small pieces

2 tablespoons carob powder or unsweetened cocoa powder

▸ Place all the ingredients in a blender.

▸ Process at high speed until smooth.

▸ Pour into a tall glass and serve immediately.

PER SERVING: 279 calories, 5 g fat (<1 g saturated), 54 g carbohydrate, 8 g dietary fiber, 8 g protein, 0 mg cholesterol, 55 mg sodium, 838 mg potassium. Calories from fat: 15 percent.

ORANGE CREAMSICLE SMOOTHIE

I like to make this refreshing drink on a summer evening when I'm craving something sweet and cool. It tastes just like an orange sherbet shake.

Serves 1

Preparation time: 5 minutes

1 cup crushed ice

3 tablespoons orange juice concentrate

1 cup vanilla vegan milk

1 teaspoon vanilla extract

▶ Place all the ingredients in a blender.

▶ Process at high speed until smooth.

▶ Pour into a tall glass and serve immediately.

PER SERVING: 203 calories, 5 g fat (<1 g saturated), 31 g carbohydrate, 4 g dietary fiber, 8 g protein, 0 mg cholesterol, 32 mg sodium, 817 mg potassium. Calories from fat: 19 percent.

BANANAS IN PAJAMAS SMOOTHIE

This is one of my morning favorites—I like to whip up one of these smoothies before work. It keeps me feeling satisfied until lunch—no midmorning snack attacks. I think bananas truly are the perfect food, and a wonderful source of potassium to boot. Depending on the ripeness of the banana that you use, this smoothie can taste either like a banana milkshake or a vanilla milkshake.

Serves 1

Preparation time: 5 minutes

1 ripe banana (yellow, not too green and not overripe), broken into several small pieces

1 cup crushed ice

1 cup vegan milk

1 teaspoon vanilla extract

▸ Place all the ingredients in a blender.

▸ Process at high speed until smooth.

▸ Pour into a tall glass and serve immediately.

PER SERVING: 202 calories, 5 g fat (<1 g saturated), 33 g carbohydrate, 6 g dietary fiber, 8 g protein, 0 mg cholesterol, 31 mg sodium, 819 mg potassium. Calories from fat: 21 percent.

GREEN (I SWEAR TO GOD IT'S GOOD!) SMOOTHIE

This very-healthy, great-tasting smoothie is perfect for when you need an energy boost. It's amazing, but I swear I can feel the energy from the enzymes, vitamins, and minerals as they go to work when I have one.

Serves 2

Preparation time: 5 minutes

1 cup crushed ice

1¼ cups water or apple juice

¼ cup (1 scoop) vegan protein powder

2 ripe bananas (yellow, not too green and not overripe), broken into several smaller pieces

1 tablespoon flax oil

2 tablespoons wheat germ

2 tablespoons powdered green supplement such as Green Magma, which is powdered barley grass juice

▶ Place all the ingredients in a blender.

▶ Process at high speed until smooth.

▶ Pour into a tall glass and serve immediately.

PER SERVING: 247 calories, 8 g fat (<1 g saturated), 41 g carbohydrate, 4 g dietary fiber, <1 g sugar, 5 g protein, 0 mg cholesterol, 86 mg sodium, 931 mg potassium. Calories from fat: 30 percent.

BERRY DELICIOUS SMOOTHIE

Just the thing for a quick, nutritious morning breakfast or a healthy ending to any meal. Here's a helpful hint: If you use the berries when they are still frozen, you will make a thicker smoothie.

Serves 1

Preparation time: 5 minutes

1 cup crushed ice

1 cup apple juice

¼ cup water

1 cup frozen berries (blueberries, blackberries, or raspberries)

1 ripe banana (yellow, not too green and not overripe), broken into several small pieces

▸ Place all the ingredients in a blender.

▸ Process at high speed until smooth.

▸ Pour into a tall glass and serve immediately.

PER SERVING: 285 calories, 1 g fat (<1 g saturated), 71 g carbohydrate, 11 g dietary fiber, 2 g protein, 0 mg cholesterol, 8 mg sodium, 949 mg potassium. Calories from fat: 4 percent.

PINK PASSION SMOOTHIE

This smoothie is another healthy way to start the day or to use as a sweet, delicious ending to any meal.

Serves 1

Preparation time: 5 minutes

1 cup frozen strawberries

1 cup crushed ice

1 cup apple juice

¼ cup water

1 ripe banana (yellow, not too green and not overripe, broken in several small pieces)

▸ Place all the ingredients in a blender.

▸ Process at high speed until smooth.

▸ Pour into a tall glass and serve immediately.

PER SERVING: 270 calories, 1 g fat (<1 g saturated), 67 g carbohydrate, 6 g dietary fiber, 2 g protein, 0 mg cholesterol, 10 mg sodium, 1014 mg potassium. Calories from fat: 4 percent.

CARIBBEAN CRUISE SMOOTHIE

This smoothie will tickle your taste buds with its smooth, rich-tasting combination of coconut and pineapple. If you kick back in your backyard or patio with this drink, you'll feel like you're on vacation.

Serves 1

Preparation time: 5 minutes

1 cup crushed pineapple, drained

1 cup crushed ice

1 cup vegan milk

2 tablespoons unsweetened shredded coconut

¼ teaspoon coconut extract

▶ Place all the ingredients in a blender.

▶ Process at high speed until smooth.

▶ Pour into a tall glass and serve immediately.

PER SERVING: 327 calories, 14 g fat (9 g saturated), 47 g carbohydrate, 7 g dietary fiber, 9 g protein, 0 mg cholesterol, 37 mg sodium, 727 mg potassium. Calories from fat: 35 percent.

RED BARON SMOOTHIE

I created this smoothie when I was having a snack attack and it definitely did the trick.

Serves 1

Preparation time: 5 minutes

1¼ cups vanilla vegan milk

1 cup crushed ice

1 cup frozen, pitted cherries

2 tablespoons carob powder or unsweetened cocoa powder

▶ Place all the ingredients in a blender.

▶ Process at high speed until smooth.

▶ Pour into a tall glass and serve immediately.

PER SERVING: 241 calories, 7 g fat (<1 g saturated), 44 g carbohydrate, 13 g dietary fiber, 10 g protein, 0 mg cholesterol, 42 mg sodium, 889 mg potassium. Calories from fat: 25 percent.

RICH HOT COCOA
(SINGLE SERVING)

Remember the warm feeling you get from a cup of hot cocoa on a cold winter day?
You can recapture that same good taste and warm feeling with this vegan version.
The recipe below is for one serving and is so easy because it's made in the microwave.

Serves 1

Preparation time: 5 minutes

1 cup vanilla vegan milk

1 teaspoon vanilla extract

2 teaspoons sugar

1 tablespoon unsweetened
   cocoa powder

PER SERVING: 137 calories, 5 g fat
(1 g saturated), 16 g carbohydrate,
5 g dietary fiber, 8 g protein, 0 mg
cholesterol, 31 mg sodium, 434 mg
potassium. Calories from fat: 33
percent.

▸ Heat the milk in a microwave-safe mug in a microwave until it is steaming but not boiling (1 to 1½ minutes, depending on the strength of your microwave). Add the vanilla and sugar and stir. Put the cocoa powder into another small cup. Add a small amount of the warm milk mixture to the cocoa. Stir to mix. Add more of the warm milk and stir.

▸ Pour the cocoa mixture back into the rest of the milk in the mug and stir well.

▸ Serve immediately.

RICH HOT COCOA
(FOUR SERVINGS)

If you're having friends over and want to make hot cocoa, this recipe is easier to use than making it one cup at a time. Same good taste as the single serving recipe!

> **Makes 4 servings**

Preparation time: 5 minutes

4 cups vanilla vegan milk

1½ tablespoons vanilla extract

2 tablespoons + 2 teaspoons sugar

¼ cup unsweetened cocoa powder

PER SERVING: 122 calories, 5 g fat (1 g saturated), 12 g carbohydrate, 5 g dietary fiber, 8 g protein, 0 mg cholesterol, 31 mg sodium, 435 mg potassium. Calories from fat: 36 percent.

▶ Heat the milk in a small pan until hot (steaming), but not boiling. Add the vanilla and sugar and stir. Put the cocoa powder in another small cup. Add a small amount of the warm milk mixture to the cocoa and stir to mix. Add more of the warm milk and stir.

▶ Pour the cocoa mixture back into the rest of the milk in the pan. Stir well.

▶ Serve immediately.

FROSTINGS, TOPPINGS, AND CRUSTS

This chapter contains frosting, topping, and pie and tart crust recipes for many of the dessert recipes in this book. I have paired each cake with a frosting or topping as indicated in each recipe. Please feel free to mix and match cakes with toppings or frostings and create your own masterpieces.

....

Note: It is a good idea, whenever possible, to prepare any tofu-based frosting the day before to allow the frosting to set. It will be firmer and easier to use.

CHERRY FILLING

2 cups fresh cherries, pitted
and halved

½ cup apple juice

1 tablespoon arrowroot

½ cup water

PER SERVING: 25 calories, <1 g fat
(<0.1 g saturated), 6 g carbohydrate,
<1 g dietary fiber, <1 g protein,
0 mg cholesterol, <1 mg sodium,
66 mg potassium. Calories from fat:
0 percent.

▶ Place the cherries in a saucepan with the apple juice.
Bring to a boil and allow to simmer until the cherries are
soft, about 10 minutes.

▶ Dissolve the arrowroot in the ½ cup of water. Add to the
hot cherries and heat until just thickened—do not boil.

Recommended for:
Cherry, Cherry Not Contrary Cake, page 45
Triple Cherry Treat, page 87
Cherry + Chocolate = Delicious Cake, page 97

CHERRY TOPPING

1 cup fresh cherries, pitted and
chopped

¼ cup apple juice

1½ teaspoons arrowroot

¼ cup water

PER SERVING: 13 calories, <1 g fat
(<0.1 g saturated), 3 g carbohydrate,
<1 g dietary fiber, <1 g protein,
0 mg cholesterol, <1 mg sodium,
33 mg potassium. Calories from fat:
0 percent.

▶ Place the cherries in a saucepan with the apple juice.
Bring to a boil and allow to simmer until the cherries are
soft, about 10 minutes.

▶ Dissolve the arrowroot in the ¼ cup of water. Add to the
hot cherries and heat until just thickened—do not boil.

▶ Refrigerate until ready to use.

Recommended for:
Banana Split Cake, page 72
Cherry Vanilla Dream, page 86

WHIPPED CHERRY TOPPING

> Makes twelve ¼-cup servings

1 pound (16 ounces, or 1⅓
  [12-ounce] packages) firm
  silken tofu

1 cup powdered sugar

2 teaspoons cherry extract

¼ cup unbleached all-purpose
  flour, or 2 teaspoons xanthan
  gum (optional for thickening)
  (see Note)

½ cup fresh cherries, pitted and
  chopped

▶ Place the tofu in a food processor and process until
smooth, scraping down the sides as necessary. Add the
powdered sugar, cherry extract, and flour and process
until blended. Stir in the cherries.

▶ Refrigerate until ready to use.

Recommended for:

Triple Cherry Treat, page 87

Cherry Vanilla Dream, page 86

Cherry, Cherry Not Contrary Cake, page 45

PER SERVING: 74 calories, 1 g fat
(<0.1 g saturated), 3 g carbohydrate,
<1 g dietary fiber, 10 g sugar, 3 g
protein, 0 mg cholesterol, 14 mg
sodium, 40 mg potassium. Calories
from fat: 2 percent.

Note: Xanthan gum will produce a slightly softer frosting, but will not
give the mild flour taste that you may get if you use the flour.

WHIPPED CHOCOLATE FROSTING

> Makes twelve ½-cup servings

1 pound (16 ounces, or 1⅓
  [12-ounce] packages) firm
  silken tofu

1 cup powdered sugar

2 teaspoons vanilla extract

2 cups melted vegan chocolate
  chips (use a microwave or
  double boiler)

▶ Place the tofu in a food processor and whip until smooth,
scraping down the sides several times.

▶ Add the sugar and vanilla and process.

▶ Pour the melted chocolate chips into the tofu mixture
and blend completely.

▶ If refrigerating the cake overnight before serving, you
may use the frosting right away. If planning to frost the
cake and serve it immediately, make the frosting a day
ahead of time and refrigerate overnight to allow it to set.

Recommended for:

Cherry, Cherry Not Contrary Cake, page 45

Nuts About Chocolate Cake, page 50

Chocolate-Covered Gold, page 53

Chocolate-Covered Mint, page 69

PER SERVING: 214 calories, 9 g fat
(5 g saturated), 28 g carbohydrate,
2 g dietary fiber, 25 g sugar, 5 g
protein, 0 mg cholesterol, 36 mg
sodium, 25 mg potassium. Calories
from fat: 14 percent.

CHOCOLATE CREAM CHEESE FROSTING

Makes twelve ½-cup servings

12 ounces (1 package) firm silken tofu

1 (8-ounce) container vegan cream cheese (such as Tofutti, which has no casein)

3 cups powdered sugar

¼ cup unbleached all-purpose flour

1½ cups melted vegan chocolate chips (use a microwave or double boiler)

▸ Place the tofu in a food processor and process until smooth, scraping down the sides as necessary. Add the cream cheese and continue to process until smooth. Add the powdered sugar and flour and process.

▸ Add the melted chocolate chips to the other ingredients and mix.

▸ Refrigerate overnight for best results, so the icing has time to set.

Recommended for:
> Double Chocolate Delight, page 84
> Chocolate-Covered Gold, page 53
> Mellow Yellow Cake, page 54
> Mint Madness, page 85

PER SERVING: 237 calories, 7 g fat (4 g saturated), 46 g carbohydrate, 1 g dietary fiber, <1 g sugar, 2 g protein, 0 mg cholesterol, 6 mg sodium, 22 mg potassium. Calories from fat: 22 percent.

VEGAN CHOCOLATE SYRUP

Makes ten 1½-teaspoon servings

¼ cup pure maple syrup

2 tablespoons unsweetened cocoa powder

▸ Combine the maple syrup and cocoa powder in a small bowl. Stir with a wire whisk until the mixture is the consistency of commercial chocolate syrup. If it is too thick, you may add a little water. If it is too thin, add a little more cocoa powder.

Recommended for:
> Cherry, Cherry Not Contrary Cake, page 45
> Nuts About Chocolate Cake, page 50
> Just Loafing Around (pound cake), page 51
> Banana Split Cake, page 72
> Triple Cherry Treat, page 87
> Cherry + Chocolate = Delicious Cake, page 97

PER SERVING: 19 calories, <1 g fat (<0.1 g saturated), 5 g carbohydrate, <1 g dietary fiber, 4 g sugar, <1 g protein, 0 mg cholesterol, <1 mg sodium. Calories from fat: 0 percent.

VANILLA TOFU WHIPPED TOPPING

8 ounces (¾ [12-ounce] package) firm silken tofu

½ cup powdered sugar

1 teaspoon vanilla extract

2 tablespoons unbleached all-purpose flour, or 1 teaspoon xanthan gum (optional, for thickening) (see Note)

▶ Place the tofu in a food processor and blend until smooth and creamy. Add the powdered sugar and vanilla and blend. Add the flour, if necessary.

▶ Refrigerate.

Recommended for:

Banana Split Cake, page 72

Long on Flavor Shortcake, page 74

Chocolate Lover's Pudding, page 225

Peanut Butter and No Jelly Pudding, page 227

Bahama Mama Pudding, page 228

The Berry Best Pudding, page 229

Creamy Rice Pudding, page 230

Orange Chocolate Chip Pudding, page 231

Tangy Lemon Pudding, page 232

Strawberry Fields Pudding, page 233

PER SERVING: 44 calories, <1 g fat (<0.1 g saturated), 6 g carbohydrate, <0.1 g dietary fiber, 6 g sugar, 2 g protein, 0 mg cholesterol, <8 mg sodium, 3 mg potassium. Calories from fat: 1 percent.

Note: Xanthan gum will produce a slightly softer frosting, but will not give the mild flour taste that you may get if you use the flour. If you are making the Banana Split Cake as a wheat-free cake, you should use the xanthan gum instead of the flour.

VANILLA GLAZE

¾ cup powdered sugar

2 tablespoons vegan milk

½ teaspoon vanilla extract

▶ Mix all the ingredients together. Pour over the cake before slicing.

Recommended for:

Just Loafing Around (pound cake), page 51

You Can't Catch Me I'm the Gingerbread . . . Cake, page 60

Cinn-sational Apple Cake, page 76

"P" is for Pumpkin Cake, page 77

Rootin' Tootin' Raisin Spice Cake, page 96

PER SERVING: 31 calories, <1 g fat (<0.1 g saturated), 8 g carbohydrate, <0.1 g dietary fiber, 2 g protein, 0 mg cholesterol, <8 mg sodium, 8 mg potassium. Calories from fat: 2 percent.

PUMPKIN WHIPPED TOPPING

1 pound (16 ounces, or 1⅓ [12-ounce] packages) firm silken tofu

1 cup powdered sugar

1 teaspoon vanilla extract

⅓ cup pure pumpkin puree

1 teaspoon ground cinnamon

▶ Place the tofu in a food processor and process until smooth, scraping down the sides as necessary. Add the rest of the ingredients and blend.

▶ Refrigerate until ready to use.

Recommended for:
   "P" is for Pumpkin Cake, page 77
   Pumpkin Pie, page 168

PER SERVING: 52 calories, <1 g fat (<0.1 g saturated), 12 g carbohydrate, <1 g dietary fiber, <1 g sugar, <1 g protein, 0 mg cholesterol, 11 mg sodium, 54 mg potassium. Calories from fat: 1 percent.

STANDARD CHOCOLATE FROSTING

8 ounces (¾ [12-ounce] package) firm silken tofu

½ cup powdered sugar

1 teaspoon vanilla extract

1½ cups melted vegan chocolate chips (use a microwave or double boiler)

▶ Place the tofu in a food processor and whip until smooth, scraping down the sides several times.

▶ Add the powdered sugar and vanilla and process.

▶ Pour the melted chocolate chips into the tofu mixture and blend completely.

▶ If refrigerating the cake overnight before serving, you may use the frosting right away. If planning to frost the cake and serve immediately, make the frosting the day before and refrigerate overnight to allow it to set.

Recommended for:
   Chocolate Raspberry Celebration Loaf, page 47
   Mellow Yellow Cake, page 54
   Double Chocolate Delight, page 84
   Peanut Butter Kandy Kake, page 93
   Chocolate-Covered Gold, page 53

PER SERVING: 145 calories, 6 g fat (4 g saturated), 18 g carbohydrate, 1 g dietary fiber, <0.1 g sugar, 3 g protein, 0 mg cholesterol, 23 mg sodium, 2 mg potassium. Calories from fat: 10 percent.

COFFEE FROSTING

1 pound (16 ounces, or 1⅓
[12-ounce] packages) firm
silken tofu

1 cup powdered sugar

1 tablespoon instant coffee
granules or grain "coffee"
such as Roma

1 teaspoon coffee extract
(optional, to give a more
intense coffee flavor)

¼ cup unbleached all-purpose
flour, or 2 teaspoons xanthan
gum (see Note)

▶ Place the tofu in a food processor and whip until smooth,
scraping down the sides several times.

▶ Add the powdered sugar, coffee granules, and coffee extract and process. Add the flour. If possible, refrigerate
overnight so the frosting can set.

Recommended for:

Mocha Madness Cake, page 49
Nuts About Chocolate Cake, page 50

Note: Xanthan gum will produce a slightly softer frosting, but will not
give the mild flour taste that you may get if you use the flour.

PER SERVING: 73 calories, 1 g fat (<0.1 g saturated), 12 g carbohydrate,
<0.1 g dietary fiber, 10 g sugar, 3 g protein, 0 mg cholesterol, 14 mg
sodium, 35 mg potassium. Calories from fat: 2 percent.

CREAMY PEANUT BUTTER FROSTING

1 pound (16 ounces, or 1⅓
[12-ounce] packages) firm
silken tofu

1 cup powdered sugar

¾ cup creamy natural peanut
butter

¼ cup unbleached all-purpose
flour, or 2 teaspoons xanthan
gum (see Note)

▶ Place the tofu in a food processor and whip until smooth,
scraping down the sides several times. Add the powdered
sugar and peanut butter and process.

▶ Add the flour and mix.

▶ If possible, refrigerate overnight so the frosting can set.

Recommended for:

Nuts About Chocolate Cake, page 50
Mocha Goober Cake, page 52

PER SERVING: 167 calories, 9 g fat
(2 g saturated), 15 g carbohydrate,
1 g dietary fiber, <12 g sugar, 5 g
protein, 0 mg cholesterol, 76 mg
sodium, 135 mg potassium. Calories
from fat: 14 percent.

Note: Xanthan gum will produce a slightly softer frosting, but will not
give the mild flour taste that you may get if you use the flour.

FLUFFY ORANGE FROSTING

Makes twelve ¼-cup servings

1 pound (16 ounces, or 1⅓ [12-ounce] packages) firm silken tofu

1 cup powdered sugar

2 teaspoons orange extract

¼ cup unbleached all-purpose flour, or 2 teaspoons xanthan gum (see Note)

PER SERVING: 74 calories, 1 g fat (<0.1 g saturated), 12 g carbohydrate, <0.1 g dietary fiber, <10 g sugar, 3 g protein, 0 mg cholesterol, <14 mg sodium, 28 mg potassium. Calories from fat: 2 percent.

▶ Place the tofu in a food processor and whip until smooth, scraping down the sides several times. Add the powdered sugar and orange extract and process.

▶ Add the flour and mix.

▶ If possible, refrigerate overnight so the frosting can set.

Recommended for:
Citrus Orange Cake, page 55
Cherry Vanilla Dream, page 86

Note: Xanthan gum will produce a slightly softer frosting, but will not give the mild flour taste that you get if you use the flour.

LIGHT RASPBERRY FROSTING

Makes twelve ¼ cup servings

1 pound (16 ounces, or 1⅓ [12-ounce] packages) firm silken tofu

1 cup powdered sugar

¼ cup raspberry jam

¼ cup unbleached all-purpose flour, or 2 teaspoons xanthan gum (see Note)

PER SERVING: 90 calories, <1 g fat (<0.1 g saturated), 17 g carbohydrate, <1 g dietary fiber, <13 g sugar, 3 g protein, 0 mg cholesterol, 16 mg sodium, 32 mg potassium. Calories from fat: 2 percent.

▶ Place the tofu in a food processor and whip until smooth, scraping down the sides several times. Add the powdered sugar and raspberry jam and process.

▶ Add the flour and mix.

▶ If possible, refrigerate overnight so the frosting can set.

Recommended for:
Mellow Yellow Cake, page 54
Double Chocolate Delight, page 84

Note: Xanthan gum will produce a slightly softer frosting, but will not give the mild flour taste that you may get if you use the flour.

WHIPPED LEMON FROSTING

1 pound (16 ounces, or 1⅓ [12-ounce] packages) firm silken tofu

1 cup powdered sugar

2 teaspoons lemon extract

¼ teaspoon turmeric (for color only)

▸ Place the tofu in a food processor and whip until smooth, scraping down the sides several times. Add the powdered sugar, lemon extract, and turmeric and process.

▸ If possible, refrigerate overnight so the frosting can set.

Recommended for:
Mellow Yellow Cake, page 54
Lemon Times Two Cake, page 75

PER SERVING: 48 calories, <1 g fat (<0.1 g saturated), 10 g carbohydrate, <1 g dietary fiber, <1 g sugar, <1 g protein, 0 mg cholesterol, <1 mg sodium, 26 mg potassium. Calories from fat: 6 percent.

TOASTED COCONUT PECAN FROSTING

12 ounces (1½ [8-ounce] containers) vegan cream cheese

1½ teaspoons tahini

1½ cups powdered sugar

1½ teaspoons vanilla extract

¼ cup unbleached all-purpose flour

¾ cup toasted unsweetened shredded coconut (see Note)

1 cup chopped pecans

▸ In a food processor, combine the cream cheese and tahini and puree until smooth. Add the powdered sugar, vanilla, and flour, and process.

▸ Stir the toasted coconut and pecans into the frosting by hand.

Recommended for:
Mellow Yellow Cake, page 54
Toasted Coconut Pecan Cake, page 57
Double Chocolate Delight, page 84

PER SERVING: 182 calories, 11 g fat (2 g saturated), 19 g carbohydrate, 1 g dietary fiber, <15 g sugar, 2 g protein, 0 mg cholesterol, 49 mg sodium, 57 mg potassium. Calories from fat: 39 percent.

Note: To toast the coconut: Line a cookie sheet with aluminum foil and coat with nonstick cooking spray. Spread the coconut in a thin layer on the baking sheet and broil. Stir as the coconut begins to brown. Remove from the broiler immediately when golden brown.

WHIPPED COCONUT CREAM FROSTING

Makes twelve ¼-cup servings

1 pound (16 ounces, or 1⅓ [12-ounce] packages) firm silken tofu

1 cup powdered sugar

2 teaspoons coconut extract

¾ cup unsweetened shredded coconut

PER SERVING: 70 calories, 2 g fat (4 g saturated), 12 g carbohydrate, 1 g dietary fiber, <11 g sugar, 3 g protein, 0 mg cholesterol, 14 mg sodium, 59 mg potassium. Calories from fat: 2 percent.

▸ Place the tofu in a food processor and whip until smooth, scraping down the sides several times. Add the powdered sugar and coconut extract and process. Stir in the coconut by hand, reserving about 2 tablespoons for a garnish.

▸ If possible, refrigerate overnight so the frosting can set.

Recommended for:
　Mellow Yellow Cake, page 54
　Tropical Mango Cake, page 59

COCONUT CREAM CHEESE FROSTING

Makes twelve ⅓-cup servings

6 ounces (½ [12-ounce] package) firm silken tofu

12 ounces (1½ [8-ounce] containers) vegan cream cheese

1 cup powdered sugar

1 teaspoon coconut extract

½ cup unsweetened coconut

¼ cup unbleached all-purpose flour, or 2 teaspoons xanthan gum (optional for thickening) (see Note)

PER SERVING: 86 calories, 4 g fat (1 g saturated), 13 g carbohydrate, <1 g dietary fiber, <1 g sugar, <1 g protein, 0 mg cholesterol, 49 mg sodium, 11 mg potassium. Calories from fat: 7 percent.

▸ Place all the frosting ingredients except the coconut in a food processor and process until smooth. Stir in the coconut by hand.

▸ If possible, refrigerate overnight so the frosting can set.

Recommended for:
　Tropical Fruit Cake, page 67
　White on White Tropical Cake, page 80

Note: Xanthan gum will produce a slightly softer frosting, but will not give the mild flour taste that you may get if you use the flour.

MEGA-COCONUT CREAM CHEESE FROSTING

Makes twelve ½-cup servings

9 ounces (¾ [12-ounce] package) firm silken tofu

16 ounces (2 [8-ounce] containers) vegan cream cheese

1½ cups powdered sugar

1½ teaspoons coconut extract

¼ cup unbleached all-purpose flour, or 2 teaspoons xanthan gum (optional for thickening) (see Note)

1 cup unsweetened coconut

PER SERVING: 127 calories, 6 g fat (2 g saturated), 18 g carbohydrate, <1 g dietary fiber, <1 g sugar, 1 g protein, 0 mg cholesterol, 66 mg sodium, 30 mg potassium. Calories from fat: 11 percent.

▸ Place the tofu in a food processor and whip until smooth, scraping down the sides several times.

▸ Add the cream cheese and powdered sugar and process. Add the coconut extract and flour and process until combined. Stir in the coconut by hand.

▸ If possible, refrigerate overnight so the frosting can set.

Recommended for:
Mellow Yellow Cake, page 54
Coconut-Covered Delight, page 92

Note: Xanthan gum will produce a slightly softer frosting, but will not give the mild flour taste that you may get if you use the flour.

CREAM CHEESE FROSTING

Makes twelve ¼-cup servings

1 (12-ounce) package firm silken tofu

1 (8-ounce) container vegan cream cheese

1 cup powdered sugar

1 teaspoon vanilla extract

PER SERVING: 47 calories, <1 g fat (0.1 g saturated), 10 g carbohydrate, <0.1 g dietary fiber, <10 g sugar, <1 g protein, 0 mg cholesterol, 66 mg sodium, 19 mg potassium. Calories from fat: 5 percent.

▸ Place all the ingredients in a food processor and process until smooth.

▸ If possible, refrigerate overnight so the frosting can set.

Recommended for:
You Can't Catch Me I'm the Gingerbread . . . Cake, page 60
Hold the Wheat Carrot Cake, page 61

Vegan Cream Cheese Glaze

4 ounces (½ [8-ounce] container) vegan cream cheese (such as Tofutti, which has no casein)

½ cup pure maple syrup

½ teaspoon vanilla extract

▶ Blend all the ingredients together in a food processor until smooth.

Recommended for:
Hold the Wheat Carrot Cake, page 61
Applesauce Applause Cake, page 65
Cinn-sational Apple Cake, page 76
"P" is for Pumpkin Cake, page 77
Rootin' Tootin' Raisin Spice Cake, page 96

PER SERVING: 36 calories, <1 g fat (<0.1 g saturated), 9 g carbohydrate, 0 g dietary fiber, 8 g sugar, <1 g protein, 0 mg cholesterol, 3 mg sodium, 27 mg potassium. Calories from fat: 5 percent.

Maple Cocoa Frosting

⅓ cup whipped tofu (see Note)

½ cup pure maple syrup

1 cup unsweetened cocoa powder

▶ Place the tofu in a food processor and blend until smooth.
▶ Add the maple syrup and cocoa powder and continue blending until the mixture is smooth and creamy.

Recommended for:
Death by Chocolate Brownies, page 36
Nuts About Chocolate Cake, page 50
Bold Banana Cake, page 63
Double Chocolate Delight, page 84

PER SERVING: 51 calories, 1 g fat (<1 g saturated), 13 g carbohydrate, 2 g dietary fiber, 8 g sugar, 1 g protein, 0 mg cholesterol, 3 mg sodium, 137 mg potassium. Calories from fat: 2 percent.

Note: Use a mini food processor or blender to whip a slice of soft tofu from a 12-ounce package. Measure out ⅓ cup after it is whipped.

WHIPPED CREAM CHEESE FROSTING

6 ounces (½ [12-ounce] package) firm silken tofu

1½ (8-ounce) containers vegan cream cheese

1 cup powdered sugar

1 teaspoon vanilla extract

¼ cup unbleached all-purpose flour, or 2 teaspoons xanthan gum (optional for thickening) (see Note)

- ▶ Place all the ingredients in food processor and process until smooth.
- ▶ If possible, refrigerate overnight so the frosting can set.

Recommended for:

Applesauce Applause Cake, page 65
Orange Creamsicle Cake, page 66
Granny's Cranberry Cake, page 68
Cherry Vanilla Dream, page 86
Ten-Carat Gold Cake, page 88

PER SERVING: 78 calories, 3 g fat (<1 g saturated), 12 g carbohydrate, <0.1 g dietary fiber, <0.1 g sugar, <1 g protein, 0 mg cholesterol, 48 mg sodium, 4 mg potassium. Calories from fat: 16 percent.

Note: Xanthan gum will produce a slightly softer frosting, but will not give the mild flour taste that you might get if you use the flour.

CHOCOLATE DECORATIVE TOPPING

6 ounces (½ [12-ounce] package) firm silken tofu

½ (8-ounce container) vegan cream cheese (such as Tofutti, which has no casein)

1 cup powdered sugar

2 tablespoons unbleached all-purpose flour

½ cup melted vegan chocolate chips (use a microwave or double boiler)

PER SERVING: 78 calories, 2 g fat (1 g saturated), 15 g carbohydrate, <1 g dietary fiber, <0.1 g sugar, <1 g protein, 0 mg cholesterol, 39 mg sodium, 2 mg potassium. Calories from fat: 9 percent.

▶ Place the tofu and cream cheese in a food processor and process until smooth and creamy. Add the powdered sugar and flour and process until combined. Add the melted chocolate chips and process until smooth and creamy.

▶ If possible, refrigerate overnight so the frosting can set.

Recommended as a garnish for:
Nuts About Chocolate Cake, page 50
Chocolate-Covered Mint, page 69
Richer Than Fort Knox Cake, page 78
German Chocolate Cake, page 81

German Chocolate Coconut-Pecan Frosting

Makes twelve ¼-cup servings

1 cup coconut milk

1 cup brown sugar

⅓ cup canola oil

¾ cup water

2 teaspoons flax powder

1½ tablespoons arrowroot

1 cup chopped pecans

1⅓ cups unsweetened shredded coconut

1 teaspoon vanilla extract

½ teaspoon salt

PER SERVING: 241 calories, 20 g fat (6 g saturated), 22 g carbohydrate, 2 g dietary fiber, 13 g sugar, 2 g protein, 0 mg cholesterol, 105 mg sodium, 167 mg potassium. Calories from fat: 31 percent.

▸ Heat the coconut milk, brown sugar, and oil over medium heat until it is steaming. In a small cup, mix the flax powder and ½ cup of the water. Add to the coconut milk mixture.

▸ In another small cup, mix the arrowroot and the remaining ¼ cup of water. Add to the coconut milk mixture and heat until thickened (do not boil—the mixture will thicken more as it cools).

▸ Stir in the pecans, coconut, vanilla, and salt. Allow to cool completely.

Recommended for:

Nuts About Chocolate Cake (use ½ recipe), page 50
Mellow Yellow Cake, page 54
German Chocolate Cake, page 81

FLUFFY MINT FROSTING

1 pound (16 ounces, or 1⅓ [12-ounce] packages) firm silken tofu

1 cup powdered sugar

¼ cup unbleached all-purpose flour, or 2 teaspoons xanthan gum (optional for thickening) (see Note)

1 teaspoon peppermint extract

PER SERVING: 58 calories, <1 g fat (<0.1 g saturated), 12 g carbohydrate, <0.1 g dietary fiber, <1 g sugar, <1 g protein, 0 mg cholesterol, <1 mg sodium, 28 mg potassium. Calories from fat: 6 percent.

▸ Place the tofu in a food processor and blend until smooth and creamy.

▸ Add the powdered sugar, flour, and peppermint extract and continue to blend.

▸ If possible, refrigerate overnight so the frosting can set.

Recommended for:
Chocolate-Covered Mint, page 69
Mint Madness, page 85

Note: Xanthan gum will produce a slightly softer frosting, but will not give the mild flour taste that you might get if you use the flour.

Buttercream Frostings

These frostings taste just as delicious as their traditional counterparts—they are simply made without the dairy. Totally scrumptious!

....

Pink Peppermint Buttercream Frosting

Makes sixteen ¼-cup servings

1 cup peppermint candies (see Note)

¼ cup soft vegan butter spread, preferably tub style, at room temperature. (If using stick butter, soften it in the microwave until it is the consistency of tub butter. Do not melt!)

¼ cup vegetable shortening (preferably unhydrogenated, such as Spectrum or Earth Balance)

½ teaspoon peppermint extract

1 teaspoon vanilla extract

4 cups powdered sugar

¼ cup plus 1 tablespoon water

▶ Place the peppermint candies in a blender. Blend until they are the consistency of fine dust.

▶ Using an electric mixer, cream the butter, shortening, peppermint extract, and vanilla until creamy. Slowly add the powdered sugar, peppermint candy "dust," and water. Beat until light and fluffy.

Recommended for:
Candy Cane Cupcakes, page 102
Peppermint Patty Cupcakes, page 103
Mint Madness, page 85

PER SERVING: 137 calories, 4.8 g fat (1.5 g saturated), 23.9 g carbohydrate, 0 g dietary fiber, 23.5 g sugar, 0 g protein, 0 mg cholesterol, 24 mg sodium. Calories from fat: 7 percent.

Note: Read the ingredient list on peppermint candies. Some are made of a lot of artificial stuff. Try to find candies with real ingredients.

CHOCOLATE BUTTERCREAM FROSTING

¼ cup soft vegan butter spread, preferably tub style, at room temperature. (If using stick butter, soften it in the microwave until it is the consistency of tub butter. Do not melt!)

¼ cup vegetable shortening (preferably unhydrogenated, such as Spectrum)

1 teaspoon vanilla extract

4 cups powdered sugar

⅔ cup unsweetened cocoa powder

½ cup water

▸ Using an electric mixer, cream the butter, shortening, and vanilla until creamy. Slowly add the powdered sugar, cocoa powder, and water. Beat until light and fluffy.

Recommended for:
Just Like Grandma Used to Make Cupcakes, page 110
Chocolate Covered Gold, page 53
Chocolate Covered Mint, page 69

PER SERVING: 179 calories, 6.5 g fat (2.1 g saturated), 31.9 g carbohydrate, 0.1 g dietary fiber, 29.5 g sugar, <1 g protein, 0 mg cholesterol, 31 mg sodium. Calories from fat: 10 percent.

PEANUT BUTTER BUTTERCREAM FROSTING

¼ cup soft vegan butter spread, preferably tub style, at room temperature. (If using stick butter, soften it in the microwave until it is the consistency of tub butter. Do not melt!)

⅔ cup peanut butter

¼ cup vegetable shortening (preferably unhydrogenated, such as Spectrum)

2 teaspoons vanilla extract

4 cups powdered sugar

¼ cup plus 2 tablespoons plus 2 teaspoons water

▶ Using an electric mixer, cream the butter, peanut butter, shortening, and vanilla until creamy. Slowly add the powdered sugar and the ¼ cup of water, then the additional water 1 tablespoon or teaspoon at a time. Whip between each addition. Stop adding the water when the frosting is the desired consistency. Beat until light and fluffy.

Recommended for:

Vanilla Peanut Butter Cupcakes, page 105
Chocolate Peanut Butter Cupcakes, page 104
Mocha Goober Cake, page 52

PER SERVING: 157 calories, 7.6 g fat (2 g saturated), 21.4 g carbohydrate, 0 g dietary fiber, 20.3 g sugar, 1.8 g protein, 0 mg cholesterol, 53 mg sodium. Calories from fat: 15 percent.

VANILLA BUTTERCREAM FROSTING

¼ cup soft vegan butter spread, preferably tub style, at room temperature. (If using stick butter, soften it in the microwave until it is the consistency of tub butter. Do not melt!)

¼ cup vegetable shortening (preferably unhydrogenated, such as Spectrum)

2 teaspoons vanilla extract

4 cups powdered sugar

¼ cup plus 1 tablespoon plus 1 teaspoon water

▶ Using an electric mixer, cream the butter, shortening, and vanilla until creamy. Slowly add the powdered sugar and the ¼ cup of water, then the additional water 1 tablespoon or teaspoon at a time. Whip between each addition. Stop adding the water when the frosting is the desired consistency. Beat until light and fluffy.

Recommended for:

Just Like Grandma Used to Make Cupcakes, page 110
Orange Creamsicle Cake, page 66

PER SERVING: 114 calories, 4 g fat (1.2 g saturated), 20 g carbohydrate, 0 g dietary fiber, 19.6 g sugar, 0 g protein, 0 mg cholesterol, 20 mg sodium. Calories from fat: 6 percent.

FUDGE ICE CREAM TOPPING

This rich fudge topping tastes great smothering a scoop of vanilla vegan ice cream. If you want a real treat, try making I Can't Believe They're Not Sinful Brownies, page 35, and top a piece while it is still warm with a scoop of vanilla vegan ice cream nestled under this delicious fudge topping. Being a vegan never tasted so good!

Makes six ⅛-cup servings

Preparation time: 5 minutes

½ cup unsweetened cocoa powder

¾ cup pure maple syrup

1 teaspoon vanilla extract

▸ Place all the ingredients in a bowl and mix until smooth and creamy.

▸ Heat the topping on full power for 10 seconds in a microwave. Stir and heat for another minute. Repeat until the sauce is at a temperature to your liking.

PER SERVING: 121 calories, 2 g fat (<1 g saturated), 30 g carbohydrate, 2 g dietary fiber, 23 g sugar, 2 g protein, 0 mg cholesterol, 8 mg sodium, 286 mg potassium. Calories from fat: 2 percent.

CARAMEL ICE CREAM TOPPING

This gooey sweet caramel-like topping tastes great on many of the nondairy frozen desserts that are now available at most supermarkets and health food stores.

Makes ten 1-tablespoon servings

Preparation time: 10 minutes

⅓ cup corn syrup or agave nectar

⅓ cup brown sugar

3 tablespoons vegan milk

2 teaspoons vanilla extract

¼ teaspoon salt

▸ Place the corn syrup and brown sugar in a small pan and heat to a boil.

▸ Simmer until the mixture reaches the soft-ball stage (240°F on a candy thermometer).

▸ Remove from the heat and stir in the milk, vanilla, and salt. Allow to cool to room temperature before serving.

PER SERVING: 50 calories, <1 g fat (<1 g saturated), 12 g carbohydrate, <1 g dietary fiber, <1 g protein, 0 mg cholesterol, 24 mg sodium, 8 g sugar, 47 mg potassium. Calories from fat: <1 percent.

STANDARD VEGAN
SINGLE PIECRUST

> Makes 1 single piecrust, 10 servings

1¼ cups unbleached all-purpose flour

⅛ teaspoon salt

¼ cup canola oil, or coconut oil if desired

½ cup + 2 tablespoons cold water or apple juice

PER SERVING: 110 calories, 6 g fat (<1 g saturated), 13 g carbohydrate, <1 g dietary fiber, 2 g protein, 0 mg cholesterol, 8 mg sodium, 31 mg potassium. Calories from fat: 44 percent.

▸ Put the flour and salt in a small bowl. Add the canola oil and stir into the flour until the dough forms pieces no larger than a pea. (If using the coconut oil, which is solid at room temperature like vegetable shortening, cut into the flour with two knives until the dough forms pieces no larger than a pea). Add the cold water and mix just until the mixture forms a ball (add more water if necessary). Refrigerate for 10 minutes.

▸ Place the ball of dough on a piece of floured waxed paper. Sprinkle the ball of dough with a little more flour. Place another piece of waxed paper on top of the ball of dough and push down to flatten. Using a rolling pin, roll out the dough as thinly as possible between the two sheets of paper.

▸ Remove the top sheet of paper carefully. Flip the piecrust onto the pie plate. Carefully remove the second piece of waxed paper. Fit the crust into the pie plate, allowing the edges to hang over the edge. Cut the edges of the dough with a sharp knife. Crimp the edges of the crust with your fingers and prick the bottom of the crust with a fork.

Standard Vegan Double Piecrust

2½ cups unbleached all-purpose flour

¼ teaspoon salt

½ cup canola oil, or coconut oil if desired

1¼ cups cold water or apple juice

▶ Put the flour and salt in a small bowl. Add the canola oil and stir into the flour until the dough forms pieces no larger than a pea. (If using the coconut oil, which is solid at room temperature like vegetable shortening, cut the oil into the flour with two knives until the dough forms pieces no larger than a pea). Add the water. Mix just until the mixture forms a ball (add more water if necessary). Refrigerate for 10 minutes. Divide into two equal balls.

▶ Place one ball of dough on a piece of floured waxed paper. Sprinkle the ball of dough with a little more flour. Place another piece of waxed paper on top of the ball of dough and push down to flatten. Using a rolling pin, roll out the dough as thinly as possible between the two sheets of paper.

▶ Remove the top sheet of paper carefully. Flip the piecrust onto the pie plate. Carefully remove the second piece of waxed paper. Fit the crust into the pie plate, allowing the edges to hang over the edge of the pie plate. Set the dough-lined pie plate in the refrigerator until ready to fill.

▶ Roll out the other half of the piecrust between two sheets of floured waxed paper and set aside. If possible, place on a cookie sheet and refrigerate until ready to use.

PER SERVING: 220 calories, 12 g fat (<1 g saturated), 26 g carbohydrate, <1 g dietary fiber, 4 g protein, 0 mg cholesterol, 16 mg sodium, 62 mg potassium. Calories from fat: 44 percent.

TART CRUST

Makes 1 tart crust, 12 servings

1½ cups whole wheat pastry flour

¼ cup granulated sweetener

¼ cup canola oil

¼ cup + 2 tablespoons water

1 tablespoon pure maple syrup

▸ In a small bowl, stir together the flour, granulated sweetener, and oil until it resembles coarse crumbs. Slowly stir in ¼ cup of water until the mixture forms a ball in the bowl.

▸ Place some flour on a piece of waxed paper. Put the ball of dough onto the floured waxed paper and roll in the flour to coat. Put another piece of waxed paper on top of the ball of dough. Roll the dough between the two pieces of waxed paper until very thin. Remove the top piece of waxed paper.

▸ Flip the dough onto the tart pan. Press the dough around the bottom and up the sides of the pan. Cut to fit at the top of the pan. Place pie weights in the bottom of the pan and bake for 15 minutes. (If the piecrust is not weighted with commercial pie weights or dried beans placed on foil, the crust will bubble and shrink during baking.)

▸ Combine the maple syrup and 2 tablespoons of water in a small bowl. After 15 minutes, brush the maple syrup mixture over the crust and bake for 5 more minutes to glaze. Set on a wire rack and allow to cool in the pan for 10 minutes. Remove from the pan and allow to cool completely before assembling.

PER SERVING: 111 calories, 5 g fat (<1 g saturated), 15 g carbohydrate, <1 g dietary fiber, 1 g sugar, 2 g protein, 0 mg cholesterol, <1 mg sodium, 20 mg potassium. Calories from fat: 37 percent.

METRIC CONVERSIONS

The recipes in this book use U.S. measurements and oven temperatures. The following tables will help you to convert if you use another standard of measure.

General Formulas for Metric Conversion

Ounces to grams	→	ounces × 28.35 = grams
Grams to ounces	→	grams × 0.035 = ounces
Pounds to grams	→	pounds × 453.5 = grams
Pounds to kilograms	→	pounds × 0.45 = kilograms
Cups to liters	→	cups × 0.24 = liters
Fahrenheit to Celsius	→	(°F − 32) × 5 ÷ 9 = °C
Celsius to Fahrenheit	→	(°C × 9) ÷ 5 + 32 = °F

Linear Measurements

$\frac{1}{2}$ inch	=	$1\frac{1}{2}$ cm
1 inch	=	$2\frac{1}{2}$ cm
6 inches	=	15 cm
8 inches	=	20 cm
10 inches	=	25 cm
12 inches	=	30 cm
20 inches	=	50 cm

Volume (Dry) Measurements

$\frac{1}{4}$ teaspoon = 1 milliliter
$\frac{1}{2}$ teaspoon = 2 milliliters
$\frac{3}{4}$ teaspoon = 4 milliliters
1 teaspoon = 5 milliliters
1 tablespoon = 15 milliliters (3 teaspoons)
$\frac{1}{4}$ cup = 59 milliliters
$\frac{1}{3}$ cup = 79 milliliters
$\frac{1}{2}$ cup = 118 milliliters
$\frac{2}{3}$ cup = 158 milliliters
$\frac{3}{4}$ cup = 177 milliliters
1 cup = 225 milliliters
4 cups or 1 quart = 1 liter
$\frac{1}{2}$ gallon = 2 liters
1 gallon = 4 liters

Volume (Liquid) Measurements

1 teaspoon = $\frac{1}{6}$ fluid ounce = 5 milliliters
1 tablespoon = $\frac{1}{2}$ fluid ounce = 15 milliliters
2 tablespoons = 1 fluid ounce = 30 milliliters
$\frac{1}{4}$ cup = 2 fluid ounces = 59 milliliters
$\frac{1}{3}$ cup = $2\frac{2}{3}$ fluid ounces = 79 milliliters
$\frac{1}{2}$ cup = 4 fluid ounces = 118 milliliters
1 cup or $\frac{1}{2}$ pint = 8 fluid ounces = 237 milliliters
2 cups or 1 pint = 16 fluid ounces = 473 milliliters
4 cups or 1 quart = 32 fluid ounces = 950 milliliters
1 gallon = 3.8 liters

Oven Temperature Equivalents,

Fahrenheit (F)	Celsius (C)	Gas Mark
250°F	120°C	$\frac{1}{2}$
275°F	140°C	1
300°F	150°C	2
325°F	160°C	3
350°F	180°C	4
375°F	190°C	5
400°F	200°C	6
425°F	220°C	7
450°F	230°C	8

Weight (Mass) Measurements

1 ounce = 28 grams
2 ounces = 55 grams
3 ounces = 85 grams
4 ounces = $\frac{1}{4}$ pound = 125 grams
8 ounces = $\frac{1}{2}$ pound = 240 grams
12 ounces = $\frac{3}{4}$ pound = 375 grams
16 ounces = 1 pound = 454 grams

ACKNOWLEDGMENTS

I'd like to thank my family, friends, co-workers, and neighbors who were faithful and honest taste testers. Without all of you, this book could never have been completed.

INDEX